Falsely Accused?

Mike Tyson and the Rape Trial That Destroyed a Champion

Mark Shaw

Copyright © 2011, Mark Shaw

All rights reserved. No part of this book shall be reproduced in any form by any means, electronic or mechanical, including photocopying, recording, or by any information storage or retrieval system, without written permission of the publisher, Six Dogs Books, 2855Rock Creek Circle #223, Superior, Colorado 80027. Although every preparation has been taken in the completion of this book, the publisher and author assume no responsibility for errors or omissions. No liability is assumed for damages resulting from the use of the information contained herein.

Publisher's Cataloging—In—Publication Data

Mark Shaw 1945—
Falsely Accused
by Mark Shaw
p. cm.

ISBN-13: 978-1460943052; ISBN – 10: 1460943058

1. Shaw, Mark 1945—
2. Mike Tyson
3. True Crime
4. Boxing
5. I. Shaw, Mark II. Title

10 9 8 7 6 5 4 3 2 1

Printed in the United States of America

Mark Shaw Books

Falsely Accused?
Road to a Miracle
Beneath the Mask of Holiness: Thomas Merton and the Forbidden Love Affair that Set Him Free
Melvin Belli, King of the Courtroom
No Peace for the Wicked
Dandelions in the Moonlight
Clydesdales: The World's Most Magical Horse
From Birdies To Bunkers
Miscarriage of Justice: The Jonathan Pollard Story
Larry Legend
Testament To Courage
Forever Flying
Bury Me In A Pot Bunker
Jack Nicklaus, Golf's Greatest Champion
The Perfect Yankee
Diamonds In The Rough
Down For The Count
Let The Good Times Roll
How To Become A Published Author "Idea to Publication"
Book Report
Grammar Report
Poetry Report
Writers' Report
Self-Publishing Report

Injustice anywhere is a threat to justice everywhere.

Martin Luther King, Jr.

For whatsoever a man soweth;
that shall he also reap.

Galatians 6: 7-9

"I'm an insane individual."

Mike Tyson to filmmaker James Toback

Note:

This book was originally released by the author in 1993 under the title, *Down for the Count*. This edition is updated both as to fresh observations about Tyson's trial and subsequent events involving all of the significant players involved in the case.

Preface

During the period of a year that began in the fall 1991, five national events resulted in trials or hearings that captivated the imagination of millions of people around the world.

In October, Federal Judge Clarence Thomas was charged with sexual harassment by the University of Oklahoma Professor Anita Hill during his Senate confirmation hearing to become an Associate Justice of the United States Supreme Court. Later that year, one of the famed Kennedy clan, William Kennedy Smith, appeared in court after being prosecuted in Palm Beach, Florida for the alleged rapes of thirty-year-old single mother Patty Bowman.

In January 1992, former heavyweight boxing champion of the world Mike Tyson was forced to stand trial for the alleged "date rape" of eighteen-year-old beauty contestant and college student Desiree Washington in Indianapolis, Indiana. During the summer months that followed, four Los Angeles Police Department officers were charged in California state court with savagely beating motorist Rodney King. And finally, in fall 1992, seventeen-year-old Lemrick Nelson, Jr. was prosecuted for killing Jewish scholar Yankel Rosenbaum in the volatile Crown Heights neighborhood of Brooklyn, New York. Thomas, Tyson, and Nelson, Jr. were African-American while Smith and the L.A.P.D. officers were Caucasian.

Four trials and one hearing. Five emotionally-charged, high-profile cases that consumed the media for days on end. The outcomes – four not-guilty "verdicts," and only one conviction, that of Michael Gerard Tyson, convicted of rape and sentenced to six years in prison.

Why was Mike Tyson convicted and not the absolved of the charges? Was he truly guilty beyond a reasonable doubt and justice done? Or was the deck stacked against the boxing champion for any number of reasons, overzealous prosecutors out to "get" the famous black celebrity and make a name for themselves, incompetent defense counsel, a pro-prosecution judge named Patricia Gifford, or the climate pervading in conservative Indianapolis, Indiana, just a stone's throw from the former hotbed of the Ku Klux Klan? Did the jury really provide Tyson with a fair shake, or was the verdict a knee-jerk reaction to Tyson's reputation as a "bad boy," and based more on guesswork and supposition than the actual evidence in the case? Most important, did the entire criminal justice system fail denying Tyson of a most precious constitutional right, the right to a fair trial by jury by his peers?

These questions and more loom large as one begins to try to understand the fateful circumstances that led to Tyson's shocking conviction and the subsequent imprisonment of the twenty-five-year-old who rose from the slums of Brooklyn to earn the coveted title of champion of the world, the youngest ever to do so. Examination of the trial records and those on appeal including competent legal analysis of the trial proceedings indicate many similarities and some striking differences between the Tyson case and the other four incidents. Certainly, history would show that his conviction led the boxer on downhill spiral from which he could never recover concerning both his boxing career and his personal life. No, when Tyson entered prison, he was doomed to failure, his career destroyed, his life ever altered for the worse through the events in Indianapolis both in and out of the courtroom.

As the media coordinator for Tyson's trial and a legal analyst for such noteworthy outlets as *USA Today, CNN, ABC, ESPN*, and *British Channel 4*, this author enjoyed a front-row seat to the Tyson trial like no one else. From my perspective as a former criminal defense attorney with experience in rape cases, it was amazing to watch Tyson's case rolled forward. In the end, there is much to learn from it, especially when placed in context with the mood of the country in the early 1990s. When Tyson's trial and subsequent conviction are analyzed alongside the four important events surrounding his trial, it is no wonder he was convicted and sent to prison despite the potential that he was falsely accused. In the end, Mike Tyson paid for past deeds as well as current ones as he truly reaped what he had sowed.

Prologue

It was 1:15 p.m. on Monday, the tenth of February 1992. Seated around a rectangular table were twelve strangers who had been collected for only one reason: to decide for the world whether Michael Gerard Tyson, the former heavyweight boxing champion, was guilty of raping eighteen-year-old Miss Black American beauty contestant Desiree Washington on July 19, 1991.

Included among the jury were eight men and four women, ten Caucasians and two African-Americans. Among them was Ken, a black behavioral specialist who would later be quoted as saying "the case was rigged"; Michael, a computer services expert who became known as "Kentucky Lucky" when he was crowned the jury pool champion; and Steve, an auto parts manager who had stunned Judge Patricia Gifford and the rest of the courtroom by bravely raising his hand to receive permission to go to the bathroom during a crucial portion of high-powered defense lawyer Vincent Fuller's final argument to the jury.

Strangers seventeen days before, the twelve were not only bonded by their duty to perform justice by weighing the evidence against Tyson fairly, but by their having survived a mysterious fire that had consumed their hotel on the fifth day of the trial. Two firefighters and a businessman had been killed in the blaze and one of the two black jurors had been replaced with yet another Caucasian.

While the twelve had agreed with one juror's statement that Tyson was to be judged as if his name were Smith or Jones, all of them knew the world was anticipating their verdict since the famous boxer would either be acquitted and walk out of the courtroom a free man or become a convicted felon likely destined for prison. As the jurors began their deliberations, they also knew that a media mass was poised outside the courtroom and the City-County Building ready to alert the world to Tyson's fate. These included reporters from far, really far, and near as representatives from the local media outlets joined those from the *Italian LaGazzetta Dello Sport,* the *Spanish Corriere dello Sport-Studio,* the *London Daily Telegraph, News Limited of Australia, The New York Times, Sports Illustrated, Newsweek,* the *Village Voice,* and the television programs, *Inside Edition* and *A Current Affair* in watching every noteworthy event occurring during the trial and now during the deliberations. Each of the American networks, *ABC, CBS, NBC, CNN, and ESPN,* were represented with the *London Daily Telegraph* the only foreign media with a seat inside the courtroom. Others present included reporters from the *Los Angeles Times, the Boston Globe, the Atlanta Constitution, Time Magazine, Reuters,* and *U.S. News and World Report.* In all, more than one hundred reporters were dosing the latest Tyson trial news to readers, listeners, and viewers around the world. Now each waited patiently while the twelve jurors decided Tyson's fate.

The first order of business in the jury room was to elect a foreman. Closely gathered around the table in the small, cream-colored, sparsely furnished jury room located adjacent to Judge Gifford's courtroom, the jurors voted Tim, the note-taking IBM salesman, their leader. He was the one who had passed out breath mints to fellow jurors during the trial. One juror later labeled the ex-Marine to be

11

"much more conservative than the rest of us, more straight, a real redneck."

Procedures for evaluating the evidence, garnered from forty-five witnesses and more than 100 exhibits, were the next order of business but later some jurors expressed surprise that many on the jury wanted to know how their fellow jurors felt regarding Tyson's innocent or guilt. Discussion regarding this point, without a shred of evidence being debated, resulted less than fifteen minutes into the deliberations of small slips of notebook paper being distributed around the table. Each juror indicated their preference and then the slips of paper were neatly folded and place in a bowl in front of the jury foreman.

Foreman Tim then drew the slips out one at a time and spread them neatly on the table for the jurors to see. Eyes focused closely on the writing as a sense of suspense pervaded awaiting the results of the first vote. When Tim announced the tally, six members of the jury had voted to render a guilty verdict while six had not. If this was to be the final tally, then Mike Tyson would be a free man. But more votes would be taken causing jurors to flip-flop as to their belief regarding his innocence or guilt. In the end, the vote would be unanimous and the world would hear whether Tyson could resume his boxing career or whether that career was over.

Chapter One
The Grand Jury

Most trial observers witnessing the events transpiring during the course of the Mike Tyson case were not surprised with the ultimate verdict. Through a series of miscalculations, poor choices, bad decisions, and an ill-conceived trial strategy, none of which was the boxer's fault, he had been put at risk in an unfavorable manner. When 1992 ended, Tyson's trial would take its place with the most noteworthy events of the year including the Washington Redskins Super Bowl victory over the Buffalo Bills, President George H.W. Bush and Arkansas Governor Bill's Clinton's victories in the primaries triggering their match for the presidency in November, Hurricane Andrew's $26.5 million dollar damage infliction to the state of Florida, and Clinton's victory over Bush to capture the presidency.

Anyone familiar with criminal cases knows that they are won and lost many times not due to the evidence, but peripheral matters that in the end influence a jury to reach its decision. Similar to the election process, strategies are designed with one goal in mind, ultimately persuading each jury to vote guilty or not guilty. In most cases, and certainly Tyson's, the actual evidence becomes a bit player in the theatrical drama presented in the courtroom. During a trial, the judge, the attorneys, the accused, the accuser, and the jurors become actors on a stage where the defendant's very freedom hangs in the balance. It is a scary process, one where twelve strangers, who bring all of their life experiences, pro and con, to any deliberations, finally decide the fate of the accused. Pinpointing how to influence these strangers is the job of the prosecution and defense and requires hard work using every skill the attorney's possess.

During the Tyson case, the Marion County prosecutor Jeffrey Modisett, and Tyson's manager, Don King, were faced with difficult decisions to make as a result of the rape charges. Each required a strong game plan toward the ultimate goal, Tyson's conviction for the prosecution, and his acquittal by the defense. The make-up of the prosecution and defense teams was the first order of business as a trial date loomed.

For the ambitious Modisett, he had the dubious challenge of prosecuting one of the most famous African-Americans in the world. When he first heard of Washington's rape allegations against Tyson, he called a meeting of his political advisers to discuss the risks involved. On the one hand, prosecuting the boxer would certainly propel Modisett's name into the national limelight and provide him with more high-profile publicity than he could ever have imagined possible. An unlikely politician to begin with, after narrow victory in his race for prosecutor against his Republican opponent Drew Young, Modisett had higher ambitions on his mind. Perhaps he could follow in the footsteps of Stephen Goldsmith, his predecessor who had used the prosecutor's office as a stepping-stone to becoming mayor of Indianapolis.

While the potential to boost Modisett's career loomed large, there were also downsides to going after Tyson. The boxer, despite his rocky road, was extremely popular in the Africa-American community. A disastrous performance in Tokyo, resulting in the loss of his heavyweight crown to the bumbling Buster Douglas had damaged Tyson's unbeatable persona, but his stock was on the rise again since he was scheduled for a thirty million dollar bout with heavyweight champion Evander Holyfield. To the black community Modisett courted politically, Tyson was viewed as hero of sorts due to his rise from obscurity to the championship. His break from the Brooklyn ghettos was well documented, and Tyson was huge favorite with the media. Wherever he traveled, the boxer was front page news, and Don King made certain that his precious breadwinner was ready and willing to appease the press. Successful prosecution of "date rape" cases was tough enough, but any attempt to convict Tyson of such a crime was indeed formidable.

From the outset, Modisett knew that King would hire a million-dollar plus defense team to face the prosecutor, an inexperienced trial lawyer with mixed results. Tyson was estimated to be worth $80-100 million, securing the opportunity for the best and brightest defense attorney to be by his side during the bout of his life. Could Modisett battle such a worthy foe? Even if he won, how would the victory play out when election time occurred?

Another factor weighing on Modisett's mind was the initial reaction of his advisers that the case against Tyson was weak, a true "he said, she said," type of legal battle. Losing the case would tarnish the prosecutor's record, but perhaps this wasn't as bad as winning since if he won, then reaction would center on why Tyson was treated so harshly causing a backlash when Modisett ran for re-election. To use the old cliché, Modisett was "damned if he did

15

[convict Tyson], and damned if he didn't [convict Tyson]."

In the end, Modisett discovered the perfect solution for a prosecutor weary of offending a constituency that could cost him any election. After accepting all ideas from every corner of his political team, he opted to send the case to a special Marion County Grand Jury under a special Indiana Code Section. Doing so permitted Modisett the perfect political play. If six members on the jury decided Tyson should not be charged, so be it. If they returned an indictment, then it was their doing and the prosecutor had to follow through. Either way, Modisett was protected, since he would stay on the sidelines until the Grand Jury spoke. It was perfect, with Modisett wavering as to what was better politically for him, that Tyson be charged, or not.

The Special Grand Jury was convened on August 13, 1991. Delighted with his decision, Modisett assigned deputy prosecutor David Dreyer to handle the prosecution's case to the jurors. Desiree Washington was told of the decision, and Dreyer began to formulate the presentation of evidence. While this was occurring, Modisett still hoped the Tyson case might go away but this was not to be thanks to a gift provided by none other than the nationally known attorney Don King would choose for Tyson.

To King, the rape charges were just another in a long series of scrapes with that the law threatening the ex-champ's career. Despite attempts to segregate Tyson from any potential disaster ending his career, King knew full well of his client's volatile personality and unpredictable mood swings, one causing him to behave like an obedient child/schoolboy one minute and a violent, raging maniac the next. These mood swings, King believed, were a direct result of Tyson's early years in the Brownsville section of Brooklyn. An early-age product of a broken home, Tyson was headed straight to hell until a gentle man named Bobby Stewart at the Tryon School for Boys took a liking to, not only to the young Tyson, but his potential boxing prowess, as well. When Stewart introduced Tyson to the legendry boxing trainer Cus D'Amato, who had squired Floyd Patterson and Jose Torres during their respective rise within the boxing ranks, Tyson was saved from a life that would surely had ended in prison, if not an early, violent death. After Tyson's boxing ability led him to some early success, Don King decided to steal the young brawler from his managers, Bill Cayton and Jim Jacobs. Soon, the Tyson/King era began.

  When King informed Tyson of the potential criminal charges against him, Tyson paid little attention. King, a veteran of legal skirmishes himself (he had been imprisoned for manslaughter), knew the seriousness of the allegations especially since Tyson was in trouble not in New York City, or Los Angeles, or even Chicago, much more liberal settings for a trial, but in the conservative belt of American, Indianapolis, Indiana. Longtime relationships with members of the city's black community told King to watch out since Tyson would be judged in an 80-percent, ultra-conservative, Dan Quayle-type area where the Klan had deep roots. Unlike William Kennedy Smith, who would be tried in Palm Beach, Florida where Caucasians dominated the population, or Los Angeles, where there a good racial mix assured a fair shake for the officers accused of beating Rodney King,, or in Brooklyn where the African-

American population guaranteed a black young would be tried before a jury of his peers for killing a Jewish leader, Tyson was on unsafe ground in a city where African-Americans comprised only one-fifth of the population.

While King was confident the rape charges by Washington were just another attempt by a scorned woman to steal part of Tyson's multi-million dollar bounty, he still recognized that his client needed the very best criminal defense attorney money could buy since the stakes were high. A conviction meant prison and King's meal ticket couldn't earn millions fighting from a prison cell.

King's selection process covered the gamut. He considered African-American attorneys, but quickly dismissed this potential and moved down a list of the most well-known and most formidable lawyers available. One was Howard Weitzman, the L.A. lawyer known for representing carmaker John DeLorean and basketball great Magic Johnson. Others of note who could easily have represented Tyson were F. Lee Bailey, Gerry Spence, and Roy Black, the Miami attorney with a terrific reputation who had successfully defended William Kennedy Smith. He was studious, personable, and a very imaginative trial lawyer who knew how to play his case to a jury. Lawyers who knew him told reporters that Black was a master at cross-examination and highly skilled at dealing with sex crime – cases where the outcome often hinged on the cross-examination of the accuser.

While King apparently considered many attorneys to represent Tyson, his final selection was a shocker. Fiercely loyal to those who had befriended him, King contacted the offices of the prestigious law firm, Williams and Connolly in Washington, D. C. and asked to speak to sixty-one-year-old Vincent Fuller, a man of full face, medium height, graying hair, spectacles, and a slight paunch around the mid section. He enjoyed wearing expensive suits and shoes; his appearance reminded one of a politician, a professor, or perhaps a retired judge.

Don King had complete confidence in Fuller's ability since the expensive lawyer had freed King from the arm of the law when the IRS charged the controversial promoter with the wild hair and big smile with tax evasion in 1984. In a Philadelphia courtroom, King watched with admiration at Fuller's brilliance. Without King having to testify, Fuller had won a swift acquittal on all charges. What was good enough for King, the promoter reasoned, would be good enough for Tyson. But this decision, arguably more than any other King made, would turn out to be disaster since while Fuller was a competent attorney, he had never experienced what defense lawyers call the "down and dirty" arena of the legal field, one where the nastiness of allegations of such crimes as rape prevail. These cases do not occur in the federal courts, but in the rough and tumble county courts where procedure and even the law are less important than a "seat of the pants" style of lawyering that is more personalized according to the conditions existing within each venue. County courts are where the action is, with hundreds, even thousands, of cases clogging the system. Judges are overworked and underpaid and their chief duty has to be to move the cases along as quickly as possible. To do so, there normally exists a "good old boy" network, attorneys well known to a specific court who appear most every day. Each knows the bailiffs and other personnel on a first name basis and each is especially savvy to the way the court works to expedite the cases. These attorneys know the judges, oftentimes drinking or eating with them after work hours. They are especially knowledgeable of the judge's views and feelings about different types of cases, how they may rule on evidentiary matters, and especially their sentencing proclivities, whether they are tough or soft on certain type of crimes. Due to this familiarity, judges play favorites with certain attorneys, perhaps giving a break to this one or that based on past experiences. All this occurs with an eye toward re-election since most judges fear ever returning to private practice once they have enjoyed the benefits of being a judge - the power, the steady money, the prestige.

    Most citizens, everyone a prospective juror, are also aware of these attorneys, since they are the ones most often mentioned in the local newspapers and on television. Normally there are a dozen or so of these "connected" attorneys, ones who are known to handle the tough cases. Each has established a reputation for not being afraid to go to trial if necessary resulting in more plea bargains than those who are known to shun the courtroom either out of fear or because they do not want to spend the considerable time preparing for trial. Judges, prosecutors, bailiffs, even probation officers, know who the select few are and many times, even direct someone in trouble to them since they know these attorneys will provide the finest representation possible.

    Nowhere was this atmosphere more prevalent than in Marion County's City/County

Building where six criminal courts handled the felony charges. Among the elite group of seasoned and professional defense attorneys were Owen Mullin, Rick Kammen, Robert Hammerle, Arnold Baratz, Denny Zahn, and James Voyles. Some were terrific tacticians, some gifted orators, and others clever, imaginative lawyers who used more hunches than law books to persuade a judge or jury their client was not guilty.

The six judges who manned the criminal courts were as different as the type of clothes they wore under their black robes. When the distinguished Judge John Tranberg retired, Judge Gifford became the most sought after one due to her reputation for being fair even to defense lawyers despite her prosecutorial background. She was bright, knowledgeable of the law, and courteous to those appearing before her. All a defense lawyer may promise his client is a fair shake, and Judge Gifford provided such a chance whether the charge was murder or a narcotics violation.

Among the lawyer community that spent their days in the criminal courts, Judge Gifford was known as a no-nonsense judge who understood how defense lawyers worked their cases. She realized a chief strategy was to stall as long as possible before even approaching any outcome. This not only permitted attorney's time to receive payment for their services (known as the "Rule in Shelley's case"), but also to hope that the delay would permit the ultimate goal, dismissal or a plea to a lower offense so no trial, before a judge or jury, was required. Any crafty lawyer, and there were many familiar to the Marion County criminal court judges, realized during a delay, triggered by several "Motion to Continue" filings based on any number of reasons, some legitimate, some not, witnesses disappeared or died, victims changed their minds about testifying, and some moved away. The memories of witnesses could also be affected, but most important, a case that appeared to be unbelievably important when it was filed didn't seem quite as important after a few months time had passed since more cases had been filed in the interim. This was especially true if the case had ended up in the media causing a fuss with a general public demanding immediate action. Time usually cooled this demand, resulting in likely plea bargains or the best result for the defense lawyer, dismissal of the charges altogether.

    These practicing in the criminal courts during the 1990s, and the municipal courts where the lesser crimes were resolved, were normally not the fancy, three-piece suit type wearing wing tips and carrying a leather briefcase. Instead, the band of brothers held a few files in their hands stuffed with court papers since many tried two and three cases in the municipal courts before heading for various hearings or trials in the criminal courts. A daily schedule might work like this: an early visit to the county jail to see clients, old and new, a hearing on a drunken driving case and an assault and battery before a "muni" judge followed by a hearing on the validity of a search warrant, a court trial involving possession and distribution of heroin, and a sentencing hearing based on a plea bargain where a robbery charge had been reduced to assault with a deadly weapon. Once the courtroom cases were over, the lawyer might head to a card or dice game where fellow defense lawyers, prosecutors, a judge or two, and even a homicide detective might appear. This type of camaraderie might surprise the general public, but inside the courtroom, the lawyers and judges were pure professionals; outside friendships grew and lasted without any talk about the cases currently pending in the courts.

From trial experience, these lawyers who worked the criminal courts on a regular basis also had the advantage of being able to "read" a jury based on knowledge of the community mix. Since any jury trial is simply the throw of the dice based on the unpredictability of those deciding the fate of a certain person accused of a crime, knowing who was who and from where made a real difference. Sometimes jury experts would assist trial attorneys with such things, but for the most part the lawyers in the Marion County criminal courts simply used their gut hunches to decide who would make a good juror. And who would not.

The king of the criminal courts for a vast number of years had been the silver-headed barrister, Owen Mullin. He was the best of the best at controlling his cases and arguably one of the finest trial lawyers who ever lived. He was especially imaginative and innovative in dealing with county court juries, swaying them with his melodic voice and ability to search for and locate that one piece of evidence, large or small, that would influence the jury verdict his way. He was also a master of manipulation, one whose cross-examinations were classic. Mullin believed jurors paid as much attention to whether they liked the defense lawyer as they did the accused, and he thus always referred to his client and him as "we," never as "I" this or that. This way he personalized his client; made him or her seem real, not just a clay statute of some sort charged with a horrendous crime. Oftentimes, the wily defense lawyer would place his hands on the shoulders of his clients so jurors knew he wasn't afraid of them.

Mullin made it a point to learn the names of each juror and when final argument occurred, he repeated each one to let them know how important he thought they were. He also knew it only took one not-guilty vote to save his client and he thus focused on that one juror he felt could take his side of the argument. Mullin was truly an actor on stage, one who captivated the courtroom with his rhetoric. He could make a mass murderer seem like the friendly guy or gal next door.

One trait Mullin shared with the other elite Marion County Criminal Court lawyers was his crusade to force the jury to focus on anything *but* the evidence. Certainly the idea in a criminal case is to search for the truth, but Mullin was a genius at attempting to persuade jurors that *he* knew the truth and nothing else made any difference. He also knew that jurors needed one piece of evidence to hang their verdict on since when they left the courtroom since family, friends, and fellow workers would ask them why they decided the case one way or another. Throughout the trial, Mullin searched relentlessly for that piece of evidence.

If Don King had done his homework and understood the machinations of the Marion County Criminal Courts, and especially Criminal Court #4 where Judge Gifford presided, he would have chosen a local attorney with experience before her as Tyson's chief defense attorney. But King apparently felt that his famous client needed a rather famous attorney, and he thus chose Fuller, a competent lawyer but one whose experience defending tax evasion charges in Federal Court surely did not quality him to try a rape case in a county court. In fact, Fuller had no experience at all with sex crimes cases, none whatsoever. The fact that he accepted the rape case at all bordered on malpractice; and was the first mistake of many that would follow by King and his collective band of Tyson enablers.

No matter, the outsider, the white-collar crime, silk stocking attorney from the nation's capital did accept the case with a reported $500 per hour fee. Flanked by partner Kathleen Beggs and associate Lane Heard, neither of whom had experience with sex crimes cases in county courts, Fuller marched into the case like Patton ready to take on the Germans. When the case was over, the total cost for Tyson approached a million dollars.

To his credit, Fuller employed the services of James Voyles as local counsel, but Voyles, well-versed in the law, well-known in the community, and well-liked among his peers including Judge Gifford, was strictly backup, and he knew it. When prosecutor Modisett learned of King's choice of Fuller, and a background check told them of his inexperience, shock waves permeated the sixth floor offices in the City/County Building. What a gift this was since instead of a formidable local attorney heading the defense, the big shot defense lawyer from the world of white collar crime would be calling the shots.

Meanwhile, assistant prosecutor David Dreyer readied his case for the Special Grand Jury. At most, he believed there was a 50-50 chance he could secure an indictment. Charged with convincing five of the six jurors there was enough evidence to charge Tyson, Dreyer prepared his case carefully, based on the testimony of Washington and of Virginia Foster, the black driver of the limousine that transported Tyson and Washington from the Omni Hotel in downtown Indianapolis to the Canterbury Hotel where Tyson was staying and where the alleged rape occurred. Medical testimony and other corroboration for Washington's story would be presented as well, but Dreyer knew full well any chance at an indictment hinged on Washington's believability. If the grand jurors thought she was credible; Tyson would be charged; if not, he would escape being forced to defend himself against the serious allegations.

    Within three weeks of the grand jury convening to hear the case, Modisett, sitting in his office preparing to attack a busy court calendar, was shocked to learn that another gift was about to come his way. Even though Tyson was not required to testify before the jurors due to his constitutional right against self-incrimination, Fuller and company informed him that the boxer would do so. And this was to occur without any guarantee of immunity regarding statements Tyson made thus opening up the potential for the prosecution to use the statements if they conflicted with Tyson's later trial testimony. Modisett and Dreyer were nearly delirious with joy at the defense's willingness to parade Tyson, known for his awkward, often dismal appearances in courtroom proceedings or before the media, into the grand jury room. More important, Dreyer knew he could cross-examine Tyson, appearing without benefit of counsel, regarding any and all facts about the Washington encounter. This would provide the perfect opportunity to see first hand what type of witness he might be at trial if Fuller permitted him to testify in his own defense.

    When James Voyles learned of the decision, one he had no part in making, he was livid. Try as he would, the decision was not reversed even though Voyles recognized the risks involved. Fuller never spoke to the reasons why he allowed Tyson to testify, but he must have believed the boxer could sway the jury with his version of the Washington incident and knock out the State's case with one heavy blow. Unlike William Kennedy Smith, whom the savvy attorney Roy Black kept silent prior to his initial legal proceedings; Fuller had convinced Tyson that if he told the truth, his dealings in Indianapolis were over. But, predictably, it was not to be since on August 18, 1991, Michael Tyson testified before the grand jury in an event orchestrated by Fuller to gain the most publicity possible. One day later, the grand jurors voted to indict Tyson on one count of rape, two counts of criminal deviate conduct, and one count of confinement. If convicted, the ex-heavyweight champion of the world faced sixty-four years in prison.

Chapter Two
Trials and Tribulations

Even though the Clarence Thomas Supreme Court confirmation hearing and the William Kennedy Smith rape trial were held well before the Mike Tyson trial, both cases may have had a profound effect on the eventual outcome of the ex-champ's rape trial.

Most people had never heard of either Judge Thomas or Anita Faye Hill, each African-American, prior to the Senate hearings, but Hill's strong accusations of sexual misconduct and the equally strong denials by Thomas triggered headlines around the world during the week of October 6, 1991. The Judiciary hearings were held in front of an "all-white jury" composed of United States Senators in Washington D.C. and the two combatants squared off in an action-packed Senate chamber before a mesmerized international television audience trying to decide who was telling the truth.

At issue was the question of the overall fitness of Judge Thomas to serve as an associate Supreme Court justice. But the allegations of sexual harassment by the attractive, quiet University of Oklahoma law professor dominated the scene when she accused Thomas of inappropriate, uninvited, and un-welcomed sex-related conversations with her while both were employed at first, the U.S. Department of Education, and then the U.S. Equal Employment Opportunity Commission. Thomas was Hill's supervisor, and she alleged that "He spoke about acts that he had seen in pornographic films such matters as women having sex with animals and films showing group sex or rape scenes." She also alleged that one "several occasions Thomas told me graphically of his own sexual prowess."

While there was no actual judge or jury to decide Judge Thomas's guilt or innocence, in the end the senators expressed their opinions as to the validity of the charges through both their questions of the two witnesses, and by their subsequent votes either for confirmation of Judge Thomas to the court or denial thereof. The ludicrous nature of such a proceeding was apparent as the group of Caucasians attempted to sort out the truth between two diametrically opposed stories, one of which had to be false.

When the Senate panel finally reached their decision, Judge Thomas was the winner and Anita Hill was left to wonder whether she had received a fair shot from the Senators. Regardless, the "not-guilty" verdict paved the way for Thomas to be confirmed by the full Senate by a vote of 52-48. Hill left Washington confused and befuddled with the result, but her courage in standing up and being counted was admired, especially by women who had experienced sexual harassment in the workplace.

Just two months later, on December 3, 1991, a jury was convened in West Palm Beach, Florida to decide the guilt or innocence of William Kennedy Smith, the son of Jean Kennedy Smith and the nephew of John, Robert, and Edward Kennedy. Before Dade County Circuit Court Judge Mary Lupo, the thirty-one-year-old Smith answered charges that he raped Patty Bowman, a Palm Beach resident, at the Kennedy estate during the early morning hours of March 30th. Each agreed

Kennedy-Smith had left a bar the night before and escorted Bowman and another woman to the estate. Bowman said Kennedy-Smith raped her on the beach; he alleged the sex was consensual. Three women who alleged that Kennedy-Smith had sexually assaulted them during the 1980s were not permitted to testify. The trial was televised, but Ms. Bowman's identity was kept secret until after the trial.

  The two lawyers facing off in the muggy courtroom were well-matched. Roy Black had earned his stripes in many criminal cases and tough-minded prosecutor Moira Lasch was thought to be his equal. From the outset, the two advocates locked horns time and time again as both sought to gain the upper hand prior to the trial, one involving very few minorities. During the eight-day trial, momentum shifted back and forth, especially during Bowman's emotional testimony describing Smith's alleged rape of her on the sand in front of the Kennedy estate. When Kennedy Smith countered with his version of what occurred, viewers were dumbfounded with the two versions of the incident. In the end, whether because of lack of evidence by the prosecution, a poor performance by Lasch, or because of Black's superb defense strategy, jurors swiftly acquitted Kennedy Smith of all charges on December 11, 1992. Deliberations required just seventy-seven minutes causing consternation among court observers who believed that the privileged Kennedy had been acquitted due to family heritage. Like Anita Hill, Bowman's testimony was discounted making it two celebrity, high-profile cases where the woman accuser's testimony was apparently discounted.

On January 27, 1992, just forty-seven days after the Kennedy Smith verdict, the Tyson trial began. But two months later, another trial of high interest commenced near Los Angeles in Simi Valley, California. This was the culmination of an investigation into an incident occurring during the early months of 1991 when millions of television viewers were shocked to see an 82-second videotape. Filmed by amateur photographer George Holiday, the tape showed a black motorist, Rodney King, being repeatedly beaten about the body with fists and nightsticks by several members of the Los Angeles Police Department. Public outcries over the beating emanated from the White House and fellow law enforcement officers as well as civil rights leaders who deplored the police actions.

With convictions of the four police officers (Stacey Koon, Laurence Powell, Timothy Wind, and Theodore Briseno) charged practically a foregone conclusion, the trial began in Simi Valley on March 5th. Before Judge Stanley M. Weisberg, African-American prosecutor Terry White faced four Caucasian defense attorneys who argued to the six-men, six-women jury (ten whites, a Latina and an Asian-American) that their respective clients were justified using the force necessary to take the delirious King into custody. After twenty-nine days of trial, the world was astonished when the officers were acquitted of all charges, and set free. Public reaction was quick and forceful, with deadly riots occurring not only on the streets of Los Angeles, but also in Minneapolis, Chicago and other major U.S. cities. Federal civil rights charges were filed again the policemen within days of the verdict, but these actions could not quell the deep distrust for the legal system in the African-American community. Later, two of the officers (Koon and Powell) would be convicted in federal court while the other two were exonerated of all charges.

    Far across the country, in the Bensonhurst section of Brooklyn, N. Y., another highly explosive case awaited trial before Jewish Judge Edward Rappaport. Rioting following the tragic death from an auto accident of seven-year-old Gavin Cato by an Hasidic Jew led to the brutal, cold-blooded murder on August 11, 1991 of Yankel Rosenbaum in the streets of Crown Heights. Even though bloody money and a bloody knife had been discovered on the person of seventeen-year-old Lemrick Nelson, Jr., and he had allegedly confessed after being positively identified by Rosenbaum prior to his death, Nelson's conviction was not assured. Differing versions of what had occurred by the policemen assigned to the case in effect put the police on trial even though the evidence against Lemrick, Jr. was substantial. In late October, 1992, African-American defense attorney Arthur Lewis convinced the largely black jury that his client should be acquitted. Jurors said later they did not believe the police account of the brutal killing. Nelson's acquittal sparked outrage in the Jewish community, where more than 700 angry Hasidic Jews poured into Crown Hill streets protesting the shocking verdict.

    Three juries and a Senate panel had decided the fate of a Kennedy family member, a Supreme Court nominee and his accuser, four policemen charged with brutality, and a young man alleged to have killed for racial reasons. These cases surrounded the trial of Mike Tyson and in each instance, the jury or Senate Panel "acquitted" those charged with wrongdoing. How much influence, if any, these "verdicts" would have on the eventual outcome of the Tyson trial remained to be seen as media around the world captured every dramatic moment.

Chapter Three
The Game is On

Now that Mike Tyson had been indicted by the grand jury, Prosecutor Jeffrey Modisett and Tyson defense lawyer Vincent Fuller faced difficult decisions. But Modisett would prove the more worthy of the two since he was aware of how he could steer the rape case to a judge he knew would be more inclined to agree with his point of view regarding all aspects of the case. Her name was Patricia Gifford.

Modisett's decision to convene a Special Grand jury instead of permitting the Tyson case to move through regular channels towards the usual grand jury procedure was pure genius. Few realized his intention, but he knew full well what the end result of his actions would be. This was because Modisett was aware that felony charges in Marion County proceeded in three ways. First, ones arriving in the criminal courts through municipal court "bindovers" without the need for an indictment were distributed among the judges on a rotating basis, fifty at a time. If the felony charge required an indictment, it was heard before the regular grand jury session. When the indictment was returned, the case was assigned to the presiding judge for that term as one of the fifty cases.

The third way, the only way to guarantee a certain judge would handle the case, was to convene the Special Grand Jury to be presided over by a selected judge. When Modisett selected Judge Gifford, the former prosecutor, to oversee this grand jury, he stacked the deck in his favor for when Tyson was indicted, Gifford stayed with the case since not only was she the presiding judge for the special grand jury but as fate would have it, she was also overseeing the batch of cases being filed based on indictments that term. Modisett thus had guaranteed her selection; he had also guaranteed that a female judge would preside over the rape allegations, ones brought by a female. Without any way to challenge the Special Grand Jury process, the defense had lost the first round of this heavyweight bout without a fight. Fuller might have been a big shot, but Modisett had outfoxed him. Later, defense counsel would argue on appeal that the prosecutor had gone "judge-shopping," and while not directly accusing Judge Gifford of bias toward the prosecution, allege that she was not randomly selected as prescribed by law. But this argument fell on deaf ears since Modisett had lucked out since Gifford was the presiding judge over *any* indictments during the term.

  The defense concern with Judge Gifford presiding over Tyson's case was well-founded since while she enjoyed a reputation for fairness and impartiality, and was certainly ethical, her pro-prosecution leanings were obvious. One only had to check her background to understand why she was a most controversial choice to handle the rape case.

  The fifty-four-year-old Gifford was born in Indianapolis, the daughter of an Army colonel. She graduated from high school in Athens, Georgia, and then attended the College of William and Mary. Once graduated, she taught school in Indianapolis before moving to West Germany where she was a teacher at Army Dependent Schools. Apparently unsatisfied with teaching, Gifford then opted for law school at the Indiana University School of Law in Indianapolis, continuing the line of lawyers in the family that included her grandfather and an uncle. Upon graduation, she spent several years in the county prosecutor's office where was a specialist in rape cases. Her first courtroom skirmish was against famed attorney F. Lee Bailey, whom she soundly defeated.

Passionate about rape cases, Gifford was given credit for initiating legislation culminating in the passage of a strict rape shield law protecting alleged rape victims from disclosure of their sexual history. Before passage, the accuser was fair game and defense lawyers could dive back in history to reveal sexual proclivities affecting the moral compass of the alleged victim. The ability to do so kept many from reporting crimes while the new act recognized that the accused, and not the accuser, was on trial. This protection encouraged alleged victims of rape to come forward and not fear disclosure of humiliating and embarrassing incidents regarding prior sexual conduct. Questions about such matters were prohibited so the jury would not be prejudiced against the alleged victim due to allegations of poor moral conduct. Many defense attorneys believed the law went too far, since prosecutors were able to present a woman in the kindest light preventing juries from knowledge of past deeds directly relating to the current charges. Gifford, from her perch as a prosecutor of sex crimes, obviously felt differently.

After her days spent as a prosecutor, Judge Gifford campaigned for judge as a Republican in 1978. Mother of one college-age daughter, she and her husband, an aspiring actor, for the most part kept a low profile after her election to the bench although the judge was not one to be shy when speaking about issues like the rape shield law she believed in.

Known as a judge who exercised strict control over her courtroom, the tough demeanor hid a soft-spoken, friendly woman who truly believed in the rights of the underdog. Despite her graying hair, and sometimes icy demeanor, Gifford could be jovial and even funny at times when attempting to put a witness at ease or assist an attorney appearing in her court for the first time.

When asked after the Tyson trial why she wanted to become a judge, Gifford told *Indianapolis Monthly Magazine*, "I think I have the ability to weight both sides and make a determination. I have compassion for people, and I can weigh those things that affect them. I also can have the compassion for the victims and yet not let it influence me beyond what the law says should be done." Gifford's sentencing record prior to the Tyson case indicated that she had been extremely tough with convicted rapists when excessive violence or weapons were used. But in situations where no weapon was involved, the judge's average of seven-year prison sentences was in fact below the twelve-year average for the criminal courts.

No one knows whether Judge Gifford considered not accepting the Tyson case due to her background, but it probably never entered her mind. Here was the high-profile case every judge dreams about, and to give her the credit she deserved, the judge believed she could be fair to both sides. When she accepted the case, the judge leaned on the experience gained by Judge Mary Lupo, her counterpart in the William Kennedy Smith case. Known as a strict disciplinarian, the forty-three-year-old Lupo had earned a reputation as a stern judge, who, like Gifford, exercised complete control over her courtroom. To an outsider, Lupo sometimes gave the appearance of being unsure of herself on the bench, but those who practiced in her courtroom knew that she was a no-nonsense judge. Unlike Gifford, who was felt to favor the prosecution, Judge Lupo had a reputation for a more balanced view of trial proceedings. This was also true regarding the judges handling the Rodney King case (Weisberg), and the Bensonhurst murder trial (Rappaport).

      Whether Vincent Fuller and the defense team realized the potential bias on the part of Judge Gifford at this point in the proceedings was unclear, but they must have been aware that in Marion County there was an absolute right to one change of judge *regardless* of the reason for requesting this to occur. Why they did not promptly act to disqualify Judge Gifford was unknown, another question of many that would appear during the trial and beyond. Since the ability of a judge to give both sides a fair shake is of paramount importance, one has to wonder whether the defense was negligent in requesting that she be recused. Certainly they recognized the importance of decisions Gifford would make, including all pre-trial motions as well as those during trial. If the defense did its homework, and was aware of Judge Gifford's track record regarding rape cases, it should have demanded its right to a change of judge and moved on. Perhaps Voyle's felt Gifford could be fair, but if he did, he was playing with the odds based on her prosecutorial background and passion for rape victims. Why take any chance on her being biased when there were other judges, each of them male, who were more likely to give Tyson the fair shot he deserved.

Regarding pre-trial motions, Fuller and company knew how important they could be. Many times, what was decided before trial was more crucial to the end result than what happened during trial. In the William Kennedy Smith case, for instance, one of the main pretrial matters to be decided involved whether alleged instances of sexual assault or attempted rape by Kennedy-Smith was to be admitted at trial. Admissibility of an alleged confession by Lemrick Nelson, Jr. in the Bensonhurst murder case was a pre-trial issue for Judge Rappaport, and in the Rodney King case, the judge was required to rule on whether allegations of assault or battery by the police officers charged with beating King could be introduced at trial. To indicate how these rulings affect the eventual outcome, Kennedy-Smith's past history of sexual attacks was not permitted at trial with most observers believing this led directly to his acquittal.

During the Tyson proceedings, court observers watched closely Judge Gifford's rulings to see if a pattern was clear as to whether she favored the prosecution or the defense. In the final analysis, it appeared that while she provided the defense with small victories, she was much more kind toward the prosecution regarding major rulings. Modisett must have been smiling while he watched this occur since he had been the reason behind Gifford becoming the presiding judge in the first place.

Knowledgeable that a pro-prosecution judge was onboard, Modisett turned his attention to the Tyson trial and the strategy required to gain a victory for the prosecution and send Iron Mike to the penitentiary. By presenting Washington's story as corroborated by physical evidence, medical documents, and testimony from certain witnesses knowledgeable of the case, the prosecutor narrowed his attack. Fuller and the defense would certainly counter with focusing on Washington's demeanor and her motives behind charging Tyson with rape. Whether Tyson would ever take the stand to provide his side of the story was unclear.

Surveying his chances for convicting Tyson, Modisett now focused on who from the prosecutor's team might make the best foe for Fuller and his Washington D. C. partners. Despite Fuller's lack of experience with sex crimes trials, Modisett knew the seasoned barrister was a worthy trial lawyer and required an adversary who was not to be intimidated with the big law firm name and the unlimited budget at Fuller's disposal. Discussions were once again held with members of the prosecution's political advisory group about the various selections available.

Modisett faced a similar dilemma as the one encountered by Florida State's Attorney David Bludworth in the William Kennedy Smith case. Prosecuting a celebrity represented by a top-flight lawyer (Roy Black), Bludworth needed a chief prosecutor who could fight for Patty Bowman while keeping pace with Black. He purposely chose an experienced sex crimes female attorney, forty-year-old Moira Lasch, a career prosecutor who headed up the felony division of the Palm Beach Prosecutor's Office. She had gained a reputation as its number one trial lawyer. Like Modisett, Bludworth was forced to deal with political realities and thus needed to appear ready to take on the Kennedy family name while not being perceived as overzealous in the prosecution of the famous nephew. Los Angeles District Attorney Ira Reiner, another with higher political aspirations, decided to trust the prosecution of the four police officers to Terry White, a veteran member of the prosecutor's office. Whether his being African-American played a part in the selection, only Reiner knew.

As Bludworth had done before, and Reiner after, the Tyson trial, Modisett immediately disqualified himself to be chief prosecutor, based both on his lack of experience as a trial lawyer and his advisor's belief that the Tyson case was a very delicate political matter. The most obvious "in-house" choices to carry the prosecution torch were Dreyer, the chief deputy, Mark Jones, a skillful trial staff lawyer, and Carol Orbison, a sex crimes prosecution expert with a very impressive conviction rate. Ironically, if Judge Gifford had still been a prosecutor, she would have been the logical choice to handle the Tyson case due to her experience. In fact, she would have been the perfect choice.

As the time for a decision neared, Modisett suddenly had another idea, another way to go. Greg Garrison, a former deputy prosecutor, had become as "special, for hire" prosecutor, and had gained excellent reviews across Indiana mainly for his ability to successfully prosecute big-time drug dealers. Although he was impressed with Garrison's resume and his potential ability to convict Tyson, Modisett knew the selection of the forty-four-old would be a controversial one. Some members of Modisett's staff resented the pistol-packing (he often carried a gun), gruff, arrogant attorney who had a reputation as being loud-mouthed, bombastic, abrasive, and a true cowboy-boot-wearing, slicked back red haired gunslinger. Some staff wondered why an outsider had to be brought in to handle the Tyson case in the first place. Wasn't that demeaning to capable lawyers who would relish the thought of prosecuting Tyson?

When the ambitious Garrison first heard from Modisett, he was thrilled with the chance to hit the big-time. The $20,000 fee received was certainly not grand enough to entice him. But the chance to dance on a bigger stage, to stare down the ex-heavyweight boxing champion of the world, was a temptation too difficult to resist. Was he the wrong man for the job? Certainly he knew how to prosecute, but Modisett was going to spend twenty grand of the taxpayer's money to handle the high profile case. If he won, alright, then the decision had been a good one. But if Garrison lost, opponents would question Modisett's judgment. Regardless, when the announcement was made, the prosecutor said he had too many administrative duties to handle the case himself, and worried that staff members would be consumed with the case restricting their ability to handle an already imposing caseload. A hired gun was the answer, and Garrison was Paladin to the rescue.

To assist Garrison, and keep an eye on him, Modisett chose Barbara Trathen, a serious-minded deputy to be co-counsel. Modisett would still call the shots, but Garrison and Trathen would be his foot soldiers.

Disappointed, but not devastated by the grand jury setback when the charges against Tyson became a reality, Vincent Fuller began to formulate his trial strategy, one he was certain would result in a not-guilty verdict for his famous client.

To be successful, and Fuller was to the point of being overconfident, he proposed a four-point plan designed to free Tyson from the burdens of the Indiana criminal court system. The key points were 1) show that his client had a reputation as a womanizer who used filthy language and sexual innuendoes to alert his intended prey to his intentions; 2) prove that based on Tyson's words and actions, Desiree Washington clearly knew what he boxer intended when she agreed to visit his Canterbury Hotel room; 3) persuade the jury that Washington was willing to have consensual sex with Tyson because she hoped for a long-term relationship; and 4) demonstrate that Washington filed rape charges because he treated her like a one-night stand, and was only after his money. In order to play out this strategy, Fuller made it clear to James Voyles once again that he, Fuller, was in charge, and that Voyles was set to play a minor role involving little significant work prior to, or at, trial. Voyles agreed, but his partner, Denny Zahn, a superb trial lawyer and as well-respected as Voyles, refused to become involved in the case for this reason.

Fuller's decision to basically "go it alone" made little sense since retaining local counsel was a true advantage for an attorney unfamiliar with the landscape where the trial was being held. No one knew anything about Fuller, and even his stately appearance was more of an east coast look than Midwestern. His outward appearance fit a "professor" image, but a high-priced one since Fuller enjoyed wearing $600 conservative suits. He appeared scholarly, ready to teach, to educate, perhaps on the subject of international politics. Sporting granny glasses, a square jaw, and swept black hair that was graying by the moment, Fuller's appearance contrasted severely with his rugged, tough-looking client's.

Voyles, on the other hand, was plump to the point of being jolly, gregarious, fun-loving, and simply a good fellow whom colleagues and judges admired. To basically carry the water for Fuller was a put-down to his expertise, but Fuller either didn't realize this or didn't care.

Fuller had decided to be in charge of any and all major decisions and to be chief trial counsel because there was no other way for him to become involved in a case. He wanted the responsibility because he believed he was the best attorney in the land with credentials to prove it. Fuller's firm, Williams and Connolly, was the former home of famed attorney Edward Bennett Williams, who was not only know as a supcrb trial lawyer in the ilk of Melvin Belli, Percy Foreman, F. Lee Bailey, Richard "Racehorse" Haynes, and Gerry Spence, but one of the principal owners of the Washington Redskins National Football League franchise. Located on Twelfth Street in heart of Washington, D.C., Williams was the calling card that had spearheaded the firm building its reputation for being experts in federal court practice, and with federal departments and agencies. Fuller's name was right at the top of the firm stationary since he was known as the law firm patriarch. Born in Ossining, New York, June 21, 1931, he was admitted to the District of Columbia bar and U.S. Court of Appeals for the District of Columbia in 1956. He was also licensed to practice law in New York in 1962.

Fuller had received a Bachelor of Arts degree from Williams College in 1952, and a law degree from Georgetown Law School four years later. His resume included memberships in the District of Columbia Bar, the New York State Bar, the American Bar Association, the American Board of Criminal Lawyers, and the American College of Trial Lawyers.

To his colleagues and firm members, Fuller had the reputation of being practical, highly businesslike, and quite the organized trial lawyer. Most of his clients had been upper-income, white collar businessmen, but he had also carved out a different sort of reputation through his well-conceived insanity defense of John Hinkley, charged with shooting President Ronald Reagan. Constituents believed no one was better at implementing a trial strategy than Fuller. A relentless advocate known for his booming voice, he could was a master at cross-examination using a forceful presence and quick witted strategy designed to elicit the answers required for the outcome sought. Unlike Roy Black, Fuller had virtually no experience in the county court system, and as noted, none defending a client for a sex crime. But Fuller had shined during the Hinkley case, and while he was representing Don King during his tax evasion trial.

Aiding Fuller's effort from the home front at Williams and Connolly was forty-one-year-old Lane Heard, born in Houston, Texas but a *summa cum laude* graduate from Yale with a Bachelor of Arts. He then received his law degree from Yale in 1978. A tall, thin, unassuming African-American, Heard's quiet manner belied a reputation for being a master trial inquisitor. His colleague, thirty-five year-old Kathleen Biggs, a rather matronly sort, was armed with a Bachelors Degree from Wellsley College and a Harvard Law Degree. Whether she knew it or not, Beggs, who seemed quite out of place at the trial, was apparently Fuller's answer to the prosecution having Barb Trathen on its team.

Rounding out the Tyson defense was Voyles, whose teddy-bear appearance belied a fierce competitor highly loyal to his clients. He was not afraid to try a case in front of a jury, but was better known for his ability as a "fixer," one who tried to plea bargain cases whenever possible. But there was no doubt Voyles was well-respected and the attorney whom most high-profile clients scampered to when they were in trouble.

Now the stage was set, Garrison and Trathen in one corner, Fuller, Hoard, Beggs and Voyles in the other with Judge Gifford as the referee in a high stakes showdown that would decide whether Mike Tyson continued to be a free man or was destined to live behind bars during the prime of his life. Would the boxer escape the wrath of the criminal justice system or was a championship athlete's career about to be destroyed?

Chapter Four
Pretrial Positioning

To many courtroom observers, the pretrial positioning in the Mike Tyson may have been more eventful than the trial itself. Especially during a final pre-trial hearing where Greg Garrison and Vincent Fuller squared off triggering their first real confrontation.

At issue were six motions, including Fuller's request to exclude certain FBI evidence, his motion to dismiss based on selection error regarding the various jury panels, a request that Judge Gifford reconsider her decision to permit testimony from Dr. Eugene Kilpatrck, a rape trauma expert who had knowledge of Tyson's behavior following Desiree Washington's 911 call shortly after the rape allegedly occurred, Fuller's motion to add eleven new witnesses to the defense list, and a motion to continue the trial.

The most interesting of the motions centered on Fuller's allegation that the make-up of the jury pools for both the special and regular grand jury was tainted. Co-counsel Kathleen Beggs pointed out, using voter registration rolls, that of the 179 people called as potential jurors, 160 were Caucasian while only 19 were African-American. Of the 101 finally assembled after certain disqualifications, 90 were Caucasian.

Fuller spent much of the hearing haggling with Garrison over Dr. Kilpatrick's testimony. Fuller insisted the state had erred in not including the doctor in a necessary filing. Garrison countered that the prosecutor's office did not know about the 911 call until it was disclosed by Washington during a deposition. Then it had filed a motion requesting that Dr. Kilpatrick be permitted to testify as to the alleged victim's state of mind during the call. Fuller objected, stating that rules were rules and the doctor must be excluded from the witness list. After both sides had their say, and the prosecution mentioned that Fuller and company were "paranoid" about their being a conspiracy between the local police, the FBI, and the prosecutor's office to "get" Tyson, Judge Gifford scored one for the defense when denied the state's motion to call Dr. Kilpatrick as a witness.

During the hearing, it was apparent that Fuller and Garrison were attempting to size up each other. Fuller watched Garrison's demeanor closely while keeping in mind his well-known hair-trigger temper. Garrison, in turn, glared at Fuller trying to decide whether his adversary was the skilled trial lawyer he was touted to be. What they learned was kept private, but clear was the contrast between the mild-mannered Fuller, who spoke with a Federal Court type of resolute respect and calm, and Garrison, more the "down and dirty" attorney used to the county court way to do business. What style would be more effective at trial remained to be seen.

Prior to the first day of trial, Judge Gifford provided findings on several important issues. First, Tyson's off-the-cuff statement at a press conference, "I should have killed the bitch," was excluded at the request of the defense. Second, a petition by the defense to exclude a garment worn by Washington during the alleged rape was denied. Third, a defense request to exclude any reference to Tyson's criminal history was granted. Fourth, the state's motion to exclude Washington's past sexual history was granted, and five, the state's motion to exclude reference to Washington seeking counseling due to violent behavior of her father toward her mother was granted. This motion had referred to an incident where Washington's father Donald had been arrested for assaulting his wife, charges later dismissed.

Judge Gifford's granting of the motion to exclude Tyson's "I should have killed the bitch" statement was a true victory for the defense. It had been recorded during the local CBS affiliate's coverage of a press conference and could have been quite damaging if jurors were able to see and hear it. To Judge Gifford's credit, she shed her prosecutorial skin and excluded the statement citing its irrelevance to the rape allegations.

With the pre-trial matters having been decided with some winning and losing on each side, the day approached when Mike Tyson would risk his freedom in front of a jury of twelve peers of the community. The horde of media represented readied their cameras and notebooks for action as the attorney's turned their attention toward the important matter of jury selection.

Chapter Five
Twelve Jurors

As noted, the trial of the self-styled "Baddest Man on the Face of the Planet" drew media attention from around the world. Tyson was truly an international celebrity, controversial, colorful, flamboyant, and unpredictable. The media loved him and recorded his every move at the Delaware/Market Street intersection where the City/County Building was located. Police barriers were necessary at the Market Street entrance to keep spectators at bay when Tyson and his entourage arrived for court each morning. Fans lined up hours in advance to secure a much-coveted autograph from the ex-champion.

Media credential requests had been extensive with reporters and correspondents appearing from the smallest of outlets. Those permitted a courtroom seat were charged $55 to offset court costs. Tyson was the story of the day and commentators on each of the networks predicted his fate based on what they called "inside" information from reliable sources, never named. Signs for and against Tyson were held high outside and plain folks suddenly became experts as to whether the boxer would be acquitted or found guilty of the rape charges.

In anticipation of the trial, both the prosecution and the defense had carefully scripted game plans for what type of jury they wanted to sit in judgment of Tyson. In formulating these plans, the respective counsel kept in mind age-old doctrines regarding jury selection that have been true since the beginning of the trial process itself.

The prosecution knew that to convict Tyson, they needed to carry their burden of proof, a term relating to the Latin *"semper necessitas probandi incumbit ei qui agit,* ("the necessity of proof always lies with the person who lays charges") by convincing all twelve jurors since verdicts had to be by unanimous vote. This standard was the true underpinning of judicial systems where the presumption of innocence prevailed.

The standard for conviction in a felony case was "beyond a reasonable doubt," a term not easily definable regardless of the legal definitions used in courtrooms on a daily basis. Defense lawyers wanted jurors to believe that reasonable doubt meant removing "all doubt," but this was inaccurate since few things in life were ever proved beyond all doubt. Prosecutors hoped jurors would simply use common sense and decide that reasonable doubt meant being "reasonable" so that a decision could be reached in their favor when the juror believed his or her assessment was reasonable based on the evidence presented.

During the William Kennedy Smith case, Roy Black told jurors reasonable doubt was "an abiding faith . . . something you hold tightly," while prosecutor Moira Lasch described finding "guilt beyond a reasonable doubt as never wavering or vacillating" from what one believed to be the truth. Judge Gifford would offer her own definition at the conclusion of the evidence and before the jury retired to deliberate the case.

Regarding jury selection itself, in a rape case, the prosecution will normally lean toward very conservative, take charge, male jurors who will stand up for law and order and vote their conscience no matter what sympathy they may hold for the defendant. This may surprise some who believe female jurors would better relate to the alleged victim, but time has shown that many times female jurors are less inclined to believe a woman's story than a man. Regardless of the gender selection, the prosecution certainly desires people who can made decisions, ones who will not waffle back and forth with no end in sight.

Defense lawyers will predictably seek more women jurors in a rape case, and hone in on people in general with more liberal views about human conduct in general and the criminal justice system in particular. The defense will also attempt to choose jurors who may indeed be less inclined to make up their minds as it only takes one to differ with fellow jurors to render a verdict impossible. Hung juries, where the jury cannot make a decision, are not exactly a defense victory, but a tie is certainly better than a loss.

Since first impressions are critical to a juror's perception of the accused, and their lawyers since all are a team, the sharp, experienced defense lawyer will attempt to portray himself and his clients as underdogs falsely accused of a crime never committed. Prosecutors attempt another ploy by indicating their representation of "the people," whoever they may be. The latter also attempts to let the jury know they stand for law and order while the defense cares little about the safety of the citizenry and only hopes to "get their client off," a common misnomer applied to those acquitted of a crime.

Each counsel must concern themselves with their look and demeanor, what they wear, how they sit, their mannerisms, their tone of voice, and their relationship to the judge. Jurors see the judge as the impartial truth-seeker and oftentimes will make decisions about the guilt or innocence of the accused based on what they perceive the judge's feelings are about the case. This may be discerned not so much by what the judge says, but how they treat the respective counsels, either with respect or disdain. The worst thing counsel may do is to provide the judge with a reason to dislike them or their methods so as to trigger the feeling among the jurors that the judge favors one side ahead of the other.

A trial begins when the defense and prosecution attorneys question prospective jurors. With their respective strategies in mind (in the Tyson case: prosecution – lack of consent/forced rape; defense – consent, no rape), the attorneys pose hypothetical questions to the jurors intended to establish thoughts in their minds triggering a certain response once the trial evidence is presented. As noted, many attorneys have turned to jury specialists to aid in the selection process. For a clever glimpse at how this might work in the absurd, watch *Runaway Jury*, based on the John Grisham book of the same name. These jury experts compile extensive data regarding each potential juror, and then, through research and systems analysis, provide essential information to the attorney gauging how a certain juror might vote based on a specific set of facts and circumstances. In the William Kennedy Smith case, jury consultants Cathy Bennett and Robert Hirschhorn utilized questionnaires they had developed specifically for that trial. Roy Black contended that the defense had to overcome two large obstacles, pretrial publicity and the strong negative sentiment about the Kennedy family.

To expose any biases of the respective jurors, Black used open-ended questions to elicit strong inner feelings each juror might not want to reveal. Black also did not take notes during the questioning, and instead concentrated on the answers given and on his personal feelings about whether he sensed that a particular juror would be an ally or enemy of Kennedy Smith. "If you're open and honest with them," Black said, "and show them that you are human, they'll start to like you. But if come out there with a big ego, and act overbearing and supercilious, they'll cut your legs out from under you."

In the Rodney King state case, prosecutor Terry White said after the trial that he did not get one juror he wanted for the case that ended up with the acquittal of the four officers charged with beating King. He added, "The six-man, six-woman panel would have been a perfect jury in a criminal case with a civilian defendant, but could not have been worse for a case in which law enforcement officers were charged." In the King case, the judge had granted a change-of-venue motion and the trial was moved from Los Angeles, with its variety of ethnic groups, to Simi Valley, where the population was nearly entirely Caucasian. White said he had his staff had rated the 264-member prospective jury panel from one to five, with one being best, and that they had only 27 "one's" or "two's," on the list due to the strong pro-law enforcement attitude in the region. White reported that there were only half a dozen blacks on the panel, and that, because of the order in which the names were called, just two were really considered for selection by the prosecution. White believed that the final makeup of the jury was so hostile toward the prosecution that there was little chance of a conviction. Amazingly enough, several of the jurors finally selected were either relatives of police officers, had worked in law enforcement themselves, or were security guards.

In the Bensonhurst murder trial of Lemrick Nelson, Jr., the trial location was in the predominantly African-American and Hispanic neighborhood. The final jury featured six blacks and four Hispanics, providing Nelson with truly a jury of his peers, but one that was more prone to acquittal of a fellow minority than if the trial had been conducted in another, less favorable, venue.

Vincent Fuller and his defense team, despite what they considered to her unfavorable media attention to Tyson's case, had little choice regarding any possibility for a change of venue. All of the surrounding counties to Marion had dominant conservative, Caucasian populations where racial prejudice was well known. The defense had to hope that the pre-trial publicity would not harm them and that selection of several minority juries would be possible.

The selection process itself is filled with potholes, with the major one being the fear of both the prosecution and the defense that certain people *want* to be on the jury and know how to avoid saying anything that will disqualify them. In essence, the attorneys worry more about what people *don't say* than what they do say since one may have a motive or agenda unknown to either the defense or the prosecution. Each side has unlimited challenges it may make for what is called "cause," an answer from a juror that clearly indicates a bias or prejudice causing them to unqualified to serve fairly and impartially in the court's opinion. A number of "preemptory" challenges are also permitted allowing each side to strike from the jury anyone they want without having to provide a reason.

In anticipation of trial, more than one-hundred jurors in and around Indianapolis had been notified by mail to report to the City/County Building. Among the questions included with the notice were: "Have you been a member of the National Organization for Women or other groups interested in women's issues? Have you ever had any involvement with boxing? Do you consider yourself to be more of a "thinking person" or a "feeling person?" Potential jurors were also asked whether they, family members or friends had been victims of domestic violence, involved in a lawsuit, arrested or convicted of a criminal offense, involved with law enforcement, or if they had studied psychiatry, sociology, or related subjects. One of the more unusual questions was: "What three people, living or dead, do you admire most?"

Additional questions included whether prospective jurors had read or heard about the William Kennedy Smith rape trial and about the rape allegations against Tyson. They were told to respond if they or any family member knew anyone from a list of ninety-five potential witnesses or others associated with the case. And they were queried as to their impressions of lawyers, knowledge of the Indiana Black Expo and the Miss Black American Pageant, their source of news, and their participation in any school or professional sports.

By January 27, 1992, all pre-trials matters had been concluded and Judge Gifford announced "State of Indiana vs. Michael G. Tyson, case #49G049109CF116245" to a packed courtroom. Jury selection began to choose twelve citizens that would decided whether "Iron Mike" was guilty or innocent of the crimes of rape, criminal sexual deviate conduct, and confinement. When Greg Garrison read the indictment to the prospective jurors and words and phrases such as "oral sex," and "use of a finger to stimulate sexual excitement," he made it clear to spectators and jurors alike that the evidence to be heard would be very sensitive to the point of potential embarrassment for those involved in the alleged rape. While the indictment was read, it appeared most jurors did not glance at Tyson, or if they did so, it was out of curiosity more than anything. Had this boxer, this huge hulk of a man, been falsely accused or was he truly the beast the prosecutors alleged him to be?

Meanwhile, Tyson appeared to be in a daze, his face stern as he gazed at Garrison. One had to wonder whether if permitted to do so, he would have ripped into the prosecutor attempting to take his freedom and his career away with body and face blows that would cause Garrison to bleed and suffer. Certainly, this thought must have crossed Tyson's mind.

The contrast regarding respective strategies for the prosecution and defense was apparent when one considered the questions asked to the prospective jurors by Garrison and Vincent Fuller. Examples of those proposed by Garrison focused on the elements of the crimes of rape, sexual deviate conduct, and confinement, the right of both the accused and the accuser to a fair trial, that when someone said "no," it meant "no," that a defendant in Indiana could be convicted on simply the testimony of one witness, and that a woman was in charge of her own body. Garrison also referenced his view that bad judgment should not be held against a person who was raped, that celebrities should abide by the same rules as regular folk, and the outcome of the William Kennedy Smith case had no relevance to the Tyson trial. Coming through loud and clear was Garrison's directive that "no" did mean "no," and despite perhaps bad judgment on the part of Washington, she had said "no" to Tyson and this meant he was forced to stop his sexual advances. Garrison was driving home the thrust of his defense, that when the ex-champ ignored Washington's plea to stop, and in turn confined her to the hotel room bed, committed sexual deviate conduct, and forced her to have sex, he broke the law. Game, set, and match, so Garrison believed with a verdict of guilty the only prerogative.

Vincent Fuller countered with his own theories as promoted through questions focusing on the fact that reasonable doubt was based on reason, and involved decisions a person would make of only the highest concern to everyone, that consent was an absolute defense to rape, and that consent could either be expressed or implied. He asked questions that implied expressed consent could be verbal consent, that implied consent meant giving the impression of consent by actions or by the facts and circumstances surrounding the alleged actions, from silence or not objecting to the conduct prescribed. He added that an eighteen-year-old should be judged as an adult, a reference to Washington's age, that African-Americans relate to each other differently about sex that do Caucasians, that a boxer should not be judged more violent than other simply because he was a fighter, and that media hype was just that, and not to be judged as evidence. Fuller closed with questions relating to celebrities not necessarily being role models, and thus judged by a higher standard, that people make false accusations just as much as they make true ones, that the accused was not required to present any evidence in his or her own behalf, and finally, a curious note, that those who "go where they shouldn't go get what they deserve," a reference to Fuller's intention to show that Washington deserved the treatment she received since she knew about Tyson's reputation and regardless, decided to accompany him to his hotel room in the middle of the night. This defense strategy was indeed a risky one, as the ensuing trial would indicate to all who witnessed it.

Celebrity names such as Don King, Magic Johnson, Pete Rose, and Tyson's former wife, actress Robin Givens, floated about during the questioning. Rose was mentioned concerning whether he had been singled out for prosecution during a gambling probe, Johnson when one juror mentioned him as a personal hero but agreed that the former basketball star "got what he deserved when he contracted AIDS." Givens must have been disappointed when she heard that jurors had no idea who she was when asked about her relationship with Tyson.

The backdrop of the William Kennedy Smith case was, according to the questioning, in some juror's minds. Judge Gifford asked about the trial during her preliminary questions, and most jurors admitted knowledge of the case. Several had followed it rather closely. All knew of the date-rape allegations. Some agreed with the not-guilty verdict; others did not. Whether Kennedy Smith's acquittal would cause jurors to be suspicious of Washington's allegations in lieu of a jury not believing Patty Bowman's charges wasn't clear. This might occur or perhaps jurors would compare what Bowman said with Washington's story and believe there was the necessary evidence present to convict Tyson. Fuller and company hoped for the former; Garrison and the prosecution for the latter.

Both sides knew the reaction to the charges against Tyson had split the African-American community. Several ministers had organized rallies in support of their fallen hero, while others condemned Tyson for his actions. Some reports circulated that African-Americans hoped they would not be chosen as jurors fearing backlash regardless of the outcome.

During jury selection, Tyson sat quietly, his muscular body overflowing the seat he occupied. He doodled on a yellow pad but appeared to pay little attention to much of the proceedings. He appeared lost and though he spoke with his attorneys from time to time regarding their selection choices, he appeared distant, and far removed from the proceedings surrounding him. This demeanor was not unfamiliar to those who knew Tyson, since it paralleled conduct during press conferences or weigh-ins when he appeared to be near asleep or "not with it."

Perception of Vincent Fuller during jury selection varied. Legal expert Jim Drucker believed Tyson's chief defense lawyer appeared to be a "kindly professor," one intending to educate the jury. Charlie Steiner of *ESPN* disagreed, noting that

Fuller's impersonal touch was placing a barrier between Fuller, Tyson and the jury. Earl Gustkey of the *Los Angeles Times* found Fuller's style, "very businesslike," but Joe Gelarden of the *Indianapolis Star* thought Fuller's methods indicated "a federal courtroom manner that might not work in the down and dirty atmosphere of a county criminal court."

Since Tyson's defense team had unlimited funds to utilize in his defense, it was a surprise that no jury selection experts joined the team. Without one to guide the strategy, the defense appeared disorganized, oftentimes appearing to "wing it" when choices had to be made. Prominent local defense attorney Rick Kammen said that Fuller and company had consulted with the same jury experts used in the Kennedy Smith case, but dismissed using them when the "defense did not like what information they received from the experts." The result was disastrous, with one deputy sheriff assigned to the court commenting that there were "too many cooks." He said he heard the attorneys in a "What do you think? Well, I don't know. What do you think?" type of exchange when it came time for final jury selection.

Jury selection continued for two and a half days with many questions with much of the questioning mundane in nature. But a few personal matters were touched upon, causing some embarrassment. One jurors was forced to admit the imminent bankruptcy, while another was reticent to admit that his wife had been raped by an African-American stranger prior to their marriage. Most said they would not be embarrassed to discuss the female genitals or talk about vulgar terms if necessary. One juror admitted that many of his co-workers would describe him as "hateful," and another that he had to attend counseling classes due to a court-related arrest.

Reservations the defense had about racial imbalance of the jury proved valid. Consistent with the fact that only twenty-two percent of the Marion County population was African-American, three of the twelve jurors were black (later one would be excused); making the final count ten Caucasians and two African-Americans that would deliberate the case. Male and female representation were eight men and four women. The jurors ages ranged from twenty-one to fifty-five but most were in their 20s and 30s. In the end, twelve regular jurors and three alternates were selected. Based on observations about each, it was easy to tag each as a "leader" (those prone to lead fellow jurors during the deliberations), "followers" (those who would easily be swayed by fellow jurors"), or "unknowns" (those difficult to predict).

The jurors selected included:

1) <u>Joanne</u> – White, female, about forty, married, small children at home. Her husband worked at Allison Transmission in Indianapolis and was a firefighter. She felt the media hype for the trial was to be "expected." A follower.

2) <u>Ken</u> – African-American, twenty-five, married. Worked as a behavioral specialist with handicapped students in the Indiana Public School system. Had seen Tyson fight and loved sports. Appeared very laid back, and was perhaps a bit too nonchalant about becoming a juror. Probably a follower.

3) Beth – Caucasian, thirty-one, single. Worked for the Indianapolis Chamber of Commerce. Believed that young people looked up to celebrities and thought celebrities wanted to set an example for them. Difficult to categorize.

4) Walt – Caucasian, early twenties, married. PizzaHut truck driver. Appeared to give all the right answers to questions as if he wanted to be a juror. A leader.

5) Steve – Caucasian, about thirty, married. Parts manager at a body shop. A big fan of Indiana University basketball. Read newspaper sports section first. Follower.

6) Neil – Caucasian, twenty-one, single. Lived with his parents in a southern Indianapolis suburb. A t-shirt designer at a local printing shop. Definitely a follower.

7) Nancy – Caucasian – thirty-one, single. Worked for a title company. Had few opinions about anything. Definitely a follower.

8) Rosie – African-American, thirty-nine, single. An underwriter with an insurance company. Worked at a Black Expo booth, one that coordinated the Miss Black America Beauty Contest. Somewhat shy and reserved. A leader.

9) Tim – Caucasian – thirty-seven, married. An IBM marketing manager. Served in non-

combat capacity in the Marines. Wife was a nurse in the cancer critical patient ward at Indiana University Hospital. Very conservative appearance. Definite leader and possible jury foreman.

10) <u>Dave</u> – Caucasian – fifty-five, married. A UPS truck driver working nights, driving back and forth to Ohio. Admitted he was facing imminent bankruptcy. Coached youth baseball. Seemed to have lived the hard life. Oldest member of the jury. Difficult to categorize.

11) <u>Chuck</u> – African-American, thirty-six, married. Unemployed but formally worked in some capacity at Ice, Miller Donadio, and Ryan law firm. Had been a juror in two cases involving murder and robbery charges. In both cases, the defendant was ruled not-guilty. Knew about Tyson's relationship with Robin Givens. Believed the wrong verdict was reached in the Pete Rose case. Difficult to categorize.

12) <u>Chuck</u> – Caucasian, about forty-five. A Vietnam veteran, worked for a medical equipment company. Had served on three juries in the 60s and 70s. Two resulted in not-guilty verdicts. Difficult to categorize.

Alternate - <u>Michael</u> – Caucasian – forty-four, single. Worked for Indiana Bell Telephone. Somewhat shy. Was a boxing fan but only until heavyweight champion Muhammad Ali left the ring. Follower.

Alternate - <u>Matt</u> – Caucasian, twenty-three, single. Worked a sales manager. Believed celebrities should definitely act as role models for youngsters. Follower.

Alternate - <u>Sandy</u> – Caucasian – fifty-two. A political conservative who worked as a customer representative. Leader.

By 11:00 a.m. on the 29th of January, twelve jurors had been sworn in to decide Mike Tyson's fate. Could he receive a fair trial from these twelve strangers?

Chapter Six
For Openers

Experienced trial lawyers believe that ninety percent of the trial is over after the attorneys have concluded their opening statements. This is true since experts have discovered that most of the jury members will make their decision based on the first impression of the evidence as noted in the lawyer's opening statement.

During opening statement, the respective counsels fully present their case. Judges warn jurors that such presentations are not evidence, and should be ignored, but the impact of the attorney's words still is a telling factor in many cases and may have a tremendous influence on the final outcome of the trial.

For the jury, hearing from the respective lawyers provides a better chance of sizing them up than is possible during jury selection. First impressions linger as jurors decide whether they will believe one attorney or the other when evidence is finally presented. The "trust factor" may be compared to that of a politician. Standing before a jury, the lawyer is essentially presenting a campaign speech, promising to prove this or that as the trial continues. Often, defense attorneys will not only tout the defense they wish to present but try to plug holes in the prosecution's case. Since the state has the burden of proof, their argument is first providing them with a leg up on impressing the jury with their point of view. When the defense follows, the attorney must overcome what the prosecutor had to say to at least a point where the jurors have conflicting feelings about the guilt or innocence of the accused. While an attorney is duty bound to stay within the facts of the case, as they are most favorable to him or her, usually an attorney will attempt to emphasize his or her point of view to an extent that stretches the truth as far as it will go. Bottom line is gathering votes for guilt or innocence with the judge as referee.

Since no evidence has been presented to substantiate any claims made by either counsel, the attorney's assertions become the roadmap for jurors to follow. Many recall what was asserted in opening statements and then compare the actual evidence documented to see whether the lawyers lived up to what they told the jurors they would prove. This is probably more substantive regarding the prosecutor's claims since the state has the burden of proof and the defense no duty to present any evidence if it so chooses. This includes the defendant's right not to testify.

Greg Garrison began his statement to the jury using the same folksy demeanor they had noticed during the voir dire. His manner was direct and positive as he paraded back and forth in a nicely pressed suit symbolic of his stature as a player on the international stage. Never before had he enjoyed such celebrity status, and it was clear that he enjoyed the limelight. But now it was time to prove his case, for in the future he would either be known as the man who "got" Mike Tyson, or the one who let him go free.

The prosecutor's office decision to hold their cards close to the table and not boast of their case in chief against Tyson, contrary to the strategy employed in the William Kennedy Smith case where the state's attorney publicly raved about the abundance of evidence to be presented against the alleged rapist, permitted Garrison to map out, piece by piece, what he would prove to the jury. With a slight twang to his voice, the red-haired hired gun began by stating, "[Desiree] Washington's life experience was shaped by her father" without elaborating as to how this occurred. She was, he stated, "a follower of boxing and a fan of Mike Tyson." Washington watched Tyson fight and noted him "use his fame and prominence to dispatch opponents." Garrison then outlined Washington's story while making the point that she was unprepared to handle schemes like the one Tyson involved her in, a reference to a diabolical plan to trick her into joining him in his hotel room. He ended his short speech by stating, "Over and over again, you'll believe this in your head and your heart." Overall, the opening statement was effective, if not predictable, but Garrison had been savvy in not promising too much, too soon, as some prosecutors were prone to do. Was he being coy, or did he really wonder if he had enough evidence to convict Iron Mike?

Vincent Fuller apparently felt he had to go much further than Garrison in attempting to persuade jurors his client was falsely accused. In a staccato baritone voice, one that had earned him the nickname, "Foghorn Fuller," he reminded the jury of the age-old canons involving presumption of innocence, reasonable doubt, and the State's burden of proof. Standing erect behind the podium and acting like a professor addressing his students during the first day of class, he said there was no question sex occurred between Tyson and Washington, but that it was consensual. He spoke of "implied consent" and how it applied to this case. He said, "expressed consent" is truly rare."

Attempting to overcome Garrison's remarks about Tyson being smart enough to plan a scheme to lure Washington to his hotel room, Fuller delved into both party's backgrounds pointing out that while Tyson had little education, Washington was mature beyond her years. He suggested that in fact Washington was the one who had pursued Tyson, and not the other way around. She was looking, Fuller said, for a "long-term relationship. She was after Tyson."

Before continuing with references to the sexual encounter, Fuller shocked veteran courtroom observers by point-blank stating that "He will tell you," and then "Tyson will tell you," an obvious promise that Tyson would testify. Now the veteran attorney had boxed himself in a corner with no need to do so since the jury would now expect Tyson to tell his version of the story and if he did not, perhaps wonder why not and hold it against him. Any first year law student knew this was a serious miscalculation, one that could come back to haunt Fuller if he and his co-counsels believed the state had not proven its case based on the testimony of its witnesses, including Washington. It was a rookie mistake and when Fuller practically guaranteed that Tyson would take the witness stand, Garrison looked as if he wanted to stand up and cheer. What a gift this was for the prosecution and no evidence had even been presented yet.

Describing the sexual encounter in vague terms, Fuller expounded on his theory that Washington became upset after the sex act when Tyson would not walk her downstairs to a waiting limousine. "It was devastating to Miss Washington," Fuller told the jury. "She left not raped, but disillusioned." The defense lawyer then told the jury that Tyson treated Washington like a "one-night stand," and that "the motive for the rape charge is money," another risky move by Fuller since it cast dispersions on Washington's character, something that might not play out in the juror's minds. But he pressed on with this theory, stating that witnesses would say that Washington talked about Tyson, saying, "He's got money; did you see what Robin Givens got out of him?" Would they?

Fuller pointed out that Washington had hired civil lawyers sitting in the courtroom ready to "follow this case. If Tyson is convicted, she can file a lawsuit that will make her a wealthy woman," Fuller said.

By the time Fuller sat down, he had dealt his cards clearly on the table, and the jury would expect him to show aces when the time came. Promises would need to be kept. Could Fuller keep them or had he promised too much without the evidence to back up his claims?

Based on the respective statements, the jury understood that one side was telling the truth and the other was not. If one believed Garrison, the victim was a naïve, goody-two-shoes kid, who was lured in by Tyson and raped. In Fuller's, the victim was a scorned lover who decided to get back at Tyson by charging him with rape in anticipation of realizing millions of dollars from the ex-champ through a civil lawsuit. Who was telling the truth?

As both attorneys had spoken, Iron Mike sat attentively in his chair looking once again like he was in another world. He barely glanced at Fuller, or even at Garrison, the man who wanted to ruin his life and send him to prison. One glaring impression was Fuller's decision to stand behind the podium and never once approach his client, thus never indicating any affection for him, or positioning himself in the "we" position where he and Tyson were bonded at the hip. Instead of witnessing a true defense team where client and attorney were one, the foghorn barrister, the outsider, left a cold-fish impression more appropriate for a tax evasion case than a rape trial. Would Fuller's tactics work for his client, or was Tyson doomed to lose the case and his freedom?

Chapter Seven
Desiree's Story

When the jury deciding Mike Tyson's fate finally began its deliberations, only one issue would really take center stage – either the twelve men and women believed Mike Tyson or they believed Desiree Washington regarding their respective accounts as to what occurred on a queen-sized bed in room 606 of the Canterbury Hotel on the night in question. Additional testimony would take up much of the eight days of trial, but all would be secondary to key testimony of Washington, and if Vincent Fuller kept his promise, Tyson. Their respective stories were to be weighed just as those of Patty Bowman vs. William Kennedy Smith, Anita Hill vs. Clarence Thomas, Rodney King vs. Los Angeles Police Department officers, and Lemrick Nelson, Jr. vs. the police officers who arrested him and said he confessed to killing Yankel Rosenbaum.

With this in mind, the stage was set for Desiree Washington to tell her story. Tyson's accuser had been portrayed by the prosecutors as a shy, naïve college student who insisted on keeping her identity secret to protect privacy. And use of the rape shield law Judge Gifford had championed would prevent defense lawyers from probing her sexual history to see if she was anything but the goody-two shoes girl they wanted to parade before the jury.

Before Washington testified, the state called Kycia Johnson, a twenty-year-old Miss Black America Pageant contestant from Oklahoma to the witness stand. In a soft voice, the attractive woman told the jurors she was Washington's roommate during the pageant. Johnson said she first saw Tyson at a rehearsal in the Omni Hotel where the pageant was being contested. Washington, Johnson told the jury, was one of four contestants participating in a promotional video with the ex-champ.

Johnson said she saw Tyson and singer Johnny Gill talking with Washington and Pasha Oliver, the third roommate, near one of the poles in the rehearsal hall room. Johnson also said she saw Washington take a piece of paper out of her purse and give it to Tyson. When she talked to her roommate later, Washington said, "I'm going out with [Tyson] tonight." Johnson then described an early-morning telephone call from Tyson to the girls' hotel room. Washington then left, Johnson said, but when she returned, she said, "He's such a creep, such a jerk; he tried to rape me." Johnson told the jury that after the incident, Washington was "quiet, more distant, and she was staring into space, thinking about something." Follow-up by defense lawyers on the Washington quote, "he tried to rape me," wasn't thorough, leaving the jury clueless as to the difference between her having said that and "he raped me."

The round clock on the wall in Criminal Court #4 indicated 1:45 when the twelve jurors and the band of hungry media had their first close look at the eighteen-year-old former Miss Black America Beauty Pageant contestant from Coventry, Rhode Island. In anticipation of her testimony, and continuing her portrayal of the victim of a brutal crime, Washington was dressed in a carefully selected conservative gray suit and white blouse. One had to wonder whether she had ever worn such an outfit before, but the defense never ask any questions to sort this out. Certainly the conservative look was a far cry from the swimsuit-clad Washington who had paraded a slim, yet full-figure body in front of judges at the Miss Black American Pageant. That seductive appearance was the one that had captivated Mike Tyson from the first moment he saw her.

Washington's long following black hair was parted to one side and her distinctive features, soft, beaming brown eyes, high cheekbones, and heavy lips were concealed a bit as she took the oath to tell the truth and was seated just to the left of Judge Gifford. She appeared outwardly calm as prosecutor Garrison began to lead her through the events of the week of July 12, 1991. Exhibiting a low-key, matter-of-fact manner, Washington told the jury she was currently a first-year student at Providence College in Rhode Island. She told the jury her days at Coventry High School earned her many honors, including being named social committee chairman and receiving the Outstanding Sophomore Award. During her senior year, Washington said she had been one of thirty-four high school students in the country selected for a Hugh O'Brien Scholarship to visit the Soviet Union for two weeks in 1990.

The slight Washington's voice was strong but still youthful as she informed the jury that she had begun to enter beauty pageants in 1989. She told them she won the local Coventry pageant that year, and in 1990, was named Miss Black Rhode Island. Washington explained that she entered beauty pageants because she was tired of "blonde, blue-eyed" women always being the winners. Testifying without even a single glance at Tyson, Washington must have impressed the jury by telling them about her work with the Big Sisters

Organization. It had begun when she met a foster child, who, she said, "touched my heart." She also told being a Sunday School teacher and a church usher. Responding carefully to Garrison's leading questions, Washington explained that her being Miss Black Rhode Island qualified her for the Miss Black American pageant. Upon arriving in Indianapolis on July 12th for the competition, she had visited the historic Madame Walker Theatre in downtown Indianapolis to meet with pageant officials. Washington told of the preliminary activities for the pageant, ones causing her to arise at 4:00 a.m. Rehearsals for the talent competition and for promotional videos were then followed by appearances at businesses sponsoring the event. Washington also met the two pageant contestants who would be her roommates, Kycia Johnson and Pasha Oliver.

      With a steady stream of softball questions, none objected to by Vincent Fuller in contrast to many defense attorneys who attempt to unsettle a witness, especially the state's key one, with at least some objection even if it is overruled, a quite useful tactic, Garrison began to carefully guide Washington toward the fateful first meeting with the ex-heavyweight champion of the world. Washington told the jury that on July 12th, the pageant contestants were just finishing rehearsals at the Omni Hotel when Tyson and singer Johnny Gill arrived at the rehearsal studio with Reverend Charles Williams, an organizer of the event. The excited contestants all began to flock around Tyson and Gill, but the director of the promotional video quickly ordered the girls to scamper back to the their dancing duties.

Washington said that after the rehearsal, Tyson walked among the girls and said to her, "You're a good Christian girl, aren't you?" At the urging of a pageant official who had Tyson sing a rap song for one of the promotional videos, Washington said Tyson hugged her, and asked her out for a date. She accepted as she looked closely at Iron Mike for the first time. After a photograph session with Tyson where Washington said he insisted several of the girls sit on his lap, the two talked again while Pasha Oliver stood nearby. Washington told the jury she asked Tyson whether Pasha could go out with Gill, causing there to be double date. Tyson agreed, Washington said, saying, "That's fine with me." At the Black Expo opening ceremonies that evening, the contestants were lined up outside the Indianapolis Hoosier Dome in two rows. Tyson arrived with the Reverend Jesse Jackson, and Washington told the jury she saw the two kneeling in prayer. Later, Washington said she showed Tyson two photographs of swimsuits she and Oliver had purchased earlier that day. They "showed us off as looking like twins," she added while explaining that Tyson was wearing a mustard colored shirt and a "Together in Christ" pin.

  During a private moment, Washington told the jury she said to Tyson, "Are we really going out?" Tyson confirmed the date. When the festivities were over, Washington headed for her hotel room where she changed into a new outfit, one given to her by a Rhode Island pageant official for "good luck." She said the outfit was a bit too big for her especially in the chest area.

  Washington testified that she then left the hotel room for the Johnny Gil concert since she "didn't feel he [Tyson] would call anyway." Once there, she said it was cold, and that her roommate Pasha did not feel well. After visiting backstage to see the rap singer, Yo Yo, she returned to the hotel room. At 11:00, or 11:30, Washington said she exercised a bit with some stretching, talked a bit on the telephone and with other contestants, and then went to bed. At about 1:00 a.m., Washington recalled Kycia Johnson arriving home, and that the three girls made small talk. At about 1:45, the telephone rang, and Kycia answered it. The caller was Dale Edwards, Tyson's bodyguard. Kycia handed the receiver to Washington and after hearing Tyson's voice, began to speak with him.

Washington told the jury, each mesmerized with her testimony, that Tyson said, "Can you come out? I just want to talk to you." Her reply: "It's late. My hair is in rollers. I'm dressed for bed." His reply: "Oh, c'mon. We'll go sightseeing." Then Pasha asked her to ask Tyson if Johnny Gil was there. He said "no." "Why don't you come up here?" Washington said she asked Tyson as her roommates told her they were not "fit to be seen."

Looking straight into the eyes of the jurors as the media copied every word she stated, her voice never wavering, Washington said, "I did not want to go out by myself" thus asking Tyson why "we couldn't go out tomorrow." But Tyson, she said, told her he had to leave later that day. Acquiescing to his demands, Washington said she finally agreed to meet the boxer in the hotel lobby. She told the jury she took her camera along so that she could take photographs while they were sightseeing. Dressing quickly, Washington said she wore the outfit she had worn to the Gil concert. She left on her pajama underpants.

Once in the lobby, Washington said she looked for the gold limousine at the front door, but it was not there. Then she saw it at the back door. When the driver opened the door for her, she said Tyson "hugged me, and kissed me on the mouth. It startled me . . . he had bad breath." Sitting not thirty feet from his accuser, Tyson laughed. Did the ex-champ have any idea how serious the rape charges against him were?

Once the limousine was rolling along, Washington said Tyson told her, "Oh, you're not like these city girls; you're a good Christian girl." Then she said Tyson explained that he "had to pick up something," and a few minutes later, the limousine pulled up in front of the Canterbury Hotel on North Capital Street, a short distance from the Omni Hotel. Without providing a detail, she testified accompanying Tyson inside to the lobby where he shook the hand of a young fan who said, "Ooh, there's Mike Tyson." Washington asked him about the fan, and said he told her, "he was sick of it . . . that people were a pain in the ass."

In answer to Garrison's question as to where the bodyguard was, Washington testified she never saw him either in the limousine or in the hotel lobby. But she was certain that Tyson escorted her to the elevator. Within a minute or two, the two stood before the door to room 606. Upon entering, Washington said Tyson walked immediately to the bedroom and turned on the television set. He placed a telephone call but she stayed in the living room before he said to "come in here . . . I want to talk to you." Despite telling Tyson she thought they were going to leave, she walked into the bedroom and sat on the right corner of the bed. He was sitting at the top of the bed, she said, beside the night stand where the telephone was stationed.

Conversation included, Washington said, Tyson asking "about my schooling in Rhode Island" and whether "I was on an athletic scholarship." She said she replied, "no." She told the jury of explaining to Tyson "I am a big sister," and he said, "he had been a big brother." Next he mentioned his having "200 pigeons," with her responding, "That's interesting. I love animals." "We talked for fifteen minutes," she testified. "He asked about "my home life, and was I daddy's little girl . . . spoiled?" He asked, she said, whether "my family liked him." She said, "They haven't met you yet." Tyson, she recalled, responded, "Parents don't like me."

As the minutes passed by in the bedroom, Washington testified Tyson asked her, "Do you like me?" She said she responded, "You seem O.K." She then told the jury Tyson's voice changed a bit, and he said, "You're turning me on." Her answer: "I'm not like that." Washington said she then told Tyson, "I want to use the bathroom; then we'll leave." Tyson's response, "OK."

Leaving her purse on the bed, Washington said she urinated in the bathroom and then discovered there was some discharge on her panty shield indicating that her menstrual period was about to begin. The beauty contestant said she took the liner off and threw it away. "I had a pad in my purse," she stated, "but I figured I could put I on later." After washing her hands, Washington said she walked out of the bathroom only to find Tyson sitting on the side of the bed wearing nothing but his underwear. After a pause to gain her thoughts, she told the jury, "I was terrified." She said she told Tyson, "It's time for me to leave." His response,

"C'mon here." She said he grabbed her arm, and holding her close, put "his tongue in my mouth." "It was disgusting," she said.

Washington testified that Tyson pulled back a bit while saying, "Don't fight me." She told the jury she "began to hit him, but it was like hitting a brick wall." She said Tyson pinned her down, placing his forearm on her chest. He removed her jacket, and the "bra" of the outfit slid down easily, she testified. He then, she said, pulled down the "jams," the lower part of the outfit. Her panties were the last to come off, she explained.

"Get off me," Washington said she told him, "please stop," while continuing to punch him as he said, "Don't fight me." "Relax," she said Tyson told her before "he put two fingers into my vagina . . . I felt a lot of pain, and tears came to my eyes. It was excruciating pain." "You're hurting me," she said she yelled, but he "laughed like it was a game . . . he licked me, and then he jammed himself into me."

Washington testified she pleaded again for him to stop, saying "I don't want to have a baby; I have a future." His response, "Don't fight me mommy." She said he "was mean, evil. I got on top and started to get away, but he slammed me down again . . . he went on until he was done, and then pulled out, and ejaculated on the bedspread." "I told you I wouldn't come," she said he told her. "Don't you love me now?" Her response: "You disgust me," she said she responded, before he rolled off of her. She got up "fast," she told the jury and dressed, "fast." She testified he told her, "you can stay if you want" Her reply, "What, so you can do this to me again?" His response: "You're a baby; a crybaby."

Washington, never losing her composure, then told the jury she asked him, "Is the limousine still here?" She said he telephoned downstairs and then told her it was. "Out the door I went carrying my shoes," she said before she was a "dark skinned man" in front of 604 with a smirk on his face. Outside the hotel, she found the limousine. The driver, she testified, said, "You seem nice and I'll give you a ride." She said she was crying at the time. Back at the Omni Hotel, Washington said she entered her room and told her roommate, "He tried to rape me." She said she took a shower because she wanted to "feel clean." Then she said she went to bed but in the morning she told the jury "it hurt to walk. I was so sore I could not even put on a tampon." But she decided to go ahead with the competition because, she said, "I am not a quitter. I wouldn't be here right now if I were a quitter." Later in the afternoon, she said she told Pasha Oliver, "He raped me."

Washington testified that later in the day, she spoke with her mother. She was staying at the airport Days Inn. When she explained that she had been raped, her mother told her she would call 911 immediately. Her mother, Washington said, reached the county 911 instead of the city 911, and due to the hotel's location it was necessary to call the city 911. Washington did so, making the report. She was then taken, she said, to Indiana University Hospital. There, she told the jury, she saw "the victim assistance nurse before the attending physician, Dr. Stephen Richardson, examined me." She admitted to the jurors that she had had only one pelvic examination before, and "pulled away when he began his vaginal examination." She said her "legs were shaking," and that the doctor told her she should have an AIDS test when she arrived home.

Regarding her competition performance, she told the jury she "performed badly, yet I still received a top-10 finish." In a soft voice, she explained, "I still have problems with what happened to me . . . I slept with my mom after the incident. She still talks to me until I fall asleep, even while I'm at college."

All told, Washington's version of the rape lasted less than an hour. Garrison said, "No more questions," and sat down apparently quite pleased with his chief witness and with himself. To all who heard Washington's testimony, her story appeared to be quite plausible. If believed, Tyson could end up in prison for more than sixty years.

Chapter Eight
Attacking Desiree

In any rape case, and especially those where there is no eyewitness, usually the case, it is essential to the prosecution that its chief witness be highly credible. Most times, conviction or acquittal will rest on whether the jury believes the victim, or whether something about the testimony permits the reasonable doubt necessary to trigger a not-guilty verdict.

Certainly anyone has sympathy for a woman raped for it is a worse crime than even murder since many rape victims never shed the horror of the experience, of having their body and soul violated. Preparing a rape victim to testify is tricky since while the prosecution wants the woman to tell the truth in her own words, there remains the chance that once the witness takes the stand, the pressure of the moment along with the embarrassment of having been violated, whether the violation constitutes rape or not, will cause inconsistencies to appear permitting the defense to poke holes in the testimony a mile long.

No one realized this more than prosecutor Greg Garrison. He and his colleagues believed Washington's story but decided a "dress rehearsal" of sorts would be beneficial so she could be more comfortable once the defense began to question her at trial. To act as the prosecutor during a "mock examination" of Washington, Garrison chose the savvy local attorney, Robert Hammerle. His appearance in the case was rooted in the representation of another key witness, Virginia Foster, the limousine driver who had taken Tyson and Washington from the Omni Hotel to the Canterbury Hotel on the night of the alleged attack.

The forty-five-year-old Hammerle had been a criminal defense lawyer for seventeen years. His wife Monica, also an attorney, handled death-penalty, post conviction matters for convicted murderers. Hammerle was known a bright, somewhat unorthodox lawyer with a quite successful track record in the county courts. He had gained the reputation of being an innovative, seat-of-the-pants defense lawyer, one who could be counted upon to offer the best possible defense to his client. It was this reputation that brought Hammerle a new client during the winter months of 1991. One day while sitting in his office working on a fresh case, he had answered the telephone to hear the voice of Foster, the owner of a brand new limousine service in Indianapolis. She told Hammerle that in July of 1991, she had received a telephone call from Indiana Black Expo officials requesting that her limousine service provide transportation Tyson during his Indianapolis stay. She explained to Hammerle that she did not accept the job, but was in fact the limousine driver the very night when Washington's alleged rape occurred.

Foster had called Hammerle since every Indianapolis media outlet was badgering her as she had become a material witness in the case. Her decision to call Hammerle was prompted by a television station report that depicted her as "being less than a reputable person." The news story charged that Foster had had her chauffeur's license revoked, and had been intoxicated when she drove Tyson around town. Foster also told Hammerle there were reports that she had been "paid off" by the defense, and that she was going to leave the city and disappear. Once the defense lawyer heard her story, he took the offensive and called Bob Campbell, the news director of local television station WTHR to complain on his client's behalf. Campbell told Hammerle that much of the problem stemmed from Foster's refusal to speak with reporters. Hammerle told Campbell he would help with communication from that point on.

Having been retained by Foster, Hammerle called the prosecutor's office to inform them that, yes, Foster would testify at trial. He also said later, "Foster told me the same story that she would testify to at trial, including the fact that Tyson had tried to physically attack her and expose himself during the time they spent together in July." Within days of Hammerle's representation of Foster, he encountered Garrison on the streets of downtown Indianapolis. Hammerle said, "Garrison asked whether I would be interested in participating in a mock cross-examination of Desiree Washington." Expounding on the offer, Garrison told Hammerle, "We're going to bring her in, and we'd like for you to participate." Soon after he agreed to do so, Hammerle said, "Sometime in December, they [the prosecutors] delivered to me a copy of Desiree's first statement to police for my review. I didn't have much time to review it the night before I was to examine her, but my impression was that there must be much more . . must be an amplification of it . . . later in the grand jury . . . I thought this might be only part of the puzzle . . . there was much more I would like to have known."

Hammerle was not paid for his assistance, but he handled the matter with the upmost professionalism. He said he did not want to meet with Washington prior to the examination since "I wanted to bring her in unprepared . . . give her a feel for what she would experience at trial . . . I wanted to take her through a rigorous cross-examination." The parties gathered for the questioning in Superior Court #5's courtroom on the fifth floor of the City/County Building. Attending were Hammerle, Garrison, Barb Trathen, Washington, her personal attorney David Hennessey, detective Thomas Kuzmik, and three other police investigators. "Prosecutor Modisett arrived later," Hammerle said, "almost as a courtesy call."

Hammerle explained that "no notes were taken, and the session was not taped. I believe this was done intentionally. Garrison sat at one table, and I sat at another along with Barb Trathen so that she could give me any information that I might need for my examination." He added, "Garrison began by taking Washington through a preliminary direct examination. My initial impression of her was that, although she was soft-spoken, the most striking thing about her . . . was that I was overwhelmed with, was her composure. She had a real lack of emotion, and a tremendous amount of composure." Several times during the examination, Hammerle related, "we stopped and Garrison or Trathen or Hennessey told her, 'Here's what you are doing,' or 'I don't want you to do that, or say that,' or 'don't move your eyes that way,' in order that Washington would learn how to testify at trial." Hammerle's assessment: "I questioned her for several hours, and didn't pull any punches. Sometimes she would look at Garrison and say, 'Do I have to answer that,' but I would interrupt her and tell her I was the one asking the questions and that she had to answer. I asked her about her financial interest in the case . . . hiring lawyers . . . one who is the courtroom today, but Dave [Hennessey] wouldn't let her answer. I wanted to get into the reason she had hired counsel . . . but I wasn't allowed to

. . . and so I dropped it. Dave claimed the attorney-client privilege. My overall impression, the most overwhelming thing . . . was that she did battle with me. I had heard that there was this eighteen-year-old, naïve lady, but I came away with the feeling that, while it [rape] could have happened, I was dealing with someone much strong who had a backbone and when it stiffened . . . wouldn't let me run over her. I couldn't figure out how all this fit with the naïve mistakes she was supposed to have made."

Hammerle recalled that he had completed the mock cross-examination by summarizing all the improbables he saw in the case. "I began by saying to her . . . 'Look, you met Mike Tyson, and you saw him all these passes at girls . . . and then you gave him a picture of you in a bathing suit, and you still didn't think he had sex on his mind?' She said, 'no,' and then said, 'He called you in the middle of the night, and you went down to the limousine, and when you got in he kissed you, and it still never crossed your mind that he had sex on his mind?' Again, Hammerle said, she answered, 'no.'" Undeterred, Hammerle continued, "Then you went to the hotel, and you went to his room, and you sat on his bed, and it never crossed your mind that he wanted to have sex with you?' She said, 'no.' And then you got up and went into the bathroom and removed the panty shield . . . and on and on. I kept asking her and she kept saying 'no.' and it didn't make sense . . but that was her story, and she stuck to it."

After the examination, Hammerle met his wife Monica for dinner. "I told her that I honestly didn't think they could get a rape conviction. I told her that this [rape] could have happened . . . she told an effective story, impressive, but that composure of hers tells me she is very good at dealing with emotions. If she was the acting the next day after the rape supposedly occurred, then as defense counsel I would say [to the jury], 'how in the world doe we know she isn't acting in the courtroom?" Hammerle then added, "After I told Monica the information about the panty shield, I remember my wife told me that story is one no woman is ever going to believe. She felt that that woman who goes into a hotel room . . . up to the room . . . is in the safe haven area of the bedroom, and then goes to the bathroom and removes the panty shield . . . well, there isn't a woman who doesn't associated with that . . . that the woman is expecting sex. And I agreed with that."

The next day, Hammerle saw Garrison. "I ran into Greg in the elevator in the City/County Building. I waited until everyone was off and then said to Greg, "You, my friend, are in a world of shit." He just looked at me and went down the hall." Whether Garrison agreed with Hammerle's assessment, he felt that the defense lawyer's rigorous examination had served its purpose, and had readied their client for the duel she would have with Vincent Fuller. Based on his performance, one had to wonder whether the outcome of the trial would have differed if Robert Hammerle had represented Tyson.

Vincent Fuller had paid close attention when Washington testified, making notes on a legal pad that stretched several pages. But what did he really think the impact of the testimony had been? Was it effective to the extent that it had mortally wounded his client, or were there just surface wounds that might not have impressed the jury. Did she appear truthful, or did the testimony seemed contrived to the point of leaving the jury with a poor impression? Evaluating what effect Washington's story had would dictate whether the defense lawyer vigorously cross-examined her or simply threw her a few stiff punches and let her go.

Anyone who has ever witnessed effective cross-examination, such a perhaps encountered in such films as *Anatomy of a Murder* or ineffective examination as portrayed in the film *The Verdict* when the James Mason character commits the worse sin a defense lawyer can make by asking a question he does not already know the answer to, knows the demeanor of the defense attorney often dictates the impression left with the jury more than the questions themselves. Sex crimes are tricky, since it is one thing to ask probing questions aimed at the truth, and ask them forcefully but with respect, and quite another to badger the witness providing sympathy for the alleged victim. There is thus a thin line between the two strategies and this is the challenge Fuller faced when the confrontation with Tyson's accuser began. Certainly the best cross-examination involves developing a strategy so that, slowly and methodically, momentum is built, question after question, sometimes with repetition, until key errors in the witness's testimony are clear to the jurors. Focusing on certain key points is essential, for the jury must be able to recall significant concerns about the testimony that simply do not make common sense causing them to discount the testimony entirely.

In a sex crimes case, the strategy employed by the defense is quite delicate since sensitive matters are being discussed to the extent that embarrassment for the victim is apparent. The defense lawyer must remember above all that the witness believes what they are saying whether it is true or not, since they have professed a certain story and most times will stick with it regardless of the inconsistencies apparent. In many cases, it becomes a matter of pride, a game of sorts, where no matter what the defense lawyer throws at the witness, he or she will not back down. The witness, especially the chief accuser in a rape case, wants to leave the witness stand a winner having shown all that she is telling the truth as to every fact presented.

In the William Kennedy Smith case, defense lawyer Roy Black was especially effective with a relentless, but carefully crafted cross-examination. After Patty Bowman, the accuser, had testified, he analyzed its effectiveness, and listed several points he knew he had to counter with one purpose in mind; expose the reasonable doubt required for acquittal. He focused on Bowman's removal of her stockings, and whether a rape would take place under the very windows where Kennedy-Smith's mother was sleeping. Black then strongly confronted Bowman with questions about these important issues, while at the same time avoiding any possibility of upsetting the witness to the point of breaking down. At the Clarence Thomas/Anita Hill hearings, Senator Arlen Spector, a former federal prosecutor, questioned Hill in a very strong, confrontational manner. This appeared to offend not only her, but many who observed the hearings as well. Spector felt that Hill was being untruthful, but his risky decision to handle the witness as he did elicited sympathy for Hill even among her strongest critics. In fact, Spector's unnecessarily rude manner almost cost him his Senate seat in the next election.

While Bowman's demeanor, (edgy, confrontational), and Hill's (very professional, aloof), differed from Desiree Washington's (calm, controlled), Vincent Fuller needed to tread the fine line between, in effect, calling her a liar, and showing the jury that she was simply telling only *part of the truth* based on their having been consensual sex. He thus could choose to focus only on this issue, spend time on her knowledge that Tyson's "bad-boy" reputation should made her aware of his intentions to have sex with her, delve into the area regarding how Tyson's sexual innuendos made it perfectly clear that he wanted her, visit the question of her dubious behavior in agreeing to leave her hotel room and go with Tyson in the middle of the night, or inspect the idea that Washington was simply "money-hungry" and was accusing Tyson of rape in anticipation of her lawyers filing a multi-million dollar civil lawsuit against him? Or would he simply blow her story wide open, as Hammerle or another top notch defense attorney might have done, by showing the ludicrous nature of accompanying Tyson to his hotel room, sitting on his bed, and then removing the panty shield?

Vincent Fuller's march toward unwinding Washington's story began not with a pointed question intended to catch the alleged victim off guard, as is the tactic of many defense lawyers, but with softball questions permitting her to feel at ease with him. One question that might have been used would have been, "You mean to tell the jury you went to Tyson's hotel room, and then to his bed, and never thought he had sex on his mind?" Such a question, in all likelihood, answered with a "no," would have caused Washington to realize the cross-examination was going to be rough and tough, with Fuller challenging her story at every turn. Only by doing so did he have a chance to ruffle the calm demeanor she had exhibited during direct examination. Even if Garrison objected, and any objections were sustained, both he and Washington would have been put on notice that she was about to taken to task for accusing Tyson of rape.

Instead, Fuller began with easy questions that dealt with her background, focusing on her high school years and achievements. Then he hit her modeling career, with Washington telling the court how in sixteen weeks of training, she learned how to "walk, work with hair and makeup, and to improve my public speaking." Follow-up was weak, with Fuller never delving into Washington, in effect, becoming an actress of sorts, a fact important to the Tyson defense since the jury might feel an actress could fake her testimony to sway them. Fuller's questions did expose that Washington had worked with a date-rape law at her Rhode Island high school. She and some other students had formulated a model legislative bill for a school project, and forwarded it to the State Legislature. "We never heard back, so the idea died there," she said. Would Fuller point to this unusual fact during final argument, that Washington was thoroughly knowledgeable of date rape laws? How many eighteen-year-old girls could say that?

Turning to the Miss Black America Pageant, Fuller elicited Washington's answers regarding the time when the rehearsals were occurring. She said a pageant official encouraged Tyson to "Just play with them a little," apparently meaning that Tyson was to engage in some fun with the girls. Shortly after this occurred, Washington said "All at once, he was staring straight at me, and then he asked me for a date." Did Tyson say, "I want you?" Fuller asked. Washington: "No." Pursuing the point further, the defense lawyer asked whether she had said, "That's rather bold of you," after he said, "I want you?" Washington told Fuller, "That's not what happened."

Washington explained to Fuller and the jury that when she saw Tyson with Reverend Jesse Jackson at the pageant's opening ceremonies, she thought Tyson was a "good person." Did she hear Tyson utter a vulgarity, as heard by another contestant, when Jackson asked Tyson to join him? Washington: "No." Fuller then asked about the photographs Washington showed to Tyson. Did he reply, "I have the advantage . . . now I've seen you in a bathing suit." "No," Washington said with no follow-up from Fuller. When he asked her whether she told Tyson, "We're going out on a date, right?" the alleged victim said, "No, I didn't say that." Fuller then asked her about her interest in music that had sexual overtones. She testified she was familiar with the music of the rock group Digital Underground and that the song "Sex Packets" was one of the main songs she heard. Would Fuller play this song to show Washington's passion for sexual matters?

93

Turning to the events taking place at the Johnny Gill concert, Washington admitted that pageant official Alita Anderson reprimanded she and her roommates for being a "groupie." The girls were told to avoid being backstage. In one of the few follow-up questions Fuller asked, Washington surprised some by admitting that she did not know what the term meant. But then Fuller did not follow-up with another question, perhaps one examining why an eighteen-year-old girl appeared to be attempting to convince the jurors she was so naïve that she did not know the meaning of that term. Instead, apparently intent on establishing Washington's obsession with sex and sex-oriented music, Fuller turned his attention to the words of some music from Yo-Yo, the popular black rap group. Fuller mentioned the lyrics, "You can't play with my yo-yo," but Washington only admitted faint interest in the song. Re-visiting the pageant, Fuller gained the information from Washington that she arose between 4:00-5:00 a.m. each day, depending on which one of her roommates arose first. Asked whether she cared about being out all night, Washington answered, "No" without Fuller following up again to discover why, if Washington was so dedicated to performing well at the pageant, as she had testified during direct examination, she would attempt to do so with little or no sleep.

To the question, "Did you have a hope of a relationship with Tyson?" Washington testified, "Never thought I'd ever see him again." She said Tyson had "begged" her to leave her room and come see him. She recalled his voice being "a bit strange." "What did she mean by that?" was the logical follow-up, but the question was never asked. Instead Fuller, as if performing from a set script packed with his list of question, one causing him to concentrate on the next one without really listening to the witness so as to follow-up where necessary, a common mistake among rookie defense lawyers, inquired, "Weren't you alarmed when Tyson kissed you on the lips in the limousine?" Washington's answer: "No." Attempting to discredit Washington, Fuller directed his attention to when the bodyguard was with them on the night in question with Washington admitting that she had said he wasn't with them only to say he had been because she was "traumatized, in a foggy state," and "couldn't remember." Use of the word "traumatized" was such an unusual term for someone like Washington to use sounding more like a word a prosecutor might use. But Fuller never asked why she had used the term. Did he know about the Hammerle mock cross-examination? Is that where she might have heard that word?

Regarding whether she and Tyson went directly to his bedroom after entering the Canterbury Hotel room, Washington admitted providing two different accounts. She said she had told Indianapolis Police Department Detective Thomas Kuzmik that she had gone directly to the bedroom, a version differing with her having said that she waited in the living room until Tyson called to her. Without any follow-up as to this important point, one that could have provided the jury with wonderment about her veracity, Fuller moved on to questions about whether the garment she wearing had been altered by either her or her parents. Washington denied this. He then proceeded to question Tyson's accuser about whether she had intentions of filing a civil suit for monetary damages against the ex-champ. Her answers caused many to wonder after the trial whether she had committed perjury.

Washington recalled that it was Walter Stone, a lawyer, who called her and her parents, and not the other way around. "You are going to need help with the media," she quoted him as saying. "They are going to drive you crazy." When the family agreed they might need help, Stone said he had a conflict but recommended Ed Gerstein, a Providence, Rhode Island attorney. Washington admitted that Gerstein, and David Hennessey, an Indianapolis attorney, accompanied her to the Grand Jury testimony. They were all present at this trial, she admitted. As to specifics, Fuller and Washington had this exchange:

> Fuller: Do you know what financial arrangement you have with Mr. Gerstein representing you?
> Washington: No
> Fuller: You have no idea whatsoever?
> Washington: No. He never said anything like that. He just said he would help us with the media, and that, you know, he was . . . I asked my parents if I could pay him back little by little.
> Fuller: Do you think he has some retainer agreement with your parents?
> Washington: I don't know what retainer means.
> Fuller: Do you think he has some fee arrangement with your parents?
> Washington: I don't know.
> Fuller: Have you heard them explain or discuss with you a contingent?
> Washington: What's contingent mean?

> Fuller: Fee payable on a contingent that he's successful in some way.
> Washington: No. The only I know, they have to pay for his flights out here.
> Fuller: His expenses.
> Washington: Yes.
> Fuller: They are like liable to pay him anything else?
> Washington: I don't know what else they pay him.

Amazingly, Fuller never simply asked Washington point blank, "Do you have a contingency agreement? (a lawyer represents the client taking no up-front fee but instead a percentage of any monetary damages awarded) in any possible civil suit against Tyson?" Gaining a "yes or no" answer to that question would have left no doubt in anyone's mind as to the arrangements, and set Washington up for contrary evidence to be presented.

A final exchange between Fuller and Tyson's accuser produced the following:

> Fuller: You never met Mike Tyson before July 18, 1991?
> Washington: Right
> Fuller: Within minutes of the time when you first met him, he's hugging you.
> Washington: Uh-huh.
> Fuller: And you said, "Sure?"
> Washington: Uh-huh.
> Fuller: He awakened you at 1:30 in the morning, and you accompany him out, right?
> Washington: Correct.

Fuller: You join in the limousine, and he hugged you and kissed you.
Washington: Uh-huh.
Fuller: You willingly drove to his hotel.
Washington: Yes, not that I knew where we were going, but yes.
Fuller: And you willingly went to his suite?
Washington: Yes.
Fuller: And you went to this bedroom, and to his bed.
Washington: Yes.
Fuller: You remained on that bed until Mr. Tyson made a statement which you understood to be an explicit sexual remark.
Washington: Yes.
Fuller: And then you proceeded to go to the bathroom which is around the other side of the bed, and chose not to go out the door, which was directly across the end of the bed.
Washington: Uh-huh.

    With this, Desiree Washington's testimony had ended. Prosecutor Garrison, sensing that Fuller had done little, if any, damage to her story, asked a few follow up questions but nothing of any consequence. Fuller sat silent - the long-awaited cross-examination of Washington complete.
    Court observers attempted to assess the success or failure of Washington's testimony. Everyone agreed that the actual physical attack, the alleged rape, had been sidestepped by both attorneys. Washington had merely provided shadow information about how Tyson had raped her during direct examination, and Garrison never added to the information the jury might need to make its decision. More than anything, he must have

believed that her summary of the events in the hotel room was enough to show that rape had occurred, and decided to leave her testimony at that. Fuller, on the other hand, left the rape sequence alone, apparently either uncomfortable asking Washington about it, or because he did not see it as that important. The former appeared more logical since Fuller, an older man, especially one who as an attorney had never handled a sex crimes case, may have been reticent to dive into the particularities of the rape itself because he would have been as embarrassed to do so as Washington was to talk about it. But if this was the reason, then Fuller let his client down for a forceful, probing examination was required to pinpoint the details of the rape in an attempt to present inconsistencies, slight as they might be, in the jury's mind. This was in keeping with the notion that "little things mean a lot" in such cases especially when it is one person's word against another.

    In effect, Fuller was the kindly gentleman used to performing in federal court where manners are sometimes more important than an all out effort to seek the truth through tough, rough and tumble witness examination. This was disappointing since Washington's testimony had opened so many opportunities for Fuller to dive in the fray and seek explanations for her lack of detail about many of the events occurring. He also failed to note that when Washington was confronted with any inconsistency, her voice level appeared to change, her body language was altered, and she spoke more rapidly than usual. Letting her get away with "yes" or "no" answers was also a mistake as Fuller time and time again did not follow-up on important points necessary to prove that Tyson had been falsely accused. Certainly Bob Hammerle had seen the holes in the dike regarding especially the entire panty shield matter. Why Fuller did not pursue this line of questioning was a mystery.

Washington's most uncomfortable moments appeared to occur when she was questioned about financial matters regarding the retention of an attorney to file a civil lawsuit if Tyson was convicted. But Fuller, while asking surface questions about it, never nailed Washington or her parents down as to what arrangement there was with Gerstein and Hennessey. Surely, these attorneys were not spending their days in an Indianapolis courtroom for nothing. Wasn't it thus important that any physical documents detailing any agreements be provided? Shouldn't the defense have requested these, or other information showing the jury that Washington's true motive was to seal Tyson's fate and then sue him for millions of dollars in court?

Perhaps it was Fuller's chosen style for the trial that seemed the most lacking. Instead of the rapid-fire pace of questions asked earlier by Hammerle designed to put Washington on the defensive, Fuller was the nice guy appearing to make friends with Washington's accuser. In effect, he left her off the hook time and time again, especially when she made remarks such as not knowing what the term "groupie" meant. Could not the defense, in anticipation of presenting evidence to the contrary, have probed her about this point, a minor one in some eyes, but important since it involved Washington's whole persona as a naïve goody-two-shoes who had no idea what Tyson had in mind during their fateful encounter at the Canterbury Hotel. Fuller simply failed to dent the image projected by Washington that she was too young and too naïve to understand Tyson's intentions to have sex with her. Fuller also never probed such critical areas as the panty shield question, details regarding the oral sex that allegedly occurred, how Tyson had kept her pinned to the bed while this happened, whether Washington screamed or not, and if she did, why no one heard her, and why there was a lack of bruises on Washington's slim 108-pound body even though the burly Tyson had roughed her up while the rape was occurring. Fuller also ask little about how Washington was simply permitted to leave the hotel room. If Tyson had actually committed rape, would he have let her leave without any objection? Would he not have warned her to keep her mouth shut, or else? But Fuller left this area alone, and he did many others that would have shed more light on what occurred in the hotel room.

Most blatant was Fuller's inexcusable conduct of not focusing on motive, not so much the monetary motive, but why Washington filed the rape charges in the first place. One had to recall from her direct testimony that she never called 911 until after she told her mother of the rape. Could this action have been caused by Washington having had consensual sex with Tyson, and then felt scorned when he did not accompany her to the limousine and then to her hotel when she had expected more than a "one night stand?" Certainly, this proud woman had to be embarrassed at her naiveté in having fallen into the ex-champ's web of deception by ending up in his hotel room. If she wanted to have sex with Tyson, and if then he was rough with her, and then if she felt slighted after it was over, certainly the possibility existed that she considered herself to have been raped when Tyson was merely rough with her and did not stop even when she may have said "no" because her actions spoke louder than words and he felt she was simply resisting when she really did want to have sex with him. This was a perfect example of "implied consent," an argument Fuller could have made if he had only examined Washington further about the rape itself.

  To give Fuller one benefit of the doubt, perhaps he and his colleagues felt that Washington had not been that strong of a witness, and thus rigorous cross-examination was not required. Maybe he felt that going over and over the incident only imprinted it more in the juror's minds, and thus decided less cross-examination was better cross-examination. Perhaps he felt that if he went too far, the jurors would sympathize with Washington, feeling the defense attorney was brow-beating her. But the soft-soap examination of Tyson's accuser had left many questions unanswered, ones that could only be cleared up or expounded upon by her. Now her testimony was completed, and Garrison, Gerstein, and Hennessey must have jumped for joy at the ineffective manner of Fuller's performance. This was not a tax evasion case but a rape trial and Fuller had shown he was way over this head in the down and dirty criminal courts. He simply did not have the temperament to go toe-to-toe with Washington, who was intent on destroying Tyson's career, sending him to prison, and earning millions through a civil lawsuit. No, Fuller had been too nice of a guy, ill-equipped, and a superb disappointment.

  This performance was in contrast to the one Roy Black delivered in the William Kennedy Smith case. Like an experienced surgeon, Black honed in on critical areas of Patty Bowman's direct testimony, and then dissected them thoroughly especially those dealing with the stockings and whether it was logical to believe Kennedy Smith would commit rape below the room where his mother was sleeping. Slowly and methodically, and by carefully listening to Bowman's responses to his questions so he could follow-up where necessary, Black had raised questions for the jury to ponder during deliberation. In the Rodney King case, defense lawyers for the police officers had broken down the infamous videotape to show frame by frame how King had fought back triggered the beating that ensued. By doing so, they were able to neutralize the accusations against the officers resulting in their acquittal. But Fuller had either been ill-prepared, or simply not up to the task, and when Desiree Washington walked out of the courtroom after her testimony, Tyson was in deep trouble. To most observers, Washington had told a plausible story and because Fuller had failed to disturb that story, the rest of the trial would an uphill climb.

Chapter Nine
In Support of Desiree

Confident that Desiree Washington had made an excellent witness impressing the jury, prosecutors Greg Garrison and Barb Trathen now readied themselves for presentation of the remainder of the State's evidence. During Washington's testimony, Mike Tyson had barely glanced at her as if she didn't exist. Jurors watched his reaction closely and must have wondered why he was not more defiant, perhaps by shaking his head, at the accusations. They were left with the impression that either Iron Mike didn't care, or had been schooled by his attorneys to show little emotion. If this occurred, it was a mistake since it is important for jurors to sense an indignation on the part of the accused as the accuser levels what they believe to be untrue charges at them.

Realizing that motive was still a key element to the case, Garrison and company felt it is crucial to plant in the juror's minds the idea that the naïve Washington was truly intent on "sightseeing" with the ex-champ on the night he picked her up at the Omni Hotel. What she actually thought she would see, a matter left unanswered through direct testimony, or most surprising, cross-examination, was unclear, especially in the dark at 1:30 a.m. Showing that Tyson had tricked the gullible, star-struck, wide-eyes, college freshman into believing the sightseeing would occur was thus paramount to the State's case. In effect, the prosecution intended to show that Tyson's used his fame to set a trap for Washington tantamount to kidnapping her.

Prosecutor Moira Lasch had intended to use the

104

same strategy in the William Kennedy Smith case by portraying the accused as the rich nephew of a famous family as sex-starved, night-club rover who had only one thing on his mind when he picked up Patty Bowman at the Au Bar nightspot in Palm Beach, Florida. Based on Bowman's testimony, one alleging that Kennedy Smith began to remove his clothes on the pretense of swimming at the beach where they ended up on the fateful evening, Lasch sought to show that Kennedy Smith had lured and manipulated Bowman into a compromising situation where no escape was possible. This, in turn, led to the prosecutor's assertion that nothing Bowman did after this was consensual since even if she "cuddled" with Kennedy Smith, when she said "no" that meant "no" and the subsequent advances and intercourse constituted rape.

    While Garrison was aware that this strategy had failed, he believed Tyson's situation quite different. Kennedy Smith and Tyson might both be famous, Garrison admitted, but that was where the similarities ended since Tyson, Garrison believed the evidence would show, had deliberately hoodwinked Washington into believing there would be sightseeing when he had not intention of this occurring but was instead focused on sex with his young prey. Thus false pretenses existed, Garrison believed, and this meant he had to show Tyson's evil ways so the jurors could pin the subsequent rape on him. Garrison began his scheme by calling to the witness stand Laticia Moscrip, the Canterbury Hotel general manager to introduce telephone records. No explanation was offered as to why this relevant but certainly the impression provided was that these records would be of interest to the jury regarding calls Tyson and his bodyguard made from the hotel room on the night in question. Next, the prosecution produced McCoy Wagers, the Canterbury Hotel night auditor. He first explained that Tyson's representative had reserved two rooms from the 17th of July through the 21st before stating that at about 1:30 to 1:45 a.m. Tyson had entered the lobby "happy and smiling, cheerful, and said hello." A woman was "two or three steps" behind him, Wagers said.

At about 2:00 a.m., Wagers said Dale Edwards Tyson's bodyguard was in the hotel parlor and "asked for an outside line to make a long distance telephone call." Wagers also said the bodyguard said he had an important call coming in and he wanted to know when this occurred. Edwards then ordered room service for room 604, the room beside Tyson's. When Edwards asked for airline telephone numbers, Wagers gave him the one for U.S. Air. Wagers said he never "saw the woman who accompanied Tyson again," and only saw Tyson when he checked out at 4:00 a.m. Wagers told the jury the ex-champ looked "tired," and there were no smiles or hellos. Next to testify was Chris Lowe, a hotel bellboy. "Between 1:45 and 2:00 a.m.," he stated, he saw Tyson and shook his hand. He testified the woman with Tyson was only in the hotel forty to forty-five minutes. Vincent Fuller's cross-examination produced testimony from Lowe that Tyson had departed the limousine after the woman had done so and that Edwards, the six-foot, three-hundred-pound bodyguard followed them. When Tyson and Edwards checked out so quickly, Lowe was concerned about whether they had done so thoroughly. He entered room 606 and discovered "money on the table and a shirt on the bed."

Having set the stage for what occurred at the Canterbury, Garrison was now ready for Virginia Foster, the limousine driver, to testify. Prior to her doing so, a hearing outside the presence of the jury was conducted as to whether she could testify about Tyson's conduct during her hours as the limousine driver. During the hearing, the prosecution told Judge Gifford Foster would testify that Tyson "lured" her up to the hotel room in a manner similar to that alleged with Washington. Foster would also say that Tyson tried to touch her and exposed himself to her as well. To her credit, Gifford denied the State's request that Foster testify about these matters since when, according to Indiana law, consent was a defense, prior conduct by the accused was inadmissible. Besides the question of whether the evidence was relevant, Gifford said that Tyson was not denying that it had occurred, only that the sex was consensual. The fact that he made advances on Foster was thus excluded from her testimony.

Owner of the Sold Gold Limousine Service, the fifty-one-year-old Foster, appearing much younger than her age with a certain flair and edge to her character, testified that she had a master's degree and had taught previously in the Indianapolis Public School System. She said she had also worked with behavioral problem children and young kids. Foster first confirmed that the telephone call from Tyson to Washington at about 1:35 a.m. on July 18th. She stated she heard Tyson ask "the girl to come out and talk." Foster said "he was begging – he obviously wanted a woman." Foster said she picked up Washington and then transported she and Tyson to the Canterbury where she "helped the pretty lady out first." She recalled that the lady "had a real pretty hairdo; that was what stood out about her." At 3:10 to 3:15. a.m., Foster said she saw "the lady rushing out of the hotel." Foster said she got in the limousine, and then the bodyguard arrived and told Foster to take her back to the hotel. "Any conversation?" Foster was asked. "Yes," she replied. "The lady said, 'I don't believe him – who does he think he is."

At the Omni, Foster testified that she helped the lady out of the limousine. Regarding her appearance and demeanor, Foster said, "her hair wasn't as neat; she looked frantic, in a state of shock, dazed, disoriented, she couldn't focus." She appeared "scared," Foster said to no objection from the defense despite the opinions being offered.

Back at the Canterbury, Foster said the bodyguard told her, "We'll be leaving." At 4:15, he brought the luggage. The limousine then traveled to a West 65th Street address, the house where Tyson's girlfriend, singer B Angie B lived. When a knock on the door produced no one, a call was then placed to the Holiday Inn South to see if the singer was there. When Foster was asked whether she could drive to the hotel and then the airport by the time Tyson's flight was scheduled to leave, her answer was "no."

Cross-examination was mild with Foster sticking to her story. Apparently the defense did not believe the limo driver had reported any conduct inconsistent with consensual sex. Why they felt his way, especially regarding Foster's belief that the lady, Washington, was "frantic, in a state of shock, dazed, disoriented, she couldn't focus," and appeared "scared," was incidental was beyond reason. Certainly the jury must have believed Foster leaving little wiggle room regarding any defense challenge to her important testimony since here was a corroborating witness to Washington's state of mind after leaving Tyson's hotel room. How would the defense explain such abnormal conduct? Did Washington's ruffled appearance and perplexing demeanor square up with her charge that she had been raped, or was she simply upset that she had permitted Tyson to have sex with her and the unceremoniously dumped her into the street as nothing more than a one-night stand with no intention of seeing her again? Had Washington been raped or scorned so intensely that as she thought more about what had occurred, she was certain she had been raped. And how did Foster's story mesh with Washington's statement to her roommate, "I think he raped me."

Following Virginia Foster to the witness stand was Indiana University Hospital Emergency Room physician, Dr. Stephen Richardson, a serious man whose eyes appeared to burn through Tyson when he glanced at him. An associate professor, he testified that Washington had two small abrasions on her vagina, consistent with 20-30% of the injuries prevalent in sex assault cases. This statement was not a fatal blow to the defense, but then the good doctor dropped a bombshell: only twice in his twenty years had he ever seen these types of abrasions where there had been consensual sex. Then he went further, telling the jury the abrasions could only have been caused "by forced or very hard consensual sex," a mixed bag answer. On cross, the defense made matters worse when a probing question caused Dr. Richardson to explain that in 20,000 cases, he had only seen two with like injuries where consensual sex occurred. If the jury believed the doctor, Tyson was half way, if not within walking distance, of a state prison.

Forensic crime laboratory expert James Enoch, a spritely man with an easy manner and a sense of trust to him, followed Dr. Richardson to the witness stand. He told the jury that 10:28 p.m. on July 22nd, more than three days after the alleged rape, he visited Tyson's Canterbury Hotel room. Asked to look for the existence of bodily fluids on or near the bed, he utilized a UB ultraviolet light. It could detect the presence of saliva, semen, and perspiration. The room had been cleaned since the night in question, but Enoch nevertheless testified that he was able to look at a section of the bed on the lower right hand corner where Detective Kuzmik believed the attack could have occurred. When Enoch used the UB light, it showed a certain fluorescence indicating the presence of fluids. Whether this fact impressed the jury was unclear, but if they were, then another tiny bit of the puzzle was presented toward convicting Tyson as each witness was providing damaging evidence toward the believability that rape had occurred. But there was more from Enoch.

Before he left the witness stand, Enoch testified that he discovered a sequin along the wall that separated the bedroom from the living room. He photographed the sequin and then collected it as evidence. Prosecutor Garrison then connected it to the alleged crime scene by producing the outfit Washington wore the night of alleged attack indicating where the sequin fit on the dress. Some questions existed as to whether the sequin was white or yellow were raised by the defense, but Enoch testifying that its color depended on the lighting where the sequin was inspected. Defense attorney Kathleen Beggs questioned whether the dress had been altered since it was sent back from Washington's east coast home. The expert said he had no opinion. Beggs then asked about some spots on the floor but Enoch could not connect them to either Washington or Tyson. But she stopped short of a rigorous cross-examination regarding the existence of the liquids on the bed *three days after* the crime and how they connected to Tyson, or why the presence of the sequin was related to anything other than one having dropped off of Washington's dress, if it truly did.

Dr. Richardson and James Enoch had been reliable witnesses and to follow them, Garrison and his crew chose Thomas Kuzmik, the investigating police officer assigned to the case. A member of the sex crimes unit, he told the jury he first met Washington on July 22nd at the Child Advocacy Center on East Ohio Street. He described her as being "nervous and unable to focus. She would begin a sentence, and then trail off. She was apprehensive, confused, and had problems keeping every thing in sequence."

The detective told the jury that he asked Washington whether she still had the clothing she wore the night she was allegedly attacked. She told him her brother had returned it to her Rhode Island home. This prevented any examination of the clothing immediately after the alleged rape preventing a key element of the accusations against Tyson to be presented. Compounding the problem for the prosecution was Detective Kuzmik's admission that he had asked the Tyson family to return the clothing, loaned to Washington by a local pageant official, in tact but that he was overruled by the prosecutor's office causing the clothing to be sent after Washington's father tore sequins from the dress and cut a patch away before sending it to Indianapolis. He said nine sequins were sent yet only seven were present in the envelope produced at trial. Vincent Fuller tried to make a big deal of this, but he never showed why this was of importance.

One small point Fuller raised could have been significant if pursued further. On direct examination, Washington testified that one could not see the television from the end of the bed. Fuller thus asked the detective whether photographs had been taken from the viewpoint at the end of the bed whether Washington said she sat. Kuzmik said they had not and Fuller left it at that. Had the defense gone to the trouble of securing photographs for the detective to consider? Apparently not.

When asked whether Washington had "time to review the statement she gave to him," his reply was a stern, "Yes." This, the defense appeared to conclude, permitted her time to change her statement if she so desired. But once again follow-up questions were not asked regarding what may have been changed, leaving the jury to wonder if she had done so. Clarity was the issue with the defense apparently believing the significance of their questions was quite clear while court observers wondered why they did not tie up matters so there was no room for confusion. Perhaps Fuller intended to do so later with other witnesses or in final argument.

Mohammed Ahira n additional forensic expert, was the next prosecution witness. In a low tone, but with authority, the handsome Ahir told the jury he had inspected Washington's panties for fluid specimens. He testified that while there were semen and blood samples on the panties, he could not say whether he could separate regular blood from menstrual blood. No mention was made as to whether the semen present was Tyson's and the jury was left to wonder about this fact.

The prosecution's obsession with the sequin discovered in Tyson's hotel room was pursued with their final expert witness, forensic expert Dirk Shaw. Comparing the sequin found with those on Washington's outfit, he testified they were identical. Cross examination was nil with the chance to show the jury how insignificant this piece of evidence was since a sequin could have dropped off Washington's dress without their ever having been a sexual attack. And since three days had passed before the sequin was discovered, its placement was subject to conjecture. But the defense let the sequin evidence pass in the wind without worrying about it. They should have.

When Dirk Shaw left the witness stand, one had to assess the damage done to the defense by the string of witnesses, especially Virginia Foster. The prosecution had proceeded in an orderly fashion while realizing that Fuller's promise that Tyson would testify loomed in the background. If this occurred, then small bits of evidence potentially insignificant on the surface might play larger roles in putting the noose around his neck later on.

Far and above the most telling testimony had been provided by Virginia Foster. Garrison and company were quite pleased with her performance while the defense appeared unable to realize its strong significance. Without the jury's knowledge that she had been harassed by Tyson and even lured to his hotel room in a manner similar to that of Washington, if one believed her story, there was no reason, no motive, as to why Foster lied. But the defense was prevented from showing bias since they did not want the jury to know of Tyson's treatment of Foster. They thus were stuck with attempting to discredit her without any ammunition to do so. Fuller's cross-examination was thus fruitless. He thus did not experience the same success that Roy Black had in the William Kennedy Smith case when a witness named Ann Mercer was called by the prosecution. She was present to tell what she and her boyfriend observed when they picked up Bowman at the Kennedy estate shortly after the alleged rape. Mercer told of Bowman's disarray, but on cross-examination Black was lethal in tearing apart her story and casting doubt for the jury on the credibility of the testimony.

Similarly, defense attorneys shined when they cross-examined police officer Melanie Singer during the Rodney King trial. She had been called to testify that Sergeant Stacey Koon had taken over the arrest of King from her without cause, and that officer Lawrence Powell had repeatedly struck King with head shots, causing severe injury to his face. But defense lawyers wrecked Singer's credibility when she admitted that she was quite inexperienced. And photographs of King's injuries inconsistent with her portrayal of his injuries made her testimony difficult for the jury to believe. In both the Kennedy Smith and King cases, rigid cross-examination had won the day. Thus far in the Tyson case, the same had not occurred.

But far and above other matters, it was Virginia Foster who had landed a good right cross to Tyson's chin. The impersonal nature of Fuller's cross-examination appeared to inflame her and even without mentioning the sexual harassment she said occurred, the defense lawyer could have discredited her with pointed questions since it was clear that she disliked the ex-champ. By dancing around the harassment, Fuller could have cleverly exposed why Foster had nothing good to say about Tyson thus providing the jury with the innuendo that she was biased against him. Without listening carefully to her answers, and then following up with questions designed to probe her true feelings toward Tyson, Fuller missed a critical chance to cast some doubt on her story, one that was powerful in nature. One example occurred when Foster was asked to describe the relationship between Tyson and Washington in the back seat of the limousine. She said she saw little or nothing, but was that true? During the ride from the Omni to the Canterbury, was it possible that she observed nothing?

    One had also to wonder whether the jury knowing of Foster's allegations that Tyson was mean to her, tried to touch her, lured her to his hotel room, and exposed himself might have seemed absurd to the jury poisoning the testimony. Foster was not un-attractive but was it credible to believe that Tyson, with a bevy of younger, more attractive, available, he had tried to romance Foster? Perhaps the defense should have considered permitting her to vent against Tyson taking the chance that doing so would clearly show why she lashed out against him. But this never occurred and Foster left the witness stand unmarked and may have very well resulted in the moment when jurors began to truly believe that Tyson was guilty of rape.

    More to the point of indicating defense ineptness with the string of prosecution witnesses was Fuller's shocking behavior in asking Dr. Richardson questions Fuller clearly did not know the answer to, the fool's gold that every first year law student knows can be condemning. The most blatant example had been Fuller's question that solicited Richardson's answer that in 20,000 cases he had never seen consensual sex consistent with the abrasions apparent on Washington's vagina. When this answer was given, it was if a five thousand pound bowling ball was dropped on Criminal Court #4. Certainly the jury must have wondered why Fuller had suddenly become a member of the prosecution team. This was especially crucial since jurors, while suspect of the testimony of ordinary citizens, are prone to buy the testimony of experts such as Dr. Richardson. This is because they have little reason to lie despite working for the prosecution. This makes it even more important that the defense strongly challenge them during the time they testify and not wait until expert testimony may be introduced to counter what the jury has heard. Such is true since the later expert testimony may prove to be ineffective.

    Greg Garrison certainly indicated a positive vibe toward the jury for he believed his parade of witnesses thus far had been most effective. He objected now and then to defense questions but it appeared more to interrupt the flow that to make any important points. He was clearly showing a take-charge attitude in the courtroom, one of his greatest strengths and why prosecutor Modisett had hired him.

    Vincent Fuller, on the other hand, had done little to help his client by rarely showing a feistiness indicating the fighter in him. Once, when he misplaced his notepad, it showed a crack in his armor, a human sort of thing that made him appear less plastic. But his errors in judgment regarding the questioning of prosecution witnesses was glaring and a shock to those who believed the polished lawyer would wipe the street with Garrison. Thus far, the gunslinger had outfought the sheriff. There was no doubt about that.

What the jury thought of their duel was unclear, but the prosecution had built an impressive case bolstered by the strong testimony of Virginia Foster and Dr. Richardson. If the jury believed Washington, even part of her story, and if they believed Foster and the doctor, Tyson might as well have been fitted for his prison garb. Now Garrison intended to close in further on the boxer by presenting beauty queens to substantiate Washington's story. Could Fuller turn the tide and gain some needed points for Iron Mike?

Chapter Ten
More Beauties

In an attempt to bolster Desiree Washington's claims about the sex-driven side of Mike Tyson, the prosecution called to the witness stand several Miss Black America Beauty contestants.

First to testify was Stacy Murphy, a Chicago State University student attempting to earn a degree in microbiology. A pleasant woman with a light-up smile, she told the jury of being one of Desiree Washington's best friends during the pageant. Avoiding any discussion of the events occurring on July 18th, she instead focused on her impressions of Desiree the day after the alleged rape. This was during the rehearsal in front of Union Station in downtown Indianapolis. "All of the contestants were sluggish," she testified, but she and Washington had time to chat during a rest period. Asked to describe further her relationship with her new friend, Murphy said the two had kidded each other since they "neither one had rhythm." She joked that they were "sisters under one rhythmless motion." Murphy said that Washington "wasn't enthusiastic that morning," but that she thought it was because of the late evening the night before. She told the jury she kidded Washington about this, but that she didn't kid back causing Murphy to wonder if something was wrong.

Finally, Murphy said, Washington spoke up. "I feel so stupid," Murphy quoted her as saying: "He raped me." Then Washington told her, "He asked me to a party, a rooftop party. When we got in the limousine, he said he had to go to the hotel to pick up his bodyguards." Murphy then added that Washington said, "she felt stupid, went to the bathroom; he was all over me." When some other girls began listening, Murphy told the jury she said, "the story [was] a nice movie" to divert their attention away from Washington's story. When a pageant producer told the girls to get in line and continue to practice, Murphy advised Washington "not to tell any of the girls, but to tell officials, tell her parents." Murphy said she tried to keep Washington's mind off the incident the rest of the day, but she wouldn't "crack jokes." Murphy added, "It wasn't like it was before." She said "looks tell so much," and "her look told it all . . . she was talking to me, but her soul was gone," she didn't look like herself . . . "she was a zombie . . . I tried to comfort her . . . but she just kept talking."

While Tyson continued doodling on a yellow pad as if he didn't have a care in the world, defense lawyer Lane Heard tackled Murphy on cross-examination. With an easy manner and congenial personality, he was proving to be the most effective of Tyson's trial counsels. More important, unlike Fuller who appeared intimidated by Greg Garrison's forceful style, Heard seemed to agitate Garrison with a strong manner and unwillingness to back down when Garrison confronted him with various objections. Proving he was savvy with cross-examination, he began with a straightforward questions relating to facts about the Miss Black America Pageant. Murphy supplied a bit of comic relief to the otherwise stoic proceedings when she said the "tension began to build," causing some of the contestants to become "upset" and "nasty" to one another. Then she related that Washington told her she had seen Tyson backstage at the Johnny Gil concert, and talked to him after pageant official Alita Anderson had reprimanded her for being a groupie. Murphy said Washington said that Tyson asked her out to a "rooftop reception," where all the other contestants would appear. Skipping to the time when Washington rode in the limousine with Tyson, Washington told her that Tyson said "he had to got pick up a bodyguard," and that after they got to the hotel, "he raped me." Attempting to present for the jury a contrast between what Washington told Murphy and what she had testified to in court, Heard bombarded Murphy with several questions designed to indicate that Washington had never mentioned such items as any hotel room telephone calls, the kiss in the limousine, the fact that she entered the bedroom and sat on the bed, any kiss on the bed, or any removal of the panty shield in the bathroom. Asked by Heard if Washington told her she had been crying when she left the hotel room, Murphy said Washington indicated she "gathered her things and left the room crying," and that she had kept saying to Tyson, "Stop. Stop." She also stated that Washington told her about going to the bathroom, and then admitted that she, Murphy, had never mentioned these things in prior statements to the prosecution.

      Whatever effect the Murphy testimony was having on the entire jury was unknown, but throughout, Neil, juror #6, the young t-shirt printer, stared at Tyson. Either he didn't believe what he was hearing, was insulted by what he was hearing about the ex-champ, or quietly condemning him for his irreverent conduct toward Washington. Other jurors, including Tim, the ex-Marine and Rosie, the African-American woman sitting next to the printer, also stared at Tyson but he never acknowledged them as he continued doodling.

After a brief pause, Heard referred Murphy back to the opening pageant ceremonies held outside the Hoosier Dome. She recalled gaining Tyson's attention, and seeing Rev. Jesse Jackson reprimand Tyson for his gaudy behavior toward the contestants. She also recalled Tyson saying "oh, shit," a comment she attributed to his feeling that Jackson should leave him alone. Describing the scene at the rehearsal hall, Murphy said "everyone flocked to Tyson. He was an octopus, with his arms around waists and touching the behinds and breasts of any girl he could fine." Murphy admitted that if "a girl didn't want to be touched," she shouldn't have been there and that she didn't like the fact that Tyson had told the girls, "If you want to have your picture taken, you have to sit on my lap." Offended by the remark, she decided not to have her photograph taken with the ex-champ.

During re-direct examination, Murphy testified that there were a great many "back-biters" among the contestants. Some "felt Desiree was too perky, and there perkiness was just part of a game." This revelation was certainly cause for further inquiry since the defense had already opened the door to arguing that Washington was an aspiring actress who could have been faking her testimony about Tyson to gain millions through a civil suit. Were her allegations part of some game, one she had conjured up after informing her mother of the sexual encounter with Tyson? Heard needed to take her statement about "a game" and pound away at it trying to discover whether this point could be pivotal in the jury's determination of Tyson's guilt or innocence. But Heard let her statement go and did not follow up. Perhaps this portion of the testimony would become part of a riveting final argument Fuller had in store for the jury.

Miss Black America contestant Charise Nelson testified that she had met Mike Tyson at New York City's Apollo several years before. She said Tyson put his hand around her waist, but when "I said stop. He did."

Regarding her contact with Desiree Washington on the 20th of July, one day after the alleged attack, Nelson said she saw Washington in the Omni Hotel lobby. Nelson noticed that Washington had "no make-up on," and that she was waiting for her mother. "I'll wait too," Nelson said she told Washington. "I'm going to the hospital," Nelson said Washington replied. "I have cramps." Moments later, Nelson told the jury Washington asked "me to promise not to say anything." Nelson said she agreed, and then Washington told her, "I was with Mike last night." "Mike who?" Nelson said she replied and Washington said, "Mike Tyson – I was with him. He raped me." Nelson said she told Washington, "take him to jail" before Washington explained that Tyson said "Come to the hotel, 'cause I'll get my bodyguard." Once there, she told Nelson, "Tyson started to take advantage of me," saying "I like girls who say 'no.'" Finally, Washington told Nelson, Tyson, referring to his body part, asked her "Am I too big?"

Next to testify for the state was Cindy Jenkins, an Indianapolis police officer who spoke to Washington following the alleged attack. She said Washington "was fidgety," and "looked down" while speaking. Jenkins told the jury Washington was "bug-eyed," her eyes were "wide-open." The woman was in "a state of shock," and very confused. Jenkins said Washington told her Tyson had promised they "would go around town" and had to go to the Canterbury Hotel to "get the bodyguards." Further, Washington told the police officer "she tried to fight him off," and "begged him to stop." She said she screamed and that Tyson said, "Don't fight me – you know you want me." Jenkins said Washington was "disoriented as to time, and would jump around from one topic to the other." Jenkins told the jury Washington informed her that she had talked to a chaplain some twenty-five hours after the alleged attack.

 Symbolic of the mixed message and inherent value of this part of the testimony against Tyson required a closer look at certain statements made by Stacy Murphy. She was the beauty contestant who said that Washington had stated, "I feel so stupid; he raped me." The prosecution could point to the statement backing up its contention that Washington was duped ("I feel so stupid"), when she agreed to join Tyson in his hotel room. But the defense might counter with the argument that 1) the comment meant that Washington knew she shouldn't have gotten involved with Tyson and she felt so stupid for having sex with him, the latter an undisputed fact, and thus 2) because she felt so stupid, and embarrassed, Washington struck back by filing rape charges against Tyson.

 While the worth of both defense arguments was being debated against prosecution claims, another area of interest for the defense should have been the inconsistencies apparent between what Washington told police and investigators and what she told fellow beauty pageant contestants. Certainly she had never mentioned rooftop parties or quotes from Tyson such as "I like girls who say no" or "am I too big" in any of her statements. More clarity as to what else Washington may have added to the mix would have been possible but defense lawyers failed to follow up with probing questions especially with Charise Nelson. She and the other beauty contestants appeared to show Tyson was indeed a "sexual animal" on the prey, and the defense did little to defend against these accusations.

In the William Kennedy Smith case, the prosecutor wasn't as intent on proving him to be a sexual deviant, but she certainly did allude to his being a swinging bachelor, and a rich one at that. But the judge there had restricted how much Moira Lasch could delve into Kennedy Smith's background especially regarding any similar incidents to that of his alleged rape of Patty Bowman. This prohibition was also present in the Clarence Thomas confirmation hearings where Thomas was spared the embarrassment of any events similar to the sexual harassment alleged to have occurred to Anita Hill. Allegations of impropriety surfaced after she made her accusations, but for the most part these were swept under the table as being irrelevant to the challenges being made to Thomas' character. But here, in the Tyson case, there was no doubt the prosecution was attempting to show that Tyson was indeed a "sexual animal" and that his pursuit of the nice, innocent Washington had emanated from his "wanting a woman," as limousine driver Virginia Foster had reported. And, amazingly enough, Vincent Fuller was mostly silent regarding opinion evidence or hearsay since he did not object to it during the examination of many of the witnesses who criticized Tyson's behavior. Was Fuller, in effect, agreeing with the prosecution that Tyson was a dangerous womanizer prowling the streets looking for someone to have sex with and thus Washington should have known better than to trust him and thus deserved whatever fate occurred in room 606 of the Canterbury Hotel? Could this possibly be part of his masterful plan to defend Tyson?

Chapter Eleven
The 911 Tape

In the Rodney King beating case, videotape played an important part in the final determination as to whether four Los Angeles Police Department officers were guilty. None was available in the Mike Tyson rape trial, but two audio tapes, one nearly forgotten, were introduced into evidence with the second playing a major part in the final outcome.

The first audiotape was predictable since it featured Mike Tyson's unfortunate, for the defense as least, appearance before the Marion County Grand Jury. It would be introduced after Tyson testified to indicate discrepancies with his trial testimony. The second audiotape was offered by the State for a different purpose, but its existence would have never been known had Desiree Washington not mentioned it during a deposition she gave four weeks prior to trial. Somehow knowledge of the tape had slipped through the cracks at the prosecutor's office until Washington's revelation.

When introduced at trial, the transcript read:
Dispatch Tape
This tape is a copy of the Indianapolis police department 911 center for the date of July 20, 1991, being recorded from recorder number 2, line number 3, reference rape investigation beginning time 01.22.08:
Dispatcher: 911 police emergency
Washington: Yes, may I please speak with Corporal Goldman?
D: Who?
W: Corporal Goldman

D: What sector?
W: excuse me
D: What sector? This is the Indianapolis police department.
W: That's what I was told to ask for when I called.
D: What's the problem? Do you have a problem?
W: Yes, I'm calling to report a rape.
D: A rape?
W: Uh huh
D: When were you raped?
W: Well, can I speak to this person?
D: Ok, ma'am.
W: Yes.
D: OK, you are the person who was raped.
W: Uh huh.
D: OK, now I can find Corporal Goldman, or whoever it is for you, I can try to find him, uh, you want to make a police report?
W: Well, I don't know.
D: OK.
W: I want someone, I don't know. Is this being recorded?
D: It is being recorded but you can still talk to me. I mean I am a human being and I can sympathize with you. I'm here to help you. I'm not here to condemn you or anything.
W: OK
D: So obviously you need some type of help and that that's what my job is and that's what I'm here to do.
W: OK
D: So
W: I can just tell you what happened and you can determine, I . . .

D: OK, why don't you tell us what happened and then we'll see, we'll tell you what you can do. Your options and then we'll let you make the decision. OK?
W: OK
W: OK
W: OK, uh, I met this person during the day, and uh, I went out with this person in a limousine that night and person told me that he had to go get his bodyguards and ask me if I wanted to come in for a second and I said, oh, OK. Fine. You know, thinking this was a nice person. And we in and the person starting attacking.
D: Uh huh.
W: Trying to take off my clothes and I was lime, well I have to leave. See, I'm not like that and so the person agreed, OK fine, it is OK, then, you know, you don't have to do anything, you are a nice girl, you are a Christian girl, and things like that. And so, uh, I was like, well, you know, I just want to get that straight that I don't want to do anything and I kept saying that over and over, and this person went on to say that's what made him want me more because I didn't want to do anything basically. He kissed me, and oh, you are turning me on because you are not like the rest of these girls. You are not a city girl. And then, uh, person tried to take my clothes off again, and succeeded and then just basically forced himself upon me.
D: Ok, you did tell him no when you said . . . ?
W: Yes, I said no, uh, I asked . . .

128

D: Do you know this person?
W: Yes.
D: Do you know him well or is this somebody you just met?
W: It is someone that 's like famous.
D: Somebody famous?
W: Uh huh.
D: Well, that's not, you know, keep them being wrong. If you are wrong, you are wrong, I don't care who you are.
W: Yeah.
D: He forced himself upon you. He was wrong.
W: It is just that it will go public, and it is, you know.
D: How old are you?
W: I'm eighteen
D: You are eighteen. Nobody else knows?
W: Uh, my parents know. I told them. And uh . . .
D: Well, hon, you know, you have to make this decision for yourself. You weren't the won that was wrong, right?
W: No. I just feel so disgusting.
D: Most rape victims feel that way.
W: I cam out of the bathroom and this person was in his underwear and he just basically kind of did what he wanted to do and kept saying don't fight me. Don't fight me. And I was like say, no no. Get off of me, get off of me please. Get off of me and he like don't fight me. Don't fight me. And the person is a lot stronger than I was and he just did what he wanted and I was saying stop please stop. And he just didn't stop. And . . .

129

D: OK, now who is wrong?
W: Well, him.
D: You told him to stop, now who is wrong?
W: Well, him.
D: You told him to stop, now who is wrong?
W: And he just staying, I'm not going to come in you. I'm not going to come in you and I kept saying, please stop, you are hurting me. Please stop. And then finally I go in, I said I have to leave and he was like well, you are welcome to stay, and I said well no, I said I like you because I thought you were a nice person, this morning, nut just because you were a star, and now I don't like you for either one. And I left and I was crying and uh, this person's limousine driver talked to me.
D: Do you think you can be happy knowing that he did this and he is going to get away with it? What do you want to do about it? Your decision, what do you want to do about what he did to you?
W: I don't want, I'm afraid to go public, because, it is just, a I have a title and everything and I'm so afraid.
D: But you need to talk to somebody about it, right?
W: Uh huh.
D: Well there are a few suggestions I have for you. And I can tell you.
W: Uh huh.
D: Well you are 18, you are considered an adult now. You can make your own decisions, I can't make them for you. Your parent's can't make them for you. You'll have to find these decisions within yourself.

W: Yeah. I just feel that people think it is my fault for going to his room, but I was just naïve to believe that he was, you know, a nice person.
D: Irregardless to that, irregardless, you said no.
W: Uh huh.
D: Right?
W: Uh huh.
D: And that's where it should have ended.
W: OK
D: A lot of people go on dates, and there are people. See people in privacy or whatever, they, everybody has the right to say no and that should be respected.
W: Uh huh.
D: When you say no, it means no. It's doesn't mean maybe, and it doesn't mean yes.
W: OK, I didn't go to the doctor right away. I came home, and I took, and I cam back to my room and I took a shower and I . . .
D: When did this happen to you?
W: It happened, uh, around this time last night.
D: OK, it is still not too late to do something about it.
W: And I got my period, so . . .
D: Have you had any kind of medical attention, have yourself looked at?
W: No, I haven't. Uh, my period had begun to start yesterday, and when he started to do that to me.
D: Uh huh.
W: And I was trying to get out and then it just continued on today, so I'm afraid that,

131

like if there is any evidence of what he did to me, it would be out now.
D: Uh, huh, well not necessarily, see there a lot of different things involved in a rape.
W: Uh huh.
D: You have to consider, I'm not trying to scare you, ok.
W: Uh huh.
D: Venereal disease, and things like that.
W: Uh huh.
D: So you have to decide within yourself if you want to pursue this if somebody has done you wrong if you want to do something about it or if you just want to forget it.
W: Ever time I've seen this on television, I've always said I did want, I would do something about it, but, I just feel so scared. It is just so different when it . . .
D: You know television is not like real life.
W: To me, yeah, I know.
D: You don't know all the circumstances involved and that you have on TV or in the news.
W: Uh huh.
D: You have to decide for yourself who you are and what you want to do about it when somebody has violated you.
W: Uh huh.
D: And it want, there are your options. I'm not trying to scare you. You could speak with a police officer.
W: Uh huh.
D: Or I can give you the number to the _____ entrance.
W: Uh huh.

D: I could send somebody to talk to you or either you could call them.
W: Uh huh.
D: I mean nobody is going to force you to press charges.
W: Uh huh.
D: And it never hurts to talk to somebody about it.
W: OK
D: After you talk to somebody about it, well what are the options, if you want to pursue it, you can pursue it, and if you don't, you don't have to.
W: OK.
D: So you know, we're at the position now, where you need to tell me what to do. And then I can help you whatever you want to do, I can help you from there.
W: I want to go to a doctor and see if there is anything wrong with me.
D: Uh huh.
W: Really
D: Well if you want to go to a doctor and I feel that you need to. You have to listen to yourself.
W: Uh huh, and then I would have to take it from there.
D: Right. Well it is up to you now. You know. If you want to talk to somebody, I can have somebody call you either if they to be at your house or be at somebody else's house . . .
W: I don't live in Indiana.
D: Doesn't matter. This happened in Indiana. Right?
W: Uh huh.

D: Well, if the crime has been committed within the state . . .
W: OK
D: You're the victim. You are not the criminal
W: OK
D: You're the victim.
W: But I feel like one.
D: Well you are . . .
W: I mean.
D: So you need to let me know, you know, what you want to do.
W: Uh.
D: The only options that I have.
W: Uh huh.
D: to offer you
W: Uh huh, uh . . .
D: Hello. Hello.
W: Hello
D: Yeah, there are two of sitting here, ma'am. I'm training, there is two of us sitting here, she works . . .
D2: What's your name?
W: Do I have to tell my name?
D2: No, that's fine, but I was just listening to the conversation and personally, I'm not trying to tell you what to do. But first of all, you need to go to the doctor and get yourself checked out.
W: Uh huh.
D2: And I know you said that you saw it on TV that if something like this happened to you, that you would do something about it.
W: Uh huh.
D2: If you follow your heart, you follow your first instinct. If your heart is telling you

to do something about it, then do it. Don't let this just slide by because this could scar you for the rest of your life.
W: Uh, huh.
D2: Now just because he is a star and all this, that don't mean nothing. He's a person.
W: Yeah. That's what I said to him.
D2: So it doesn't matter know. He has done it.
W: Uh huh.
D2: And now it is up to you to do something about it.
W: Uh huh. How do you prove something like this?
D2: Really now, it is your word against his.
W: Exactly.
D2: But see the fact of the matter is you, like someone told me , you tried.
W: Uh huh.
D2: Don't, all I can, I'm not trying to tell you what to do, but don't be scared.
W: But someone nationally know against someone just like me, a regular person, I mean, people like just kind of naturally think that I'm going for the money or something.
D2: You don't know that. Cause you don't know what might happen.
W: Uh . . .
D2: You don't know that. The only way you are going to find out is to try.
W: Yeah.
D2: you are just as much a person as he is.
W: Yeah.
D2: If your heart is telling you to go ahead and do something about it, then you do something about it whether he is famous. If

135

he was the president of the United States, if you feel like he should, if something should be done, then you do it.
W: Uh huh.
D2: Is it what you want to do?
W: Part of me wants to do something, and part of me is scared.
D2: You want to talk to somebody.
W: Yeah.
D2: OK. Let me . . . do you want to leave a number or do you want somebody to come out right now?
W: Uh, I'm at a hotel right now.
D2: That doesn't matter.
W: And it is like for a pageant, so, if someone were to come talk to me, then it wouldn't look good for me.
D2: I understand.
W: Uh . . .
D2: Do you want to talk to someone on the phone?
W: Yeah.
D2: Ok. Let me give you, what's your phone number?
W: OK
D2: What's the phone number where you can be reached at?
W: Ok, I'm at the Omni Biltmore, I'm at the Omni Biltmore and the number 317-634- and I'm in room 2, I'm in room 443, but it says 2443.
D2: So you are in room 243.
W: Uh, huh. And I think the number to the Omni is 6666. Or 6661. But . . .
D2: Are you the only one there in your room?

W: No, there are my two roommates. But I told them about it already.
D2: Do you feel comfortable leaving your first name?
W: My name is Desiree.
D2: You-Desiree.
W: Uh huh.
D2: OK. I'm going to have someone call your from victim's assistance.
W: OK
D2: OK
W: Alright thank you.
D2: Uh huh. Bye.
W: Bye Bye.

Ending time is 01.35.41. This tape was recorded by Gail Larsen, Tape Research Analysis, IPD.

Before Washington's conversation was entered into evidence, admissibility of the audiotape became quite the debate between the prosecution and defense. Kathleen Beggs argued that the tape should have been submitted into evidence while Washington was testifying so that cross-examination could have been conducted. But she also argued that the tape was not relevant due to the time gap between when the alleged rape occurred and when the telephone call was placed, that because of her earlier argument, the witness was no longer available for cross-examination about the tape contents, that the strong responses from the dispatchers were highly prejudicial and that under no stretch of the rules could the taped conversation be considered an "excited utterance, and thus admissible under an exception to the hearsay rule" because of the time gap.

Prosecutor Greg Garrison countered by arguing that to leave out the contents of the tape "takes a piece out of our case" and not permit Washington from defending herself against the "hatchet job" done on her character by Vincent Fuller. Calling Begg's argument "silly," he said the tape portrayed Washington's state of mind (an exception to the hearsay rule) and therefore was highly relevant.

To this point in the trial, Judge Patricia Gifford had been quite careful not to permit any evidence peripheral in nature to the actual facts surrounding the alleged rape in the hotel room. But, she permitted the tape into evidence since the defense had brought into the case the defense of motive, by some means charging that she was money-motivated to accuse Tyson, and the conversation allegedly showed an alternative motive.

The jury was thus able to hear the tape, with some parts deleted, permitting Washington, if effect, to testify twice, the second time without cross-examination. The defense did not argue that it be permitted to call Washington again to the stand, but perhaps they felt the taped conversation indicated some inconsistencies with Washington's direct examination they could argue later in the trial. The fact that she had brought up the issue of money during the call could give the jury the feeling that Washington was fishing for information about whether such a motive would cause her problems if she filed charges. But just the fact that the issue of money was on her mind appeared significant.

Prior to trial, both the prosecution and the defense had enlarged the importance of the 911 tape for obvious respective reasons. The prosecution felt Washington's call was consistent with her direct testimony and showed she was struggling with whether to file charges because she was "scared" and wondered if anyone would believe her since Tyson was a "famous person," and she was a "regular person." But the defense could counter with the money issue and the fact that dispatcher number two, while trying to be objective, was much more persuasive toward applying pressure for Washington to file charges that her counterpart, the trainee. In the end, the jurors would decide the relevance of the tape as they heard Washington's voice for a second time. The defense was left to hear it too and without the benefit of any cross-examination. Would they pay for this in the end?

Chapter Twelve
Three Who Never Appeared

For the most part, the Mike Tyson trial had been smooth sailing for Judge Patricia Gifford. The admissibility of the 911 tape had been subject to objection by some courtroom observers, especially the "legal beagles" who were providing media outlets with expert opinion, but her handling of the trial had brought praise from most everyone who had watched whether her pro-prosecution background might sway her toward the state's way of thinking.

A test awaited her, however, when chief Tyson defense lawyer Vincent Fuller attempted to add three material witnesses to the defense list before the trial continued. His reason for doing so was explained in a written motion filed with the court:

> "These persons were present near the front entrance of the Canterbury Hotel in the early morning of July 19, 1991, and witnesses a limousine pull up in the driveway. One of the witnesses observed two people in the back seat of the limousine hugging and kissing and pointed that fact out to the second witness. One of the two persons that emerged from the back of the limousine was young black woman with prominent hair; the first witness recognized the other person to emerge as Mike Tyson, and she pointed him out to the second witness. The third witness who was on the telephone in the hotel parlor and was looking out the

window, noticed the two people holding hands after they exited the limousine and entered the hotel. The witnessed also described a heavy-set black man with golf glasses who emerged from the limousine's front passenger seat and a woman who emerged from the driver's seat."

In behalf of their motion, Fuller and company asked the court to consider that the defense had only learned about these witnesses on January 30th when contact was made with co-counsel James Voyle's office. After talking with the three witnesses, and verifying their stories, Greg Garrison was alerted to the witness's existence. The legal argument to permit their testimony was based on due process of law with Fuller stating how critical they were to defending his client.

To bolster their case that the three should be permitted to testify, the defense filed an "Offer of Proof" for each witness. The first read:

> " . . . It is anticipated that Carla J. Martin would testify that [she], along with Ms. Lawrence and Ms. Neal, attended the Johnny Gill concert at the Hoosier Dome on the night of July 18, 1991. Ms. Martin did so because she was the girlfriend of am an who was playing the drums in Mr. Gill's band on this particular tour. Because Mr. Gill's band was staying in the Canterbury Hotel, Ms. Martin had changed her closes on the day of the concert in a room in the Canterbury Hotel and left a bag with her belongings at the front desk. After the concert ended sometime after 12:30 a.m. on July 19, Ms.

Martin and her two companions went to the backstage area of the Hoosier Dome in which Mr. Gill's bus was parked. When Mr. Gill's band was fully packed on the bus, Ms. Martin said goodbye to her boyfriend and she and her companions left the Hoosier Dome. They went to Mrs. Lawrence's Nisson 300ZX.

With Ms. Lawrence driving, the three women proceeded to the Canterbury Hotel in order to pick up Ms. Martin's belongings. Ms. Martin sat crammed behind her two friends in the two-seat sports car. They pulled their car up next to the curb, just beyond the entrance to the semicircular driveway of the hotel. Ms. Martin went inside to retrieve her bag, and Ms. Neal also entered the hotel in order to make a phone call.

Ms. Martin got her bag, exited the hotel, and sat down in the passenger seat (since Ms. Neal had not yet emerged from the hotel). As Ms. Martin sat there, a limousine pulled slowly into the semicircular driveway. Ms. Martin looked at the limousine, was able to see through the tinted side windows in the back seat, and noticed a man and a woman hugging and kissing. Ms. Martin exclaimed to Ms. Lawrence that the two people were all over each other.

Ms. Martin then observed that people began to exit the limousine. The woman exited first, from the passenger door facing the

hotel, and stepped back so that her upper body was visible to Ms. Martin above the trunk portion of the limousine. Ms. Martin noticed that she was a black woman with shoulder-length curly hair. The second person to emerge from the limousine was husky black man with large glasses; he exited from the front passenger seat of the limousine. The, the driver of the limousine, who was a black female with tinted hair, existed; she began to walk around to the passenger side of the limousine. The man who had been kissing in the back seat then exited the limousine, and Ms. Martin immediately recognized him as Mike Tyson. She noted that fact to Ms. Lawrence. Ms. Observed the woman moved toward Mr. Tyson until their upper bodies appeared to be touching, and she appeared to put her arm in Mr. Tyson's. Ms. Martin then observed Mr. Tyson and the woman enter the Canterbury Hotel, at about the same time that her third friend was leaving the hotel. Ms. Martin observed that Ms. Neal bumped into Mr. Tyson and the young woman."
The Offer of Proof for witness Pamela Lawrence was of a similar nature to that of Carla Martin with a few differing details: "Ms. Lawrence then observed a young black female emerge from the rear passenger-side of the limousine. Ms. Lawrence observed that the woman had a prominent hair style of a kind not commonly seen among black women in Indiana. Then Ms. Lawrence observed a black male exit from the rear passenger-side of the limousine. Ms.

Lawrence heard Ms. Martin say that the black male was Mike Tyson. Ms. Lawrence further observed a heavy-set black man in the vicinity of the limousine. Ms. Lawrence observed Mr. Tyson and the young black woman enter the hotel together."

The Offer of Proof for witness Renee Neal paralleled that of the other two women regarding attending the Gill concert. The only new element Neal added was her observation that "the man and woman [were] holding hands as they entered the hotel." She also had seen the "heavy-set black man with gold glasses near the limousine."

James Voyles verified for the court that the three witnesses had only been discovered the previous week. He told Judge Gifford that many people had called his office since the trial had begun suggesting information but that many of them were crank calls disregarded. But when one of his associates talked to the woman and believed they were legitimate, Voyles interviewed them. He then immediately called Greg Garrison to alert him to the women. Tempers flared when Garrison questioned Voyle's veracity with Voyles shouting "You've jumped on the wrong bull's back." Garrison never backed down in his belief that the defense had been less than candid before arguing that not only had his star witness testified previously, but most of his critical witnesses as well. "Must the prosecution start over," he raved, citing the unfairness of the late witness disclosure.

No issue involving a motion to add witnesses had been heard in the William Kennedy Smith case, the Rodney King state trial, or the Bensonhurst trial. But three witnesses who could have testified about Kennedy's apparent involvement in sexual assaults similar to the one he was charged with, had been banned by the judge. This was a tremendous victory for the defense, and one of the main reason prosecutors pointed to the eventual not-guilty verdict. Here the stakes were high as well since the three women, if permitted to testify, plugged holes in Washington's testimony, especially regarding her behavior in the limousine before she and Tyson entered the Canterbury Hotel. If she was kissing and hugging Tyson as Carla Martin would testify, then a far different portrait of the hotel room events was painted, one questioning Washington's version of the story in Tyson's bedroom. The jury could certainly infer that if the beauty contestant was being less than candid about this part of her story, it cast down on the entire story she had told him while testifying.

For the first time in the trial, Judge Gifford appeared rattled by the sudden turn of events letting her emotions get the better of her. Before making a ruling, she explained that she did not appreciate being put in the current position. She told the lawyers strict discovery guidelines had been set up, and the personal banter between the attorneys was not welcome in her courtroom. Normally, when any important ruling was required, she took her time and consulted with David McNamer, her savvy court commissioner, but this time she did not. Instead, with what appeared to a less than judicial manner, she summarily denied the defense's right to present the three witnesses stating that their appearance would cause "substantial prejudice to the State's case." She also explained that this prejudice could not be cure by a recess or a continuance since the State's witnesses had already testified. More than anything, she appeared quite offended by the antics of Fuller and Voyles in testing her judgment with such a request. The judge also never mentioned that the prosecution had already interviewed the three women and would have their chance to cross-examine them before the jury. Where was the search for the truth, Tyson's attorneys wanted to know? Did not these three witnesses need to be heard so as to learn that truth?

Indianapolis Star legal expert, retired judge John Tranberg, was skeptical of the decisions, stating, "I will not second-guess Judge Gifford, but the two questions were close calls." Regarding the 911 tape, he added, "[It] bolsters the victim's claims. It was really a dramatic moment in the case as we were able to listen to [Washington's] voice talk about how she wanted to report the rape but was afraid that because her attacker was a celebrity, that she would come under fire." Concerning the exclusion of the three witnesses, the respected Tranberg said, "Garrison really wanted that evidence kept out and it got almost personal. The evidence must have been damaging to the victim's story."

In retrospect, the decision to exclude the testimony of the three witnesses, especially Carla Martin, one that appeared to be quite personal in nature, was arguably the most important one she made at trial. As an afterthought, Judge Gifford later labeled the anticipated testimony "cumulative" when it clearly was not. But her decision stood, and Tyson was dealt a critical blow to his chances of being acquitted. Three witnesses - none of whom appeared to be biased - would never be heard by the jury. In effect, the judge had given prosecutor Jeff Modisett the exact sort of ruling he was hoping for when Judge Gifford ruled against admitting relevant testimony. Most courtroom observers, including the legal beagles, were shocked not only by the decision but the personal nature of it. This was by far the judge's darkest hour, the moment when she had failed to provide Tyson with a fair trial for what appeared to be more of a problem with inconvenience to her than to the trial itself.

 The ruling rekindled thoughts on the part of many that Judge Gifford should have never accepted the case in the first place but disqualified herself as being the wrong judge to be hearing Tyson's sex crimes case. To be certain, the judge was well-intentioned when it came to serving up justice, and quite competent with most matters affecting the law, but her prosecutorial background, especially in the sex crimes arena, made it nearly impossible for her to rule without prejudice and fairly during a rape trial such as Tyson's. Now, in the eyes of many, she had embarrassed herself, and while the ruling might be confirmed on appeal, if there was one, she had denied Tyson the due process right to have important witnesses heard by the jury deciding his fate. All this, because she said, it would prejudice the state. At the end of the day, Modisett, Garrison, and Trathen had to be smiling. Judge Gifford had, in effect, become a member of the prosecution team.

 Once the hearing ended, and the attorneys settled down, the prosecution called to the witness stand Mary Washington, Desiree's mother. Her testimony was quite brief but very important since she was the one who had strongly suggested that Desiree call 911 to report the rape accusation.

Obviously quite proud of her daughter, the attractive mother testified that when she saw her daughter in the lobby of the Omni Hotel, Desiree "looked terrible." Then, with tears running down her cheeks, she said, "She's not the same daughter I sent here." She told the jury, as to whether Desiree should file charges, "this was a decision she must make, but whatever decision she made, I'll be behind her 100%. I encouraged her to do whatever is right."

When Mrs. Washington completed her direct testimony, Vincent Fuller, the nice guy from the big city, asked but two questions: "Do you consider your daughter an intelligent woman, and do you love your daughter?" The answers were a predictable "yes," and the mother was excused from testifying. Fuller had obviously decided to let her go without any testing of her daughter's story, any of the facts at all. Doing so was the easy way out, and Fuller was right that he had to be careful with Mrs. Washington, but there was questions that needed to be asked, among them ones dealing with whether the daughter feared her mother knowing about being with Tyson in the middle of the night when she faced the pageant contest the next day, accompanying the boxer to this hotel room, and so forth. Could it have been possible that Washington feared telling her mother about being with Tyson and made up the story about the rape so as to escape the wrath she knew would be forthcoming from a mother who loved her daughter dearly and might suspect that Desiree had sex with Tyson? Was the rape charge a shield against such wrath, with Washington already upset over being treated as a one-night stand? If Clara Martin was telling the truth and Tyson and Washington were hugging and kissing in the limousine, and why would she have lied, then wasn't it logical to think that Washington wanted to have sex with Tyson but when he treated her so rudely wanted to get back at him? And so when she told her mother that she had been with Tyson, a story that certainly the mother would have heard from Desiree's roommates, she finally decided in her mind that yes, she had been raped. This story then took root when she first told her roommate and then another contestant and finally took hold in her mind when she spoke to her mother. Did this then make her think that if she could prove rape, money was possible from the rich Tyson? Perhaps this explained why she had given so many different versions of what had occurred to various people as she tried to finalize her story. Certainly, this scenario was subject to conjecture, but Fuller missed a chance to at least probe areas of interest with Mrs. Washington that might fit later with evidence to prove his theories. Instead, Mr. nice guy let her off the hook with two short questions.

After Mrs. Washington exited the courtroom, Garrison played the 911 tape for the jury. Since there was no possibility of cross-examination as Washington had traveled back to the east coast, the jury heard her voice without objection and without interruption. Jurors faces craned forward listening to her every word with little doubt that the impact of her being "afraid," and hesitant as to whether to file charges against Tyson since she wondered whether a "regular" person like her would be believed against the word of a famous fellow like the ex-champ, rang in their ears. And the judge listened with everyone else without an apparent care that the best way to really serve justice was for there be a trial continuance so that Washington could be recalled to the stand and cross-examined as to her words on the tape and, if the three witnesses were permitted to testify, about the blatant discrepancies between her direct testimony about what occurred with Tyson in the limousine before they arrived at the Canterbury Hotel and what Clarita Martin and her friends witnessed. But such was never to be, and after the tape had been played, Greg Garrison announced, "The State rests," ending the prosecution's testimony against Iron Mike.

Was this evidence, on its own, enough to convict Tyson beyond a reasonable doubt since the defense had no duty to present evidence of any kind? Examining the state's case, the testimony by Washington and Virginia Foster, and the medical opinions of Dr. Stephen Richardson, were the strongest reasons to do so but certainly the 911 tape had been an added corroboration to Washington's direct testimony. Despite the strength of the state's case, many court observers, including several of the legal beagles covering the trial, believed that if the defense had rested, the prosecution's chances at conviction were at most fifty-fifty *if*, and it was a dubious if, Vincent Fuller presented a strong, lethal final argument in his client's behalf. But, based on his trial performance, and the choices he had made, there was much to wonder about whether he could come through for Tyson.

While deciding whether to present a defense is always a tough call, (many experts believe jurors expect them to do so regardless of the presumption of innocence and no duty to present any defense),

Fuller had no choice in the matter since he had promised the jury in his ill-fated opening statement that they would hear from Tyson. He had thus boxed himself in to presenting a defense unless he felt he could explain that the evidence was so weak that Tyson did not need to testify, a tricky proposition at best. In addition, Fuller caused himself problems by not outlining sufficiently his line of defense through his questioning of the state's witnesses, a common practice by experienced trial lawyers who expose their theories through crafty questions or comments leading the jury to understand what the defenses are. This is an especially strong tactic when the accused either has a terrible criminal record, or would, in the estimation of trial counsel, make a terrible witness in his own behalf for any number of reasons including a principal one – having inadequate social skills to handle the pressure of doing so. Certainly Fuller must have realized that his client fit this description since Tyson was, due to educational deficiencies and lack of social skills, unable to converse well with other members of the human race. But Fuller had promised the jury they would hear from his client, and there was thus no decision to be made – the defense would present a defense.

In the William Kennedy Smith case, Roy Black had never, wisely, committed his client to testify. In fact, Black had never permitted his client to say "word one" about the charges except to utter "not guilty" when read the charges by the judge handling his arraignment. The prosecution was left with no ability to know whether Kennedy Smith would testify but hoped the strength of their case would force Black to present him to the jury.

Black's decision to keep his client silent before the trial had also assisted the defense since there were no statements that had to be reconciled with any possible trial testimony. Expert defense attorneys know that 95% of those accused *convict themselves* through their own words since it is the tendency of human beings to explain their conduct when confronted with accusations of any kind. If people would keep their mouths shut when any accusations are made, especially by law enforcement officials, and simply say the simple words, "I want to talk to a lawyer," the prisons would be less full of people who convicted themselves through stupid statements that come back to haunt them. But people are basically blabbermouths and few have the strength to keep quiet until they receive legal counsel.

In the Clarence Thomas/Anita Hill confrontation, the two squared off in a bizarre no-rules situation with United States senators firing questions at them left and right. Neither had the benefit of counsel to object to questions, and each made statements that caused some heads to turn. Whether the question of Thomas' fitness to serve on the Supreme Court would have been decided differently if the case had been in a court of law is subject to conjecture, but a good, rigorous cross-examination of both would have certainly produced a better attempt at the truth in what amounted to a "he said, she said," argument.

The Rodney King state trial produced another instance where the appearance of a witness, in this case King himself, was the subject of a decision that was critical to the outcome of a trial. Based on King's messy past, conflicting statements, and criminal record, Los Angeles County District

Attorney Ira Reiner and lead counsel Terry White decided it was best to never present King to the jury. Hindsight proved this decision was a disastrous one since keeping King silent at trial made it impossible for jurors to humanize King while he told of his terrible beating at the hands of police. White apparently felt that the videotape of the horrible incident spoke for itself, but seeing King in person might have made quite the difference as he explained the agony he experienced. White, like all good prosecutors do when their client has questionable character, especially when they are testifying for the prosecution through a plea bargain, reveal the nastiness of the witness' background to the jury before the defense does so. Basically they are saying, "hey, yes, this guy or gal is a terrible human being, but regardless, they are telling the truth about what occurred." Juries then may weigh the veracity of the witness based on the good, the bad, and the ugly.

Faced with the decision as to whether to call their clients to the witness stand, defense lawyers for the four accused policemen decided to let the jury hear their stories. This decision was a wise one, and led to the not-guilty verdicts when the pro-law enforcement jury acquitted them of all charges.

Accused murderer Lemrick Nelson, Jr. did not take the witness stand in the Bensonhurst trial. Defense lawyer Arthur Lewis made that decision based mainly on post-arrest statements by Nelson that were, in effect, admissions of guilt. The judge had disallowed them into testimony but Lewis did not want to take a chance on Nelson being asked about the statements and instead turned the attention of the trial toward the veracity of the police officers who handled the investigation. By placing there believability on trial, he shifted the burden of proof to the prosecution causing them to defend their own witnesses accounts of what occurred on the night of Yankel Rosenbaum's murder. Lewis and Black's brilliant strategies made one wonder how Tyson's trial might have turned out if either had defended him.

Having little option as to whether there would be a defense to the charges against the ex-champ, or that Tyson would testify, Vincent Fuller prepared to launch a strategy aimed at creating reasonable doubt in the jury's mind that his client was a rapist. No one will thus ever know what the outcome might have been if the defense had startled the prosecution with the announcement, "The Defense rests." Based on the eventual verdict convicting Tyson, silence might have been the better strategy employed.

Chapter Thirteen
The Defense Attacks

In line with Vincent Fuller's opening statement to the jury, the defense intended to call witnesses designed to: indicate Desire Washington provided inconsistent statements concerning what occurred during the alleged rape; show that because of Tyson's bad behavior and lewd language, Washington must have known of his sexual intentions; point out that her appearance in his hotel room at 2:00 a.m. proved she intended to have sex with Washington; suggest that while in the hotel room she had consensual sex with the ex-champ, and demonstrate that Washington's ulterior motive for filing the rape charge was the anticipation of millions through a civil lawsuit. In hindsight, if Fuller and company had concentrated on one single issue, consent, the outcome of the trial might have been quite different.

Tyson's close friend and confidant John Horne was the first defense witness. The thrust of the Tyson loyalist's testimony was twofold: one, to show the jury that Tyson could not have unlocked his hotel room without assistance since he never carried credit cards or keys, and two, to inform jurors that he had driven from Albany, New York to Cleveland to meet Tyson when he arrived there on July 19th. The latter was intended to show that Iron Mike had not fled Indianapolis right after the Washington encounter but left as planned to travel to Ohio. Up next was Joan Bates, a hostess at St. Vincent Hospital in Indianapolis. She was the aunt of B Angie B, the rapper girlfriend of Tyson. Mrs. Bates said her niece told her Tyson would be joining her in Indianapolis during Black Expo but then would travel to Cleveland for another concert. She then informed the jury that she saw Tyson at her home on the 17th when B Angie B and Tyson walked around their neighborhood with a bodyguard. Mrs. Bates testified that she saw B Angie B the next morning, and then took her to the airport to meet Tyson for the trip to Cleveland. A missed opportunity occurred when defense lawyers failed to ask Mrs. Bates Tyson's demeanor when she saw him at the airport a few hours after the alleged rape. If he was in a good mood, this would have countered allegations by the Canterbury Hotel employees who said Tyson was in poor spirits.

Off-duty Indianapolis Police Department Sargeant Eugene Boyd told the jury he had seen Washington in the Omni Hotel lobby at approximately 1:15-1:30 a.m. on July 20th. This occurred when Washington's parents arrived at the hotel and asked if they could double-park in the entryway. When Sgt. Boyd asked Mrs. Washington why this was necessary, Boyd said she replied, "My daughter has been raped." Boyd then asked "Where?" to which Mrs. Washington answered, "At another hotel." Boyd added that he then saw two young black females in the lobby and inquired of them whether police assistance was forthcoming. He said the older of the two said, "Yes, we've called 911 and a police officer is going to assist us."

Turning to the money motive, Fuller called to the witness stand Desiree's father, Donald. "Haven't you hired civil lawyers?" Fuller first ask, followed by the questions, "Could you bring a civil suit?" and "What about the garment Desiree wore and the sequins?" To these questions, the calm Washington provided answers that were vague and somewhat evasive. But the effect was clear, Fuller believed he had scored no points by questioning the alleged rape victim's father and probably lost some with his attempt to show the money motive. Why Mr. Washington was called as a witness made no sense to anyone. In fact, legal expert John Tranberg concluded it was a big mistake, stating, "The father understandably has strong feelings about Tyson and what he believes happened to his daughter. His stare could have an effect on the jury." The latter comment was in reference to Donald Washington's having stared at Tyson so intensely that when Tyson caught his eyes, the boxer looked away. Several of the jurors must have noticed this exchange.

Fortunately the next witness, Reverend Kathryn Newlin, was a bit stronger. The resident chaplain at Methodist Hospital where Washington was treated, she replied to the questions "Was the victim in pain? In physical discomfort?" by answering, "No, she looked tired; she was quiet. Rev. Newlin then told the jury of overhearing Washington's conversation with Dr. Stephen Richardson and hearing her say that "Tyson was touching some of the girls." Regarding the alleged attack, Rev. Newlin said Washington told Richardson Tyson "was touching her breasts and panties." She then heard Washington say she told Tyson, "No more" but "Tyson continued on." "Did you get a read on what Desiree's involvement was?" Rev. Newlin was asked. Her answer: "Yes, I had a feeling there was some sense of participation." This latter statement, perhaps indication of consensual foreplay occurring, along with Rev. Newlin's testimony that Washington had allegedly seen Tyson touch other girls, definitely scored points for the defense, much needed points.

Additionally, the presence of Mrs. Washington throughout Desiree's report of the alleged rape appeared an attempt by Fuller to show the mother's influence, perhaps even pressure, to file charges. Whether this was clear to jurors or not remained to be seen.

If Fuller understood the potential strength of the gift he had been given through the, "I had a feeling there was some sort of participation" comment by Rev. Newlin, he may not have fully realized it. Based on the questionable evidence presented by the prosecution, and now this revelation, could not Fuller have simply sidestepped calling Tyson to the witness stand, called any other witnesses he felt beneficial to his case, and then resting with confidence that the state had not proven their case beyond a reasonable doubt? Of course he could have, and most experienced county court trial lawyers would have done so. But Fuller could not resist permitting Tyson to testify, could not remedy the idiotic promise he had made to the jury during opening statement that the ex-champ would be heard from, and thus he marched ahead with blinders on and his client's freedom at stake. Did he not realize that the consent defense provided the best of all possible avenues toward a not-guilty verdict? Hone in on that with further witnesses and argument, and let Tyson sit in his chair and doodle instead of taking the extreme risk of testifying and in all likelihood, based on his poor social skills, convicting himself. With the decision already made, however, a bizarre incident then occurred that caught everyone by surprise. It the Tyson trial could be judged a strange one, it was about to get even stranger.

Chapter Fourteen
The Mysterious Hotel Fire

On February 5th, a three-alarm fire raged through the third floor of the downtown Indianapolis Athletic Club where the jurors had been sequestered during the trial. One guest, and two firefighters battling the inferno were killed.

Twenty-six people in all had been evacuated from the seven-story dark brick building. Marion County Sheriff's Deputy Donald Marshall and two court bailiffs escorted all of the jurors to safety and then by bus to the City/County Building still dressed in their nightclothes. Judge Gifford's chief clerk, Joe Champion, told reporters "the jurors were in good spirits under the circumstances." Cause for the fire was deemed accidental, but due to mysterious nature of the blaze and the timing, Prosecutor Jeff Modisett ordered a grand jury investigation. The report later would corroborate the finding that the fire was accidental. Whether this was a certainty or not remained unknown, however, since some, especially those in the media, wondered whether the fire had been a warning of sort to jurors delivered by none other than Tyson's spiked-haired manager, Don King. Most important, would jurors connect this potential and if so, might it effect the trial outcome? Maybe some would be scared, and thus delivered a not-guilty verdict regardless of feelings to the contrary realizing that if he convicted Tyson, King, known as a bad guy extraordinaire, might cause them harm? But perhaps others might feel that if King were responsible, they were not about to be intimidated by King and thus would vote to convict despite feelings to the contrary just to show Tyson's manager he could not intimidate them. To ward off either result, Judge Gifford wisely questioned each juror individually to gain a sense of their state of mind. All but one, Chuck, juror #11, the African-American law firm ex-employee, told the court they wanted to remain on the jury. But his loss meant a reduction in the number of minorities on the jury. If King had been responsible for the fire, his intentions to help Tyson's cause backfired. Tyson would now be judged by only two Africa-Americans on the jury instead of three. How would this unforeseen development affect the outcome especially since after the trial some jurors admitted that they had seen flags flying at half-staff indicating to them that someone connected with the city had died in the Athletic Club blaze? Could jurors block out this most unfortunate series of events that Tyson had no control over. Now an intangible hung over the sense of a search for truth in the trial with prosecutors and defense lawyer wondering how the strange turn of events would affect their respective cases.

Chapter Fifteen
Beauties and the Beast

    Regardless of any feelings to the contrary, the suspicious nature of the fire altered security outside the 4th floor Criminal Court hallway. Metal detectors were suddenly appeared, and dogs were brought in to sniff for possible explosives. Security officers said the beefed-up security was merely a coincidence, but most knew otherwise.

    Before Iron Mike Tyson made his long-anticipated trek to the witness stand, Vincent Fuller called twenty-year-old Miss Black Expo Beauty Pageant contestant Madelyn Whittington, to testify after the one-day delay in the proceedings. To the amazement of the court, and in likelihood, the jurors, Whittington said Washington told her "she wanted money, wanted to be like Robin Givens." Whittington also said she observed Tyson and Washington hugging after Washington had danced during the rehearsal like "she wanted someone to notice her." The beauty contestant said Tyson kidded with the contestants, asking them, "Do you want to come to my room? I know I'm not gonna get nothin', but I'll ask anyway." Whittington said Tyson tried to move on her, but she said she did not want anything to do with him. When he heard this comment, Whittington said she heard Tyson say, "Who does she think she is, that little Catholic school motherf . . . ?" This comment startled everyone who heard it? Was the defense trying to seal Tyson's fate by exposing his irreverent, his demeaning behavior?

    Asked if she noticed any difference between Desiree Washington's demeanor from start to finish with the pageant events, Whittington said, "No." To the question, "Was Desiree absent from any of the competition," she repeated her answer of "No." During Greg Garrison's cross-examination, the prosecutor duplicated a Fuller mistake by fishing around for information by asking a question he did not know the answer to. This resulted in Whittington explaining that after the swimsuit competition where Washington was not one of the ten finalist, she heard Washington say, "I'm a ten, all the boys want to know my name at the beach." Certainly, Whittington's testimony added to the defense portrayal of Tyson as a known womanizer in full view of Washington and her being somewhat less than the "goody two-shoes" the prosecution and her had portrayed her to be. Amazingly enough, no mention of Whittington's testimony would ever be made during Fuller's final argument.

Beauty pageant contestant Cecelia Alexander next testified for the defense. Wearing a checked coat and black sweater and pants together with a small cross hanging from her neck, the Charleston, South Carolina resident spoke confidently as jurors gazed at her rounded cheeks, ruby red lipstick, and swept back, perfectly coiffed black hair. After telling the jury she wanted to be a dentist after graduating from college, Alexander testified that she saw "Washington's arm hit Mike" during rehearsals and that "they hugged, and she hugged back." Alexander added, "He asked her to go out" and she said, "Sure." Then, Alexander swore, Tyson kidded her for being from Georgia where "Holyfield [heavyweight boxer Evander Holyfield] was from." Later, while Alexander was in the bathroom, she said she heard Washington and a woman named "Madelyn" talk about Tyson and "his intelligence." Alexander told the jury Washington said, "He's not intelligent . . . he's dumb, ignorant; look at the money Robin Givens got." At the Black Expo opening ceremonies, Alexander said she heard Washington and another contestant chatting. According to Alexander the "other contestant" said, "Here comes your husband. He doesn't speak very well." Alexander said Washington replied, "Mike doesn't have to speak. He'll make the money, and I'll do the talking." When the words left Alexander's mouth, Ken, juror #2 looked squarely at Tyson. He showed a slight smile at the comment.

Regarding other interaction between Tyson and Washington, Alexander said Washington showed the ex-champ a photograph of her in a bathing suit. His comment, according to Alexander, "Boy – I have the advantage; I've seen you in a swimsuit." Then Alexander added that "Washington had competed in all the activities Friday, Saturday, and Sunday, and I saw no change in her demeanor." Later, Alexander told the jury she saw Washington sitting by herself. To the question of whether she was alright, Alexander said Washington told her, "she was feeling bad, had menstrual cramps." Washington also said her parents were coming, and Alexander waited with her. But Alexander also recalled that after the swimsuit competition, Washington was upset that she was not a Top Ten finisher. "I don't understand why others won; I'm no loser," was the comment Alexander recalled.

Finally, Alexander testified that when the FBI asked her if she knew anything about a rape, she asked them who the woman was. When they wouldn't tell her, she said she asked if she could guess by calling out a name. When she was told that would be acceptable, Alexander said she said, "Desiree Washington." Garrison objected to the answer, and it was sustained, but the jury had heard the response.

When the defense was through with Alexander, they must have felt a large hole had been driven in the state's case as a different Desiree Washington was being portrayed to the jury. And then they received some unexpected help since Greg Garrison's questions only served to reinforce Alexander's story. Instead of catching her in a lie or two, or at least some inconsistency, Alexander, appearing to be quite the unbiased witness, stood her ground making Garrison appear a bit foolish. In hindsight, he probably wished he had asked no questions.

Having hit a highlight with Alexander's testimony, the defense could have moved to more impressions of Washington and her behavior before and after the alleged rape. But it chose an unfortunate departure by calling two witnesses that broke the chain of testimony. The first was Iva Rogers, the Canterbury Hotel housekeeper. Extremely hard of hearing, this witness was asked about the bed, the covers, and the sheets that she found in room 606 after Tyson left. Her testimony was quite incomplete but she did add a quizzical comment when she testified that on the corner of the bed where Washington said she sat, there were spots of blood like Rogers had seen when "girls get married." What this meant to either the defense or prosecution was unclear, but the defense witness certainly corroborated Washington's testimony as to where she was on the bed. Neither counsel asked whether Rogers had seen the panty shield in the bathroom Washington alluded to providing the jury with no guidance as to this important piece of evidence.

Again deviating from the string of beauty contestants, the defense called its own medical expert, Dr. Margaret Watanobe. Her testimony proved to be so dull that two jurors, numbers two and six, actually nodded off with number six hiding his yawning behind his long hair.

Called to counteract mainly the testimony of Dr. Stephen Richardson, the Indiana University physician was too technical in nature when asked about pelvic examinations. Finally, after everyone was tired of her diatribe, defense attorney Kathleen Beggs asked the most important question: Was it possible, from the abrasions in Desiree Washington's vagina, to say that they were caused by forced sex? After pausing for emphasis, Watanobe said, "I don't know" leaving everyone in the dark as to what she meant. No one cleared this up, and soon Dr. Watanobe was excused from the courtroom.

Returning to the beauty pageant contestants, next up was Parquita Nassau, a short woman with deep brown eyes and a stately figure who wore a white top with a dark skirt. Her bangs flowed over her forehead as she told the jury that Tyson and Washington embraced and "cuddled" after they met at the dance rehearsal. "I saw them talking," Nassau said, "I saw them cuddling up to each other. They were more intimate as far as their contact and conversation. It looked like they were involved with each other." Apparently believing that Nassua's testimony hurt his case in chief, Greg Garrison badgered the witness with accusations that she had changed her story several times after being contacted by the defense, "eleven times." "You just forgot they were cuddling all these minutes behind the post," Garrison roared. Nassau fought back – "I said they were cuddling. Hugging and cuddling are the same thing to me." She then added, much to the dismay of the prosecutor that Tyson had said to the group in general, "If you don't want to go out, I can go on. I can have any one of you bitches," before adding, "I know you want me. I know you want me." Nassau completed her testimony by telling the jurors that Washington must have heard the conversation since when Nassau said, "He's asking us all out," Washington said, "Yeah, I know."

    Thirty-one-year-old Tanya Traylor, wearing a white blouse and blue suit coat, testified next for the defense. From Miami, she presented quite the contrast in terms of experience from the other beauty queen hopefuls. Asked what the keys to participating were, she said a contestant, "needed to be focused, needs to practice a great deal," and needed to "be physically fit." This said, she turned to explaining to the jurors, each paying close attention, Tyson's behavior at the rehearsal. Traylor said his words and actions caused him to be perceived as "not a nice person and that everybody said he had sexual overtones." He asked, Traylor said, "everybody to go out," and if he "got a no, then he moved on to the next girl." Tyson talked, she said, about taking girls "back to the room and that a kiss will do, but sex is better." "He was rude," she said and insisting that "girls sit on his lap if they wanted their picture taken." She refused, she said, since "I didn't want to have my picture taken that badly."

    At the opening ceremonies, Traylor said Tyson irreverent conduct continued. When "Carlina," a contestant, asked him about the size of his hands, Traylor told the jury, and how big they were, Tyson made "a very suggestive remark about 'what hands would be used for.'" When Traylor asked Tyson why he was like that, she said he told her, "People expect it, and next time you'll know me." Later, Traylor said she Tyson again at the Johnny Gill concert. Backstage with "Norma, another contestant," Traylor said another opportunity occurred for her to speak with Tyson. This time her impression of him was quite different during what she described as the hour conversation and she agreed to have her picture taken with him. "He was polite," Traylor said, "a nicer person, more down to earth." Following this line of questioning, defense counsel Lane Heard attempted to ascertain whether Traylor had heard Washington disciplined by pageant official Alita Anderson for being "a groupie," but a prosecution objection was sustained by Judge Gifford. This would not prevent a video of the entire video filmed by Traylor's husband to be shown to the jury later. It depicted Washington singing, dancing, and smiling away as she played to the camera.

Asked if she noticed any demeanor change in Washington during the final two days of the competition, Traylor said "Her spirits seemed to be the same." Cross-examination produced testimony that Traylor thought Washington was a "nice person," one whom she had invited to her Miami home. Then Traylor once again portrayed Tyson as a bad boy based on his lewd remarks and distasteful behavior noting that Washington had seen all that occur. When asked whether Tyson "grabbed her [Traylor's] buttocks when she was backstage," she replied, "No, that did not happen." Most important, while Traylor testified, juror number nine, Tim, the ex-marine, began to pass out breath mints to the other jurors as they watched a sidebar conference between the attorneys and the judge.

The impact of Traylor was the subject of much debate among courtroom watchers and the media. She appeared truthful and unbiased, and although later Garrison would cast doubt on part of her testimony through another witness, her impressions of Washington and Tyson showed a glimpse of the difficulty in deciding who was telling the truth. If Traylor and the previous beauty contestants were to be believed, each had duel personalities during their days in Indianapolis providing a snapshot for juries to evaluate based on the testimony. Only Tim had taken notes thus far during the trial; the others would have to recall through their memories the varied testimony presented.

If there was one beauty contestant that stood out among the others as being the most stunning, it was Jacklyn Boatwright. Dressed in a deep red outfit that accentuated her full figure, the Georgia native said she was a communications major who "tells it like it is." Unlike the other contestants, Boatwright said she never saw Tyson at the rehearsal. Instead, she ran into the ex-champ outside the Omni Hotel. Because she had always wanted to meet him, Boatwright crossed the street to greet him. She said Tyson told her, "You're pretty, give me a kiss on the cheek, and a hug." At the opening ceremonies, Boatwright told the jury she saw Tyson again, this time with a "Together in Christ" badge displayed. She said she watched Tyson with his arm around a contestant, as "he patted her on the rear." The reaction from Washington, standing nearby was a "look that could kill." Regarding Washington's demeanor on the Friday following the alleged rape, Boatwright said she "was the same when she last saw her." During cross-examination, Garrison enticed Boatwright to say that "had heard [Tyson] was a creep."

When popular rhythm and blues singer Johnny Gill walked into the courtroom and to the witness stand, everyone paid close attention. A minister's son, he testified that he had been performing since the age of five. Strikingly handsome with a pencil-thin mustache above his lip, the twenty-five-year-old stated that he had signed a recording contract with Atlantic Records in 1983. Five albums and five million records later, some solo and some with the group, New Edition, Gill was a humble man who hesitated to name the number of music awards he had won during his lively career. He testified that he had visited Indianapolis in July as part of his commitment to "Prom Promises," a tour concept that involved gaining promises where young people would stay away from alcohol or drugs at high school proms. He had arrived at the Canterbury Hotel on July 17th, and met Tyson the followed day when the ex-champ visited his room. He said he and Tyson were friends but "they didn't see too much of each other" although "Tyson had been to several of my concerts." When the two men had lunch at a local restaurant, Reverend Charles Williams, head of Black Expo, suggested they visit the Omni Hotel and greet the contestants. There, Gill said, "all of the girls got very excited when we came into the hall." Pictures and autographs were requested, he told the jury, and then he watched Tyson do a promotional video spot with several contestants. When Gill began to discuss comments he heard

Tyson utter during this time, the prosecution objected and Judge Gifford upheld the objections ruling that Gill could not testify to these comments unless or until Tyson testified because otherwise the testimony would involve hearsay as well since facts that were not yet in evidence. The interruption in his testimony for a hearing to decide such matters diminished the potential effectiveness leaving courtroom observers to wonder why the defense presented Gill before Tyson testified. One reason could still have been the defense uncertainly as to whether Tyson would testify but it appeared that was a foregone conclusion based on Fuller's promises to the jury. If this was true, then there was no excuse for presenting Gill when the defense knew prosecutorial objections would be sustained preventing him from providing critical testimony.

"There's twenty million dollars." This is what Prairie View A&M Graduate School student/beauty pageant contestant Caroline Jones told the jury Washington had said about Tyson during the Omni Hotel rehearsal. When she told Tyson that his hands were "pretty," she replied something about, she said, using the hands "a little horizontal, a little vertical." On the 19th, when she ran into Washington, Jones said Washington said, "I think I've been raped." Jones said she replied, "Either you're raped or you're not." Then, she told the jury, Washington said that "Tyson snapped, ripped my clothes off," and after it was over, allegedly said, "You're nothing, get out of here." Washington told Jones she told Tyson, "No, you're nothing. You're supposed to be a positive influence, a role model." Jones said Washington told her Tyson said, "What have I done?"

Jones told the jury "I was in shock," and that Washington told her "not to tell." Jones said she promised not to do so. "I had my doubts about her story," Jones said. If this answer had been left alone, certainly the jury could have inferred that Jones did not believe Washington, but instead, the defense made a mistake by requesting a clarification with Jones saying she felt that way because Washington was "confused." This took the punch out of Jones' revelation, another in a long line of defense mistakes. When Jones then testified that she told her mother, "Desiree thought she'd been raped," this left jurors wondering once again about the exact language Washington used. Prosecutor Barb Trathen committed the "never ask a question you do not know the answer to" blunder that had befallen Fuller and Garrison before when she asked about Washington's conduct during a videotaping outside Union Station. Jones told the jury, "Miss Washington was mocking the way the defendant talked." But Trathen rebounded by pointing out inconsistencies between Jones' testimony at trial and in a previous deposition where she had used the words "shocked and confused" instead of simply "confused," and that Jones had stated in the deposition that Washington told her Tyson said, "you can't hurt me" when she, "was trying to get away." Then Trathen forced Jones to admit that she had also stated Washington told her "she was crying" when the attack occurred, and that "she didn't know what to do." Here the defense was lax since it did not cover these statements during direct examination. Permitting the prosecutor to unsettle Jones' testimony through inconsistencies took the wind out of her story.

Caroline Jones' mother, Ethel, followed her daughter to the witness stand. She said she met and became friendly with eight or nine of pageant contestants. She called Washington, "intelligent, very nice, friendly, and athletic." She also described Washington as being "very aggressive," and one who always could "get to the front" at photo sessions. When she had the conversation with Caroline about Washington possibly being raped, Ethel Jones walked to the Omni. There, she told the jury, she saw Washington in the foyer. She was, Mrs. Jones said, "smiling, seemed happy. I saw nothing on her hands or body, no bruises – nothing." Later, at the swimsuit competition, Ethel Jones said she saw no bruises. On Sunday, the final day of the competition, Mrs. Jones told the jury Washington "placed overall in the top ten."

Continuing to parade witness after witness before the jury in order to prove its various theories as to why Tyson was innocent, Fuller and company called to the stand Frank Valentine, a twenty-two-year-old Moorehouse College student. He testified that his aunt, Alita Anderson asked him to work with the pageant. At the rehearsal, Valentine told the jury that Washington was "jocking on Mike," a term meant to point out how Washington was attempting to gain Tyson's attention. Later, Valentine testified that he saw Washington backstage at the Johnny Gill concert. He said he saw Anderson and reprimand both Pasha Oliver and Washington by saying, "Stop acting like groupies." Valentine also told the jury Washington never missed any part of the competition, and that she never appeared to act any differently to him from the way she had acted at the beginning of the competition.

On Sunday, Valentine said he saw Washington at about 10:00 a.m. on the Omni Hotel second floor. "Did you go out with Mike Tyson?" Valentine said he asked Washington. The reply, according to Valentine: "She looked at me strange" before asking, "Why ask me that?" Later in the conversation, Valentine said, Washington told him she "went out with him [Tyson] and got raped." "Are you sure?" he said he asked her before telling the jury, "She didn't seem sure. She told me she screamed; nobody came; there was a bodyguard outside the door." After he returned home from the pageant, Valentine said he called Washington "to see what happened." "She wasn't sure," he said. "She was hesitant. She didn't say much." On cross-examination, Greg Garrison attempted to discredit Valentine but his line of questioning focused only on erroneous dates and did nothing to dent the witness's story.

What was the overall impact of this group of witnesses? Certainly the beauty queens had provided the defense fodder for arguing that Washington had given several different versions of what occurred the early morning she was in Tyson's hotel room, and that therefore she was trying to put together a viable story based on what she recalled that truly occurred and what she may have imagined happened to verify that she had been raped. The beauty queens had also proved that all of them, but most importantly, Washington, would have to have been blind not to realize that the bad boy Tyson had only one thing on his mind with regard to the contestants: sex. The defense thus could argue that Washington, even if she was as naïve as portrayed, must have known Iron Mike wanted her body and had no interest in her mind or any future as Mrs. Tyson.

The medical evidence provided by Dr. Watanobe was disappointing, especially since the defense had unlimited funds to retain an experience physician who could counteract the strong testimony by Dr. Richardson and give the jury the knowledge that Washington vaginal abrasions could have been caused simply by rough sex and not rape. But Dr. Watanobe couldn't handle the job, and the prosecution definitely had the upper hand when it came to the issue of expert testimony, a factor sure to be strong in the juror's minds.

If Dr. Watanobe was a disconcerting witness, then singer Johnny Gill was even more so. By calling him to the stand *before* Tyson testified, and thus losing the legal battle regarding much of what he had to say that could have helped his friend, the defense lost the chance to give the jury critical evidence from a famous witness that jurors could have believed. His stature provided a certain creditability, but defense errors in judgment made him a non-factor.

When jurors weighed the impact of the totality of defense witnesses, they may have been confused by the "across the board" defense presented. By choosing to hit home Tyson's defense from so many angles, one moment it was money, the next consent, the next that Washington knew how bad a person Tyson was and should never have trusted him, etc., confusion reigned. Some defense lawyers believe the scattershot approach is the best and that throwing everything against the wall with the hope that something will stick enhances the chances for success. Most, however, are of the opinion that it is imperative that the defense hone in on one line of defense and hammer it home. Here the consensus among court watchers and legal beagles was certainly consent for it appeared that if this had been the focus, there existed quite enough evidence to show that Washington simply had consensual sex with Tyson and then decided that she had in fact been raped. This surely accounts for her saying, "I think I was raped," a clear indication that she was unsure what really did occur in Tyson's hotel room. And who could blame her, since there certainly was confusion as to what happened and whether her consent was freely given or whether Tyson hoodwinked her into having sex. But the bottom line, Fuller and company could have argued if consent were the only defense, was that there was not a rape that occurred and thus Tyson should be freed of the charges.

    Most important, if consent had been the single front and center defense, then once again Fuller could have reconsidered his promise to parade Tyson before the jury since once again, most court observers and legal beagles were of the opinion that Garrison and company had not proven their case beyond a reasonable doubt. If the defense had rested with Iron Mike never leaving his chair, the odds were in his favor regarding acquittal. But Vincent Fuller had made a promise and he was determined to see it through. Tyson, who had doodled throughout the trial with a look on his face as if to say, "What in the world am I doing here?" was about to face the most important questioning of his life, a boxing match not with a heavyweight contender, but a slender, red-haired gunslinging prosecutor who packed a mean punch and intended to take him down for the count.

Chapter Sixteen
Mike's Story

While Mike Tyson testifying in own defense at trial was no surprise, defense counsel Roy Black's decision to permit William Kennedy Smith tell a jury his version of what occurred during his night with Patty Bowman was a shocker. The crafty Black had never allowed his client to utter a word before, and the prosecution had been certain he never do so at trial. They were thus unprepared when Black stood tall in the courtroom and said, "The defense calls William Kennedy Smith to the stand."

In addition, before Kennedy Smith testified, Black had schooled him regarding a prepared script he wanted his client to follow. Day after day, Black rehearsed his client, preparing him not only for direct testimony but more important, cross-examination. When it came time for Smith to testify, he was prepared and ready to speak to the jury, just as ready as Desiree Washington had been after her rehearsal with defense lawyer Robert Hammerle. Had Mike Tyson received similar "training" regarding his impending testimony, had he been prepared, was he ready to not only tell his story but face rigorous cross-examination from a savvy lawyer bent on tricking him at every turn?

The answers to this question began to unfold on February 7th at 4:02 p.m. when the former heavyweight boxing champion of the world unceremoniously sat in the witness chair not two feet from Judge Gifford. Wearing a shiny suit that appeared two sizes small for his thick, muscular arms, Tyson, his trademark gold tooth apparent to everyone gazing at him from both the jury box and the spectator seats, appeared ready to do battle with those who had accused him raping Desiree Washington. After swearing to "tell the truth, the whole truth, and nothing but the truth," Iron Mike began to provide testimony enlightening jurors about his checkered past. First, he testified that he was born in the Brownsville section of Brooklyn, N.Y., June 30, 1966, making him twenty-five-years-old. H said he had been a professional prizefighter for seven to eight years, was a high school dropout (19th grade), and had been befriended by the legendary trainer Cus D'Amato just after a stint at reform school. The expectation that more would be divulged about the man Tyson became based on childhood experiences in what might be called a life of "hard-knocks" never occurred as Vincent Fuller stopped questioning the ex-champ about this portion of his life. The jury was thus never provided with a full understanding of how Tyson had risen from the rough streets of Brooklyn to become the heavyweight boxing champion of the world, a remarkable, inspiring story.

    Moving on, Tyson, in his wispy, almost feminine voice, said his professional record was 41-1 with 38 knockouts, and that after defeated Donovan "Razor" Ruddock, he had been scheduled to fight current champion Evander Holyfield for the championship on June 28th, 1991. This bout, Tyson told the jurors, each one glued to his face and the words spoken, had been postponed due a rib injury he had sustained. Turning to the events during July, Tyson explained using poor English that he come from Washington D.C. to Indianapolis to attend Black Expo since his girlfriend, B Angie B, was performing. Staring straight ahead at Fuller instead of the jury, as most witnesses are instructed to do so as to make eye contact, to connect, if you will, Tyson said he arrived at 4:00 a.m. on July 17th accompanied by bodyguard Dale Edwards and B Angie B, whose aunt lived in Indianapolis. Upon arrival, the threesome had traveled to the aunt's home and then to the nightclub Seville for two hours. There, Tyson hugged and kissed with the rap singer girlfriend while signing autographs. After visiting the club, the three returned to the Canterbury Hotel where all three checked in. Skipping any details as to who stayed with whom, and any interaction with hotel employees to counter accusations that he was a bit unruly, Tyson diverted his testimony to the morning of July 18th. Then, the ex-champ told the jury, he met Johnny Gill for breakfast at about 10:00, and then returned to the hotel lobby with Reverend Charles Williams, who suggested Gill and Tyson visit the Omni to say hello to the beauty contestants.

  Thus far, Tyson appeared to be following a script of some sorts Fuller had prepared without deviating from the questioning. He appeared attentive and sharp, almost like a little boy being led by his father or more likely his mother during a grade school teacher's conference. This was the Tyson who truly appeared to be helpless, childlike, and in need of care and guidance, a far cry from the violent man who knocked the daylights out of boxing opponents or was rude and unruly with women and others he did not care for. This was the opposite person to the one he said people expected him to be, the public Tyson who had to play the tough guy, the disrespectful Tyson, the roughneck who played the role Don King wanted him to play.

Continuing with an easy demeanor as if he was answering questions regarding his application for a driver's license instead of ones that could decide whether he would be free or locked away in a prison for several years, Tyson told the attentive jurors that when he arrived at the rehearsal hall, the girls there became very excited and starting hugging and kissing him while asking for autographs. When Tyson was asked to "participate in a promo," he said he agreed to do so, and proceeded to do a rap number with lyrics appropriate for the pretty girls all around him. "I'm not much of a rapper," Tyson said, and he was thus forced to "do quite a few takes" of the rap songs because, he said, "I kept messing up." At some point, he told the jury, he met the girl who turned out to be Desiree Washington and asked her if she wanted to go out. Her response, he said, was "Yeah, sure."

"To get more familiar with the girls," Tyson said, he asked them, "Want a picture, sit on my lap." "Yes," he said, "my arms were about them." He told the jury he could not recall whether Washington sat on his lap but he admitted using "explicit sexual language" and that some girls rebuffed him. After completing the promotional tape with three contestants, one of whom was Washington, Tyson said he talked to her and her roommate behind a pillar. "Would you be upset if I ask out your roommate," he said he asked Pasha Oliver, and that she said, "No." Then he told the jury he asked the same question to Washington and she said, "Well, Johnny [Gill] can come then." Tyson told Washington that was okay with him and then asked her, "Are you happy now?" To this question, he said she said, "Yes."

What followed was a rather bizarre exchange Tyson said he had with Washington. When the discussion centered on whether there might be a "movie or dinner," the ex-champ said he told Washington point blank, "I just want to be with you; I want you."

Before answering the next question Fuller proposed, Tyson was polite in saying that he could only answer "if your honor [Judge Gifford] allowed me to do so." When the judge said it was okay, Tyson uttered eleven words that may have been the most important part of his testimony for in answer to Fuller's questions about what he then said to Washington, Tyson uttered the words "I explained to her that I just wanted to f . . . her." Her reply, he said, was to say, "That's kinda bold," but then moments later, "Sure, just give me a call." To Fuller's request for an explanation as to why he would use such vulgar language, Tyson said, "That's the way I am, I just want to know what I am getting into before I'm getting into it."

To those observing the testimony, Tyson's use of the "F word" appeared to strike like a lightning bolt in the juror's faces. They had heard of his disgusting behavior but now they had seen it firsthand, from his mouth, and the effect, it appeared, was for them to suddenly see Iron Mike in a whole new light. Any aura of invincibility the ex-champ had enjoyed to that point in the trial was wiped away by the eleven words. Now he appeared to be the thug, some sort of inconsiderate and rude monster and not the man who some felt sympathy for due to his tough upbringing. He may very well have been telling the truth about what he had said to Washington, and he likely was, but just the fact that he had used the "I want to f . . . you" language with a young girl like Washington certainly seemed offensive to everyone who heard it but especially to the jurors deciding his fate.

Whether use of the 'F word" was a surprise to Fuller was unclear, but during his Grand Jury testimony, Tyson had simply said he told Washington, "I want you." And, the response to his telling Washington he wanted to f... her was met with answers that appeared unlikely based on the characterization of Washington jurors perceived through her testimony. Would Washington actually say, "That's kinda bold... Sure, just give me a call?" Such a response seemed whole unlikely and caused everyone who heard the exchange to wonder if the socially warped Tyson had exaggerated what had been said for his own purposes. Fuller certainly did nothing to explain why Washington might have responded as she did, and was thus left with juror's impressions that Tyson was the terrible person others made him out to be as well as what amounted to being a sexual predator. If Fuller wanted to pursue his line of defense that Washington should have known better to go with Tyson since she knew he was an awful human being, the defense lawyer was succeeding. The extension of his argument that perhaps Washington got what she deserved, offensive to everyone who even considered that possibility, loomed on the horizon as well.

Regarding the comment "You're a nice Christian girl," Tyson said he had picked up that line from Charlie Neal, a Black Entertainment News sportscaster. Tyson said he didn't mean anything "holy" by the comment, but only used the phrase since Neal had done so. Later in the day, the ex-champ said he tried to reach Washington at the Omni, but could not do so. At the opening ceremonies, he said one of the military men on guard gave him the Christian badge he wore. Politicians spoke but "I didn't listen," he told the jury, and then "I walked up and down and around through the contestants." When he approached Washington, Tyson said, he walked around her, and told the jury he said, "too bad you've got dresses on; I can't see what you got." Soon, Washington got his attention, Tyson told the jury, and showed him "two pictures of her in a bathing suit." He said he told her, "Good, now I know what you got."

During the evening hours, Tyson said he joined Rev. Jesse Jackson in prayer before the two had dinner. Then he headed for the Johnny Gill concert. He testified he did not recall seeing Washington backstage but recalled asking B Angie B "you gonna a make that flight [to Cleveland] or not" to which she answered, "Yeah." Once the concert had ended, Tyson said he traveled with Edwards to the Omni while telling the jury, "Edwards always sits in the front seat." At the hotel, Tyson said he wanted to pick up telephone messages. Then, the ex-champ told the jury, he and his bodyguard headed for the Omni where Edwards called Washington's hotel room after which Tyson said he spoke to Washington for about ten minutes. He said he told her to "wear something loose." When she entered the limousine on the driver's side, "I kissed her and she kissed me." Without speaking to how the limousine traveled to the Canterbury Hotel so as to clarify whether he had pre-planned to take her there (Virginia Foster was never asked about this), Tyson said he and Washington were "kissing and hugging" in the limousine on the way to the hotel," a fact that could have been verified, at least in the hotel driveway by one of three witnesses Judge Gifford banned from testifying, a decision now even more important to corroborate Tyson's story and give jurors a critical piece of information showing that Washington was already intimate before the two entered the hotel.

Regarding his entrance into the hotel, Tyson told the jury, "Me and Desiree and Dale went into the hotel," and then Edwards opened the door to room 606 with a key since "I don't carry keys." He said Washington went into the bedroom with him but didn't know where Edwards was because the door was closed but "I believe he was supposed to be in the whatchamacallit, the parlor. That where he was supposed to have been, the parlor." In the bedroom, Tyson said "We started talking about what . . . talking about Rhode Island, where I'm from; where she's from, she had a scholarship. I asked her about a fighter from Rhode Island, does she know him? She didn't know him." Concerning the respective positions on the bed, Tyson pointed to a place on a chart toward the top right corner of the bed and to her position on the right corner of the bed. Washington was sitting, he said, like a "Buddha, with her legs crossed." Regarding her clothing, the ex-champ said she had on the yellow sequined dress but as far as her pants went, he was not sure if they were yellow or pink.

Tyson said the two talked for about "ten minutes maybe" and "when we were talking, my hand was on her leg." To Fuller's question as to whether the two were kissing, Tyson answered, "Yes, I was kissing her." Asked if she was kissing him, he said, "Yes." But Tyson could not recall Washington going to the bathroom, saying, "I don't remember that."

Fuller then asked Tyson whether "there was a time when he moved Washington physically." Tyson's answer: "Just to bring her down back . . .we were kissing up . . her back was more facing the head of the bed, so I had to slide her down some." "Did you undress her?' Fuller asked but before Tyson could respond Garrison objected with Judge Gifford lecturing Fuller by saying, "He wants you to quit asking leading questions." Almost in unison, the jury seemed to appreciate the ruling as if to say, "Hey, quit putting words in Tyson's mouth. Let him testify." Perhaps they did not appreciate Fuller trying to assist Tyson as much as possible so that he would not stray too far afield and make a statement that would kill any chances of acquittal. Fuller was not much of a trial lawyer when it came to sex crimes cases, but he was no dummy and he knew the risks he was taking by permitting Tyson to testify.

As if a dam had broken, Tyson now began to disclose more details about the sexual encounter. Without Fuller's leading questions, he offered the following: "As I'm kissing her, she was moving fast. She was dropping her jacket, you know, getting her jacket off quick. And I'm just kissing on the neck, and around the ears, back of the neck and chest and nipples, the stomach. I believe she had on a white shirt as well. She was trying to get that off, so I came back while she was taking that off. She had taken off those shorts, she had . . . I'm sure she took off the shorts."

"I took my shirt off at the time she had taken off her underwear. She had underwear, and she took off her underwear, and the underwear dropped to her knees, and I pulled them all the way off. And then I took off . . . I had short pants on, and I continued kissing on the body.

"We were having oral sex for a while, and she told me to stop and told me to come up, she no, she, no, come up." Tyson said they then enjoyed sexual intercourse for "probably 15-20 minutes." When he was about to climax, he said, "She told me not to come in her, don't come in me, don't come in me. I'm not on the pill, and I pulled back, and oh, I ejaculated on her stomach and legs." He told the jury, "She went to the bathroom, I guess, to clean herself off or something." Tyson then added, "I was watching her. She had underwear on. I thought they were flowers. They looked like flowers then, but they were polka dots. She was in the mirror doing her hair, a little dance, like shoo, shoo, shoo, doing her hair . . . And I offered her to stay the night with me, because she had said, her and some other girls I had spoken to earlier, they had a 5:00 a.m. wake-up call. And it said I had to get up early as well, so perhaps she could stay with me. She didn't want to stay."

"So I informed her that my limousine was downstairs and would take her where she wanted to go. And she wanted me to walk her downstairs. I said I was too tired. I was only going to have a few hours sleep.

"She said, 'You're not going to walk me downstairs?'" And I said, "Listen, trust me, I'm tired, I'm sorry, I can't walk you downstairs. If you would like to stay, you're welcome to stay. I would love for you to stay, I really love for you to stay. If you don't want to, you can take the limousine downstairs or you can walk." To Fuller's question, "Did she express irritation toward you?" the answer was, "She was irritated because I did not walk her

185

downstairs." Ending his direct testimony, Tyson described leaving the hotel with Edwards, attempting to find B Angie B, and then the drive to airport to catch his flight.

Finally, Fuller had asked Tyson several predictable questions before he readied himself for cross-examination: Fuller: "Mr. Tyson, at any time did you force Desiree Washington to engage in sexual intercourse with you?" Tyson: "No, I didn't. I didn't violate her in any way, sir." Fuller: "Did she at any time tell you to stop what you were doing? Tyson: "Never, she never told me to stop, and she never said I was hurting her. She never said no, nothing." Fuller: At anytime, did you ever place your fingers in her vagina?" Tyson: No, I didn't." Fuller: did you touch her private parts?" Tyson: "Yes, I did." Fuller: "What did you do?" Tyson: "I just stroked her with my finger around her clitoris area."

How effective had Tyson's testimony been? Courtroom observers were split down the middle. Some believed Fuller's leading questions deflated Tyson's testimony but that appeared unfair. Leading him was a good strategy and after he felt more comfortable testifying, his own words rang out loud and clear. Certainly Tyson presented his good boy behavior with politeness and showed no anger toward anyone for being accused of rape. But Fuller had failed in some respects by not softening the blow regarding the "I want to f . . . you" comment Tyson made, or ordering Tyson not to say it that way but instead "I want you" as he had stated before the grand jury. In not doing so, Fuller was so intent on preserving the "Washington knew Tyson was a bad boy, etc." defense that he forgot it caused problems with the real defense, consent, since it got in the way. But the bigger crime Fuller committed that came back to haunt him later was his having Tyson testify before the Grand Jury in the first place since this provided prosecutors with a version of the story that could be contrasted with Tyson's testimony at trial.

    Other matters to be resolved by the jury included whether Washington would have used such language as "That's pretty bold," and "Call me," after Tyson told her he wanted to f . . . her. Was this believable or had Tyson simply been told that was what to say as it appeared those exact words were uncharacteristic of ones Washington would have used after being shocked by his vulgar language. But that didn't mean it didn't occur and it was up to Fuller to show that Washington was capable of such a response. Could he do so?

    Whether Fuller agreed or not, Tyson's comment that he had watched Washington "do her hair" was in direct conflict with limousine driver Virginia Foster's testimony providing another matter to be cleared up by Fuller. And perhaps more than anything, Fuller appeared to be trying to argue through Tyson's testimony that Washington felt scorned by Tyson's refusal to walk her down to the limousine? Would this stand up as a defense or would the jury believe it made no sense. And how was Fuller going to explain away Foster and the hotel bellhop's observation that Washington appeared to be in a state of shock and crying when she entered the hotel lobby and walked to the limousine. Could this have been caused by Tyson's simply refusing to walk her downstairs?

    More questions than answers were apparent when Tyson's direct examination was completed but certainly the jury had heard his side of the story.

Fuller had two choices when he decided to let the ex-champ testify – put him through a rigorous, almost cross-examination-like experience that would prepare Tyson for Garrison's assault while truly giving the jury the impression the accused was holding nothing back, or permit him as many leading and softball questions as possible hoping beyond hope he wouldn't screw up and then taking their chances with Garrison's cross-examination. Before trial, defense lawyers had tried to give Tyson an idea of what he might go through, but facing Garrison was totally different than facing a friendly face. In the William Kennedy Smith case, Roy Black was careful not ask leading questions but permit his client to not only answer but add substance and context to his explanation. He thus had the latitude to explain more in detail what had occurred and was comfortable with doing so. But Tyson was no Kennedy Smith either with intellectual capacity or social skills in speaking, and thus risky when given any latitude.

    The most impressive attorney in the Rodney King case had been Darryl Mounger. He represented Sergeant Stacy Koon, the one in charge of the police officers alleged to have been King. Consistent with the defense theory that if the videotape was slowed down, it showed how dangerous King had been thus triggering the need to subdue him all in the line with proper police procedures, Mounger, through his direct examination, promoted Koon as a God-fearing family man and a career law enforcement officer while de-emphasizing his intent to in any way cause King harm during the arrest. The impact was to present Koon as a friendly fellow simply doing his job. Cross-examination was ineffective based on the foundation set up by the defense. In the Bensonhurst case, attorney Arthur Lewis, knowing that the evidence against Lemrick Nelson, Jr. was strong, chose to divert the juror's minds from his client by placing the credibility of the police at issue. By employing this strategy, Lewis successfully altered the focus of the trial and succeeded without ever permitting Nelson to testify, a wise strategy if Fuller had not restricted his doing so with his promises to the jury that he would testify.

Whatever the impact of the direct examination of Tyson, the time had come when he had to walk into the ring with the gunslinger Garrison, who had been preparing for this moment for months on end. Now his time had come and he could question the ex-champ, clearly not his equal in any sense of the word, about not only the statements he had given to the jury but also at his grand jury appearance. As Garrison rose to question Tyson, there was a deep sense of anticipation and tension, but then Judge Gifford presented the prosecution with another gift by postponing cross-examination until the next morning even though Tyson's direct examination had only lasted until mid-afternoon. Instead of just a few minutes to gather his thoughts together based on Tyson's testimony, Garrison and Company would have the rest of the afternoon and the evening to inspect the testimony looking for loopholes where Garrison could pounce on Tyson's statements. Garrison and his cohorts could also review Grand Jury testimony and any other documents they had providing quite the advantage for the prosecution.

Regardless, Tyson now had given his side of the story and the jury awaited the "other side of the story" as clarified by the prosecution. Could the ill-educated, moody, socially inept Tyson handle the horse-loving, wild-west prosecutor? The answer would soon become clear.

Chapter Seventeen
Attacking Iron Mike

At 9:00 a.m. on the snowy day of February 8th, the duel began. In one corner, Michael Gerard Tyson, the ex-heavyweight boxing champion with a record of 41-1-0, and in the other, Greg Garrison, the flamboyant prosecutor who bragged that he had not lost a case since 1973. Referring, Judge Patricia Gifford, and sitting in judgment, twelve men and women sworn to uphold justice at every turn.

Challenging Tyson was not without risk for Garrison. During the Clarence Thomas/Anita Hill hearings, senator's personal questions had infuriated the Supreme Court nominee to the point that he threatened to leave the proceedings. Likewise, personal questions posed to Hill ventured beyond the bounds of good taste and angered many so much there was deep sympathy for her from spectators and television viewers alike. In the William Kennedy Smith case, prosecutor Moira Lasch performed what famed attorney F. Lee Bailey called "the worst cross-examination I have ever seen in a courtroom." Experts agreed arguing that Lasch made almost every mistake possible by angering the judge (at one point, Judge Lupo warned Lasch that "this is not a course in trial practice), and asking questions only permitting Kennedy Smith to embellish his direct testimony without any challenge to his credibility. Too many side issues were raised as well restricting the jury's understanding as to exactly what had occurred between Kennedy Smith and Patty Bowman. In California, prosecutor Terry White fell on hard times when he constantly attempted to ridicule L.A.

police officers for their lack of sense of duty by accusing them of overstating the "threat to life" defense used to show that they had to act as they did or King might have killed them. In effect, White's ineffectiveness never showed that officers feared King might have had a gun, or another weapon, or could somehow physically strike back at the policemen. The more he questioned their personal motives, the more he appeared to be challenging their integrity, an issue that did not sit well with the jury. No question existed that White was well-intentioned but hindsight showed he might have been much better off if he had not cross-examined at all and simply let the videotape speak for itself since it clearly showed an abundance of unnecessary force used to subdue the fallen King. That evidence, plus King testifying, might have changed the outcome of the trial.

For the confrontation with his savvy opponent, the man with the law doctorate as compared to his low-level education, Tyson chose an American flag outfit consisting of a blue suit, white shirt, and red paisley tie. Whether the jury might have identified more with him if he had been dressed in jeans and a T-shirt would never be known, but the suit clearly caused Tyson to look more evil that he had in his boxing shorts since he simply looked out of place, like he was faking his appearance. And this was the last thing he needed to show, any sense of being less than sincere while his freedom was on the line.

Once Tyson was situated in the witness chair, Garrison approached like a tiger ready to attack his prey. To make certain the jury knew the prosecutor was unafraid of dangerous boxer who had leveled the heads of heavyweights to and fro,

Garrison strode confidently to within about five feet of Tyson as if to say, "I'm not scared of you; you better be scared of me." Regarding his cross-examination strategy, Garrison had several alternatives. He could use the rapid-fire, machine-gun approach, designed to surprise the ex-champ, throw him off-guard, and then secure disastrous answers to questions that would secure his conviction. He could also utilize the "he said, she said," approach by contrasting Tyson's testimony with that of Washington to indicate inconsistencies that could sway the jury toward conviction. This strategy would certainly put Tyson on the defensive, and cause jurors to decide who they believed, him or his accuser. But Garrison avoided all of these strategies since he was not as interested in what occurred during the alleged rape, but more interested in the man Tyson was since he was determined to show that someone like Iron Mike was a menace to society based on past deeds as well as the Washington incident. In effect, he was going to steal a page from Vincent Fuller's playbook and show that yes, Tyson was a terrible human being and should be locked up not because Washington should have known better than to accompany him out at two a.m. but because a man like Tyson was rude, used vulgar language, had no respect for women or anyone else for that matter to the extent that they were simply playthings that he used for sex and then discarded even when he had a girlfriend who was in the very city where the sexual escapades took place. Yes, Garrison was about to attack Mike Tyson, the man, from every angle, and when he was through, there would only be shell of the fellow who was so polite and spoke with a girlish tone. Instead, the menace to society would be present for all to see including the jury and that menace would be locked away in prison for years to come. Greg Garrison would then have his scalp, having knocked Tyson out cold regardless of the evidence present indicating that he raped Washington. In effect, Tyson would pay for his sins; he would reap what he had sowed per Galatians 6: 7-9; he would be forever be known as a rapist and he would go to prison for a lengthy time, one that would destroy any boxing career possible. Basically, Garrison wanted to show the jury, "Yeah, Vincent Fuller is right. Tyson is an awful human being, one who deserves to be in prison." The end result: Mike Tyson was doomed. He just didn't realize it yet.

    Garrison began with Tyson's sordid past. Careful to avoid the boxer's confrontations with the law as a juvenile, the prosecutor chose to discuss Tyson's training with the legendary Cus D'Amato. The ex-champ's answers produced the following information: "If you listen to me," Tyson said D'Amato told him, "You will be the next champion of the world." Tyson was not yet fifteen years old at the time.

    Questioned about D'Amato's approach to boxing, Tyson said his trainer was an advocate of being "very elusive," and "having a great deal of anticipation." Garrison then asked, "How do you accomplish being elusive in the ring?" Tyson hesitated for a moment, perhaps wondering what Garrison was up to before answering, "Avoid the punches . . . Your head is so big. Some people's heads are bigger than others, and punches come in. You anticipate the punch, and put your head inside the punch." Regarding his elusiveness in the ring, Garrison asked Tyson again, "What do you do?"

Tyson: "I go forward. You go forward. You watch his shoulders, both shoulders. You can't watch his hands. You watch his shoulders, and watch if the shoulders move. And you anticipate, and you must be very relaxed."

To all who were watching the cross-examination, Garrison's aim was clear. He wanted Tyson to use the word "deceptive," but the ex-champ had not done so. Garrison then used it himself in talking about how Tyson avoided punches as he moved about the ring. One of Tyson's answers was a bit confusing: "[Cus] didn't want the guy to be able to see. He always wants you to be where he wasn't able to see the punch." Not having gained the answer he was looking for, Garrison decided to hit Tyson with a punch by referring to Tyson's grand jury testimony. The prosecutor began by mentioning Tyson's approach to women pointing out that he had told the jurors, "You don't just go right up to a girl, and say, want to screw?" Garrison then pulled out the Grand Jury and pointed to page seventy-six where Tyson, describing his conversations with Washington, was quoted as saying, "I want it to be me and you. I want to be with you alone. I said, "I want you" before Washington allegedly replied, "Okay. Just call me." Having set the stage to indicate conflicting testimony on Tyson's part, Garrison then confronted the ex-champ with his "I want to f . . . you" comment from his testimony the day before. "How come you didn't tell that to the grand jury?" Garrison asked. Tyson glared at the prosecutor before telling him that the deputy prosecutor, David Dreyer, "cut me off" before he could say anything else. Elaborating, Tyson told the jury, "You know, I didn't feel comfortable using the word at that particular time in the grand jury because there were not young kids in there my age or anything." "But you were more comfortable saying it in here yesterday?" Tyson: "No, I'm pretty much under pressure to say it. I felt very uncomfortable saying it in front of the jury, in front of the judge and my mother." Asked about Johnny Gill's statement to investigators that Tyson had "said those words to somebody," but he couldn't remember who (Garrison was trying to make the point that Tyson had not said the "I want to f . . . you" to Washington), Tyson told Garrison, "I don't know Johnny Gill's memory functions."

After an exchange where the two combatants chatted about their memories (Garrison: "Mine's not so hot sometimes – that's what my kids tell me; Tyson: "Fooled me"), the prosecutor mentioned bodyguard Dale Edwards, who Garrison noted, had not been called to testify leaving it to the jury to wonder why. Then Garrison asked Tyson, "About how much cash do you think you had on you when you were in Indianapolis," to which Tyson answered, "$30,000," a figure that appeared to shock jurors, some of whom probably didn't make that much in a year.

Still trying the ugly man he was portraying Tyson to be, Garrison brought up Rev. Jesse Jackson's name. He had baptized Tyson in 1988 and continued to be a friend. But the crux of his mention of Jackson was to note that Tyson had lied to Jackson about his promise to visit the Marion County Jail. Tyson: "As he continued to pressure me . . . he said, 'can you make it?' I said, no I've got to be somewhere. Jackson then said, 'No, you got to be there.' Finally, I said, alright." Pressed for a further explanation, Garrison asked, "When you said, 'Okay, I'll be there,' you didn't intend to go, did you?" "No way I could make it," Tyson responded. "He wouldn't take no for an answer, and he didn't understand; he didn't respect me."

Turning to the testimony of limousine driver Virginia Foster that Tyson "begged" Washington to leave her Omni Hotel room and visit him in the early morning hours, Tyson provided his version of what occurred: "She had told me, I believe that she was in bed. She was sleeping. She looked horrible. And I said, well, that doesn't matter. Throw some water on your face, and wear some loose clothes. She said, 'I'll see you tomorrow,' and I told her, "Well, I'm leaving tonight." Finally, Tyson said, she said, "I'm coming down." When asked about why he allegedly told Washington to wear something "loose," Tyson said "Because I had intentions of doing it in the limousine. I just asked her to put on something loose so I could easily get to her." Garrison: "You figured she was coming down to have sex with you?" Tyson: "Yes." Garrison: "How come?" Tyson: "I believe from our conversation we had earlier indicated that."

While some of Tyson's testimony had been a bit rambled, thus far he appeared to have had the upper hand with Garrison, whose cross-examination appeared to be ineffective. But he had scored points relating to Tyson being a bad boy and intent on having sex with Washington no matter whether it was in the back of the limousine or elsewhere. Apparently he was attempting to convince the jury that Tyson was not going to take "no" for an answer. Whether the jury would guy that argument remained to be seen. Regarding the outfit Washington wore, Garrison quizzed Tyson about the specifics with him telling the jury that he thought the outfit was pink and that the shorts in evidence, "didn't seem like the same shorts she was wearing." Garrison then read Tyson's Grand Jury testimony where he stated, "She had on very short hot pants. I believe they were very short pants. Her thighs were showing. They were tight. They were very short. She had little cut-off blouse. It was cut off to her stomach, I believe." When Garrison questioned whether the blouse "was open or not," Tyson explained, "I'm not a professional at women's attire. It was cut off to her stomach, I believe."

Asked about what he told the Grand Jury he and Washington did while in the limousine traveling to the Canterbury Hotel, ("We started hugging and kissing"), Tyson agreed with Garrison's summation that "You were touching all over her body, and you are kissing her real passionately and they were long kisses." Garrison then said, "But when you go to the Canterbury, you sit down on the bed, and you talk for fifteen minutes." Tyson explained, "I believe we both made it clear earlier that day what was going to happen when she came to my room at 2:00 a.m. in the morning. I'm sure we made it clear." Regarding the conversation itself, "It was just a conversation. I never came to say, "well, let's do it right now. It wasn't that kind of climate where we were going to make passionate love as soon as we walk in the door on the floor or something." Apparently feeling this line of questioning was getting him nowhere, Garrison returned to discussing the bodyguard Dale Edwards. "Did you know that Dale Edwards said [at the Grand Jury] that while you were in the back of the bedroom with Desiree he was in the living room of your suite?" Tyson: "I didn't know he said it that way." Garrison: "And you know three different people who worked at the hotel testified at the hearing that's not true. Edwards was all over that hotel. He made calls from 604. He placed a room service order at the front desk. He took telephone calls in the parlor. He talked to the limousine driver out front all while you were upstairs in 606. You know that to be a fact, don't you?" Tyson: "Well, no. I know he should have been in that parlor room. That's where he's supposed to be." Faced with explaining why he told the Grand Jury Edwards was in the parlor and now was changing his story, Tyson told the jurors, "I didn't know, really know. I was to believe he was in the parlor." Garrison: "King of like supposing somebody wants to have sex with you, but you don't really know, isn't it?" Tyson never answered. Garrison withdrew the question, a smart move but one that circumvented any attempt by Fuller to object. Worse, the Washington D. C. lawyer never asked that the comment be stricken from the record and the jury admonished to disregard it. Little things mean a lot in a trial, and Garrison had imbedded a thought to the jury to consider later in deliberations even though Tyson never had the chance to answer the question. Would Fuller be smart enough to ask his client to answer Garrison's question later during re-direct so as to make it clear that Tyson had no question in his mind that Washington knew he expected to have sex with her? Little by little, the savvy Garrison was trapping Tyson and the ex-champ could do little about it, especially since his trial counsel was not protecting him. Too much of a gentleman, Fuller was giving the jury the impression that either he just didn't want to fight for his client, or was inept at doing so. Since most defendants are also judged by the performance of their counsel, Tyson was losing valuable points with the jury. Not only was Garrison blemishing Tyson's persona with pinpoint precision, but Fuller was proving to be as dislikable as Garrison wanted Tyson to be. And, perhaps more important, by not fighting Garrison, Fuller was prevented from exposing the smart-alec side of Garrison that defense lawyers tried to show juries when he became upset and his temper flared. No, because of Fuller's lack of experience in county courts, Garrison was proving to be the cowboy in the white hat while Tyson and Fuller were the outlaws with Tyson the one who rode into town, raped a lovely, innocent young woman, and then left as quickly as possible knowing he had done wrong.

    Pleased with himself that he had tied the champ in knots, Garrison finally decided he had to deal with details of the alleged rape. Caring little for the delicate matter of what he was discussing, Garrison, through his questions, presented the image that if there was ten minutes of oral sex, according to Tyson's testimony, that would make, "things pretty wet down there." Then the two sparred like the two heavyweights they were. Garrison: When you injected or inserted yourself in her, did you have any trouble getting inside?" Tyson: "I don't remember if I had problems getting inside or not." Such an inconclusive answer had to resonate with the jury. Surely Tyson would have recalled such a thing. Would Fuller be smart enough to follow up so as to clear up this point? Couldn't he see that Garrison was setting up his argument that after ten minutes of oral sex, Washington, if Tyson was telling the truth, would have been wet and thus never been suspected to the abrasions discovered inside her vagina?

Leaving this arena satisfied that he had succeeded in establishing another inconsistency in Tyson's testimony when contrasted, this time, with Dr. Richardson's medical evidence, Garrison asked Tyson about his relationship with girlfriend, B Angie B. Garrison: "Did you know that she told Ms. Trathen in her deposition that when you went to the Holiday Inn [before the incident with Washington] you engaged in sex for a long time?" Tyson: "Could have been. I'm not really sure of the situation being long. I'm not really sure." Garrison: "You have forgotten whether you had sex with B Angie B at the hotel? Is this an event that was not of particular interest to you?" Tyson: "That's not necessarily true at all, no." Garrison: "You remember having sex with Desiree Washington, but you forgot having a couple of hours worth with B Angie B the day before?" Before Tyson, his face portraying someone totally confused by the question, could answer, he was asked whether he had sex twice with B Angie B." Rather than answering, Tyson turned toward Judge Gifford and said, "May I use gross, crude language for a moment, ma'am?" To this question, Judge Gifford gave the answer, "Help yourself," a totally unprofessional and unjudicial-like response that easily sent a signal to the jury that she was antagonistic toward Tyson. All she had to say was "yes," and yet she had gone out of her way to make a smart remark that Tyson did not deserve. Fuller obviously was deaf and blind for he did nothing to object, or at least request a sidebar to let the judge know he did not appreciate the remark. Once again, the pro-prosecution judge had acted in favor of

Garrison and crew. Jeff Modisett had to be smiling again.

Tyson, having been approved to use bad language, asked Garrison, "What do you mean? Do you mean every time I climaxed, that's one time? If I do it again, that's another time. What do you mean?" Garrison: "Yes, that will do." Tyson: "Then I don't know." Garrison: "Would you be surprised to know that Miss Boyd [B Angie B] has a specific recollection of all of those things?" Tyson: "Well, she must have enjoyed it a lot."

Unsure of what he thought of this answer, but assured that he had showed that Tyson remembered what he wanted to remember, and forgot what he wanted to forgot, Garrison moved on. But before he did, he noted through questions and answers that Tyson's relationship with B Angie B had deteriorated with the clear implication that she had tired of Tyson's obsession with sex to the point of excessiveness. Then the prosecutor moved to Tyson's feelings about religion by first pointing to his calling Washington, "a nice Christian girl," his wearing a "Together in Christ" button, and his prayers with Rev. Jackson. Garrison: "Those were not spiritual events in your life?" Tyson: "I don't understand what you're trying to get at." Nothing more came of this and Garrison decided to end the cross-examination on a high note by returning to what he felt, and was certain the jury would feel, was the most unbelievable part of Tyson's testimony. Garrison: "You said to Desiree Washington, eighteen years old and one month, just graduated from high school, 'I want to f . . . you,' and she said, "That's bold, call me. Is that the conversation?" Tyson: "No. She said, 'That's pretty bold." I said, well, that's the way I am. I want what

202

I want. I said, I just want to know where we stand. She said, 'Sure, call me.'" Garrison: "So this eighteen year old incoming freshman from Coventry, Rhode Island, says basically, 'You want to f . . . me? Fine, call me.'" Tyson: "Well, she told me to call her."

With this, the battle between Garrison ended. Re-direct by Fuller was weak at best, and re-cross examination merely hammered home the same points already raised. Fuller appeared quite disorganized and never could clearly show the jury the most important fact Garrison had honed in on – why Tyson talked the way he did to Washington. Fuller also left alone points Garrison scored regarding Washington being "wet," and the questions about where Dale Edwards was during the alleged assault. Was Fuller waiting to call Edwards as a rebuttal witness or would the jury be in the dark and have to decide for themselves why they had never heard from him?

Garrison, on the other hand, had been quite adept at questioning Tyson but if he truly was searching for the truth, the end goal of any trial, then his unwillingness to question Tyson more about the alleged rape was disappointing. Later, he would admit he had left out several important points he wanted to make, but believed he had pictured Tyson's dark side as best it could be exposed. And he had mixed up the ex-champ regarding his selective memory with the high point of his argument being the unbelievability of Tyson telling Washington "I want to f . . . " you and her simply saying she would expect his call. This was certain to be the final message he left to the jury in a "who do you believe" type of case. But Garrison had been effective, and more important not fallen on his face as Moira Lasch had done in the William Kennedy Smith case or Terry White had done during the Rodney King state trial. Also, Garrison had been smart not to try to show his level of intelligence advantage over the uneducated Tyson, something that might have turned off the jury and permitted them to have sympathy for him.

    The effect of Tyson's testimony would be debated by all who witnessed it. Predictably, Fuller believed he had been credible, while Garrison was waiting for final argument to pounce all over the boxer and his incredulous story. But two matters outside the evidence had weighed most heavily with those legal beagle looking for who had the edge. The first was Tyson's demeanor on the stand. Throughout the trial, the jurors had watched him intently, curious as to what kind of person he was. He had answered this on the witness stand by being calm and polite, but his facial features, ordinary for a boxer, provided a dangerous look that had to bother the jurors. He simply looked menacing, and one had to wonder whether those deciding his fate were scared of a fellow like him and if they were, then it was easy to transpose that fear to the young, innocent Washington. Some people just "look guilty, Richard Nixon comes to mind, and it is difficult for them to look any other way. Tyson had that problem because of the violent look he portrayed through no fault of his own.

    The other factor was Judge Gifford's sarcastic remark, "Help yourself," since it had indicated to the jury her displeasure with Tyson. While an attractive woman with a pleasant facial look, at times her look was a piercing one and left no doubt as to how she felt about a certain situation. This was evident when she told Tyson "Help yourself," when a simple "yes," would have sufficed. Jurors look for clues from judges as to how they feel about both the prosecution and the defense, and perhaps without realizing it to give her the benefit of the doubt, the judge's actions, the put-down of Tyson, clearly sent a signal to the jurors that she did not believe his testimony. If this was true, Mike Tyson was ready to be fitted for his prison garb, for nothing could save him.

Should Mike Tyson have testified in his own behalf? Had the risk paid off? Ultimately the jury would decide this question, and it was the only thing that mattered regardless of personal feelings about the ex-champ or conclusions reached by the spectators or legal beagles watching the trial. But did the jury have enough information to make a rational decision? Was there enough evidence presented to clearly permit them a through search for the truth? Objectively, the answer to these questions appeared to be a rousing "No," since little information was presented by either side regarding the most important aspect of the trial – the alleged rape itself. Yes, certainly, Washington and Tyson had provided their versions of what occurred, but neither spent much time on the physical act that was determinative of whether Tyson would be convicted or acquittal. Both sides danced around the particulars of the alleged rape leaving the jury with guesswork regarding exactly what occurred between Tyson and Washington. This was disappointing since either side could have probed deeper when the two were questioned so as to clearly provide a critical question – did Desiree Washington clearly say "No," and if she did, when? Determining this was elementary to the charge of rape yet no one could possibly have been clear about this point through any inference of the evidence presented. Since this was true, it appeared that the defense had the upper hand since the state had not proven the charge that Tyson had raped Washington when she resisted his advances and said "No." This would have been the norm in most cases but here, Garrison had assaulted Tyson the person so much that he was left to not be proven guilty, but to prove his innocence. He had not only failed to do this, but had helped Garrison's cause with his infamous, "I want to f.... you" comment. Combined with Judge Gifford's disparaging remark, "Help yourself," Tyson had become the evil one in the eyes of the jury while Washington still wore the white hat.

     No one will ever know what the outcome of the Tyson trial would have been if he had never testified. But there is no doubt that like a ton of others through the ages, he was helping to convict himself. More witnesses would appear, and then argument and jury instruction would follow, but when Tyson left the witness stand, the juror's faces left no doubt that he was a condemned man.

Chapter Eighteen
In Support of Tyson

While Mike Tyson rested in a chair that always appeared too small for his muscular body, the defense presented an array of witnesses designed to save Iron Mike from a lengthy prison term. First up was Johnny Gill's return trip to the witness stand.

The popular singer began by discussing the pageant rehearsal and his conversations with Pasha Oliver and Desiree Washington by the infamous "pillar." Calmly and with a professional tone, Gill confirmed Tyson's "I want to f . . . you" comment to Washington. "She never flinched," he said. The comment "shocked him," Gill told the jury, "it was from out in left field."

The corroboration by Gill of Tyson's unfortunate comment should have had an immediate impact on the jury, but by the look on their faces, it did not. It wasn't that Gil appeared to be lying, or covering up for his friend. In fact, in all likelihood he was telling the truth. But the comment was so brazen, so despicable, so rude, and so disrespectful to a lady that Gill's testimony slid by like it never occurred. Perhaps if had uttered the five words *before* Tyson testified, the blow of hearing them might have softened the shock. But when Gill did testify, Tyson's testimony was still fresh on the juror's minds and it was easy to tell that the singer's confirmation of Tyson's directness with Washington had fallen on deaf ears.

Believing that more beauty queen contestants might help Tyson's cause, defense lawyer Lane Heard questioned Tanya St. Claire

Gilles from Illinois. Wearing a dark, leather jacket, and without any trace of a smile from a face that was square in shape but accentuated by beautiful dark hair and big, brown eyes, he testified that at the rehearsal she heard Washington say Tyson "was really built," and had "a butt to hold on to." St. Clair added that Washington admitted she "wanted a man with money" before commenting that while Tyson's bodyguard was "chubby," Tyson was "just right." Then St. Claire presented another side to Washington when she recalled her having called another contestant "a bitch and a whore" after her performance before sitting down on the floor and "beating and stomping." Prosecutor Barb Trathen attempted to portray St. Claire's bias about Washington and the pageant in general by stating, "The pageant didn't go well for you."

The second beauty queen of the day who testified was Claudia Jordan, a lovely woman with a curvy figure and full lips. She testified that Washington told her "there was sex on the floor" and that "she was screaming" while Tyson attacked her. Perhaps this should have been the final contestant to be called but instead La Shauna Fitzpatrick walked to the witness stand. Cute and slim with short hair and a beaming smile, she said Washington told her "Well, he kinda, sorta, yeah, he raped me." Washington also told Jordan Tyson "restrained her," and "pushed her to the floor," statements contrary to Washington's version of what occurred. This testimony appeared to once again cast doubt on her story but the entire testimony backfired when Greg Garrison just happened to ask Jordan about Washington's appearance the day after the rape. When she said Washington "looked like death," Tyson's case had received another stab to the heart. Two jurors, Ken and Steve, #2 'sand #5, turned and looked squarely at Tyson. The looks were not ones of endearment. Tyson never blinked, doodling as always. At the defense table, Fuller looked as if he had just been hit with a right cross while Garrison sat down disbelieving how he had just been given an early Christmas present. The defense failure to uncover Jordan's damaging statement was unforgivable. Once again they had let Iron Mike down. This mistake was reminiscent of one defense lawyer Michael Stone made in the Rodney King state trial when he failed to object to prosecutors asking his client, Lawrence Powell, about statements he had made on the radio prior to the beating. Powell looked to Stone for an objection, but none was forthcoming requiring that Powell admit he had discussed a domestic disturbance involving a group of African-Americans by saying it was "right out of *Gorillas in the Mist*, a reference to the film of the same name. The inference was a killer, as Stone had not done his job in protecting Powell.

    After Claudia Jordan left the witness stand having done her damage to Tyson's case, the defense surprised the prosecution by calling Pasha Oliver as a witness. She had been one of Washington's roommates and more important, an eyewitness to the alleged conversation with Tyson and Gill when they spoke with her and Washington behind the pillar. She was also there when the 1:36 a.m. telephone call had been placed to Washington when Tyson asked her to join him in the limousine and present when Washington returned to the hotel room from her early morning date with Tyson. The State had not called her as a witness since Oliver had sued Tyson based on inflammatory remarks the ex-champ had allegedly made to her constituting sexual harassment. Fearful that a jury would see that Oliver was interested in Tyson's money, a charge the defense had made against Washington, the State had decided their case was better without her testifying. When all this was discussed with Judge Gifford at a sidebar, the defense was granted the opportunity to question Oliver as a "hostile witness." This meant the defense could use cross-examination tactics while asking her questions that could even be leading in nature. To the defense benefit, Oliver said that Tyson's comments at the pillar "made it clear that sex's what he's looking for." Regarding the early morning telephone call, she testified that she asked Washington to see if Johnny Gill was there and "can I go out with him?" Concerning what Washington told her after she returned to the hotel room, Oliver said Washington told her that she "agreed to kiss him," and then "he ripped her clothes off." She added that Tyson's "hand was over her mouth," and that "Tyson refused to take her home."

When Greg Garrison approached the witness, he appeared confused about what he intended with his questions. When he noted inconsistencies between what Oliver was saying at trial and had testified to at the Grand Jury, he finally became exasperated and said, "Do you know what perjury is?" But Oliver appeared unmoved by the strong words and kept to her story. When she was excused as a witness, Garrison appeared relieved.

To close its case, the defense presented certain portions of the videotape filmed by contestant Tanya Traylor's husband. The jury looked with interest at Washington singing and dancing, all done after the alleged rape. Also included were two comments by Washington to the effect that her ideal date "would be athletic," and that she "would reach for the highest star."

When Fuller announced to the court, "The defense rests," considerable doubt existed as to the impact of the testimony the jury had to consider. Since the defense strategy had been a scattershot one with several defenses in mind, one wondered what evidence jurors would find most credible. Certainly the presentation of the beauty queens had indicated inconsistencies in Washington's story, but were they that important to the eventual search for the truth? Did testimony as to her possible motives for filing the charges based on wanting Tyson's money truly resonate with jurors wondering about why she would lie and go through the exasperation and embarrassment of a trial just to collect money? Or would the jurors simply agree with Garrison that Tyson was a troubled and sick man who had committed rape and should be locked up in a prison so he would never commit such terrible crimes again? Certain this was what he had proved, but believing he might need a bit more ammunition, the State decided to counterattack by producing more evidence it was convinced proved Tyson's guilt.

Chapter Nineteen
The State Strikes Back

Once the defense in a criminal trial has rested its case, the State may not bring forth new evidence to bolster its accusations against the accused. But the prosecution may call witnesses to rebut testimony offered by the defense. The defense then has another short and so forth until the judge decides the pattern may not continue.

In the Mike Tyson case, the State chose to call to the stand Indianapolis Fire Department Deputy Fire Marshall Teresa Harris. Rebutting the testimony of Tanya Traylor who had termed Tyson, "friendly, gentlemanly," Harris testified that "the contestant in white," (meaning Traylor) was "gripped from behind more than four times by Tyson." Harris said she was "appalled at the behavior. It was disrespectful to women."

Next to testify was Indianapolis Police Department Detective Charles Briley. His appearance was apparently intended to clarify a remark made by Washington that was in question. It's relevance was questionable. He was followed to the witness stand by yet another beauty contestant, the reigning Miss Black America, Charmell Sullivan. She said she never saw Washington throw a tantrum or "beat on the floor" while other contestants were performing. Sullivan also noted that she did not hear any disparaging remarks made by Washington about other contestants. Commenting on this behavior were two more beauty contestants, Tasha Jarrett and Kycia Johnson. Each told the jury they had not witnessed any of the tantrums portrayed by defense witnesses.

Both women also swore that Desire would never use the dirty language attributed to her by other contestants.

To close their case, the State chose to play for the jury an audiotape of Tyson's Grand Jury testimony. At first glance, this appeared to be a mistake on the part of the state since the conversations proved that indeed deputy prosecutor David Dreyer had cut off Tyson when he wanted to continue and explain his desire for Washington. This was the good news, but the bad news implied that since the Grand Jury indicted Tyson, he must be guilty of something. When the defense did little to point this out, Tyson was left with a jury wondering what other evidence the Grand Jury might have heard so as to indict Iron Mike.

When everyone in the courtroom believed the trial was over, it wasn't. The defense called one witness, Tanya St. Claire Gilles stepfather, Anthony Rogers. His testimony was confusing at best regarding the specific language his stepdaughter had used when interviewed by deputy prosecutor Barb Trathen. Rogers thought he had heard the words "thumb, thumb," when prosecutors had alleged that St. Claire said "dick" or "penis." When this less than important point was finally considered, the evidence in the Tyson trial finished at precisely 2:01 p.m. on February 10th.

In comparison with the William Kennedy Smith, Rodney King, and Bensonhurst murder cases, the actual, relevant evidence produced in *Washington v. Tyson* that the jury would use to consider its decision, paled in comparison. To the discredit of the respective attorneys, the jury was left more with impressions rather than hard evidence to evaluate whether the ex-champ's conduct was criminal. When jurors have to guess, both sides are at risk, but here the loser appeared apparent since Tyson had take severe body blows designed to show one important point for the prosecution: Tyson might not be guilty beyond a reasonable doubt for raping Washington, but he was a dangerous man who needed to be imprisoned for who he was and probably what he had done in the past. To convict under such circumstances was against everything the judicial system stood for, but those who entangle themselves in the web of the law always assume the risk that the roll of the dice will come up double-twelve's. Being convicted on the basis of past conduct, or even the potential of future conduct contrary to the law was obscene to those who believed in the "innocent until proven guilty" credo, but such was the fate of those who were viewed as potential menaces of society, a description that unfortunately fit Mike Tyson to a "T."

Chapter Twenty
The Lawyers Speak

In view of the lack of critical evidence regarding the specifics of the rape charge leveled by Desire Washington against Mike Tyson, final arguments to the jury by the prosecution and defense took on more weighted importance.

For Greg Garrison and Barbara Trathen, each must have felt they were ahead on points but had not yet knocked Tyson out to the extent that a guilty verdict beyond a reasonable doubt was a certainty. It would thus be necessary to convinced jurors through their argument that Iron Mike was indeed a rapist, one who had taken advantage of an unsuspecting young woman who had told him "No" when he wanted to have sex with her. Then the jury could invoke the often used term, "No means No," familiar from television programs, and send Tyson where he belonged, to prison.

For Vincent Fuller, the final argument would provide a chance to redeem himself for what most all of the spectators and legal beagles believed had been a dismal performance. Whether he realized had in all likelihood lost the battle to save his client but might just pull out a win with a sensational argument to the jury was unclear, but one had to wonder whether, due to his lack of experience with sex crimes cases, he really knew his side was in deep trouble. Well-intentioned, but certainly over-confident, Fuller had alienated himself from the jury with the cold reasoning of an outsider in the ilk of an unpopular distant relative who crashes a family reunion. Garrison and Trathen were "hometowners," well-known to the jurors while Fuller was standoffish and distant with little connection to the twelve jurors who would decide Tyson's fate. But perhaps he could take a note from Roy Black, William Kennedy Smith's attorney who had superbly represented his client from start to finish but especially during final argument when he poked gigantic holes in the prosecution's case in an organized and timely manner by focusing on one defense, that Patty Bowman was simply not telling the truth. Like good defense attorneys are prone to do, he argued and argued again driving his point across that Bowman was not bruised enough to have been raped, that her clothes were not torn apart enough to have undergone the assault she described. Most important, he cut to shreds the prosecution's belief, justified or not, that Kennedy Smith would have forced sex with a woman directly below his mother's bedroom window where a screaming victim would awake everyone in sight. In effect, he was doing what competent defense lawyers do, must do, and that was to give the jurors *a reason* to acquit so that when folks, family and friends, asked them after the trial why they decided as they did, they could "hang their hat" on a piece of evidence or belief that justified their decision. Black was so persuasive that even when prosecutor Moira Lasch used the age-old, "Bowman said no, and [Kennedy Smith] didn't care," the jury did not believe her and acquitted the accused.

  To strike the first blow for the prosecution, the choice was Barb Trathen, Garrison's quite competent co-counsel. A pleasant woman with a look of truth about her, she stood before the jury at 9:25 a.m. on February 11th and began to tell the jury why she felt Tyson was guilty. Throughout the trial, she had showed trial moxie to the extent that many courtroom observers felt she had been more worthy than Garrison. Only on a couple of occasions when she either became too detailed or a bit unsettled with a witness who did not testify as she had expected, had she shown a vulnerable side.

On this morning, Trathen projected a tough persona by telling the jury that Tyson had used his fame and reputation like a thug in an alley would use a gun or knife. No objection to such a comparison forthcoming from Fuller, who appeared to be listening but not acting as he had done so many times during the trial, permitted Trathen to continue on unabated by explaining that forcible rape, "date rape," was serious and must not be considered, "half a crime." "Rape is rape, she shouted, "when there is force or the threat of force." Tyson's "tools" that he had used to seduce Washington, she argued, were the religious, not the sexual innuendos. By this, she said she meant, that his use of "You're a nice Christian girl," and the wearing of the "Together in Christ" badge made him out to be a "wolf in sheep's clothing." To emphasize her point, she moved from three or four feet in front of the jury to the first row of spectator seats where Washington sat with her mother. "Tyson," Trathen said, had been a "role model" for Washington's father, and when Desiree saw Tyson praying with Rev. Jesse Jackson, "What was this eighteen year old supposed to think?" Tyson, Trathen alleged, "had taken on the cloak of Christianity."

To Washington, Trathen told the jury, "Tyson was not a real person." She "knows how to handle young boys" back in Rhode Island, but Tyson was a different story. "It would be special to be with him," Trathen said of Washington's intentions. Turning to important medical testimony, the prosecutor mentioned Dr. Richardson's explanation that the injuries sustained by Washington were "consistent with forced sex." "In 20,000 cases," Trathen argued, the doctor had only seen "twice these types of injuries with consensual sex."

Her voice rising and falling for emphasis, Trathen asked the jury to focus on "quality" testimony, and thus discount beauty pageant evidence that may have been motivated by jealousy or mistake. Instead, the prosecutor argued, "remember the defense's motivation was that he found an impressionable young woman," one whose date with Tyson would be a "big moment" for her. Trathen then described what she called "the big lie." Could the jury imagine, she asked, that after Tyson said, "I want to f . . . you," this eighteen year old from Coventry, Rhode Island would merely go, 'ha, ha' and say, 'yeah, sure, give me a call.' That's what the defendant wants you to believe." Then she attacked Tyson saying he had "a selective memory, especially with what he remembers about sex with B Angie B." And, Trathen pointed out, Tyson never mentioned the "I want to f . . . you" statement to the Grand Jury" while Johnny Gill's "same chapter and verse" account of Tyson's words to Washington were to pat to consider worthy.

Attacking the credibility of the defense witnesses, Trathen said there was Pasha Oliver, who clearly committed perjury, Frank Valentine, who was "mixed up," and St. Claire, whose disappointing pageant results made the woman who had studied at the Little Princess Modeling School, unreliable. Tanya Traylor, Trathen argued, had not told the truth either according to Teresa Harris, the fire department witness. Summarizing, Trathen said, "Evaluate the defense witnesses," a clear insinuation that their testimony was tainted. Regarding the early morning telephone call to Washington from Tyson, Trathen pointed out that the important issue was how, "Washington wanted to spend time with Tyson." She asked him to come up, Trathen said, "she was innocent and naïve." Virginia Foster, the prosecutor argued, "was a key witness. She told you Tyson was begging and pleading for Washington to come down and talk. Washington even brought her camera." Concerning bodyguard Dale Edwards, she said "Tyson and [Edwards] were working together before insinuating that Edwards, "even waited a few minutes before getting into the front of the limousine while it was parked at the Omni." At the hotel, "what happened to Edwards?" Trathen asked. She told the jurors night clear McCoy Wagers recalled him there, and at 2:02 a. m., he was making calls in the lobby.

    Trathen noted that Tyson had testified that he watched Washington in the bathroom after the sex had taken place. She said the ex-champ said that Washington "straightened her hair, as if to say 'I've bedded the champ.'" "Does Washington's demeanor after she left the hotel room coincide with Tyson's testimony?" Trathen asked. "Virginia Foster told us what Washington was like," and "Virginia had years of training to help her determine that "the child had been raped." These strong conclusions drew no objection from Vincent Fuller. Was he really listening to Trathen or thinking too much about his upcoming argument to the jury?

    Closing her plea to the jury, Barbara Trathen emphasized that Tyson and Edward's plan was clear and Washington's "fate was sealed" when she left the Omni with Tyson. After reminding the jury that, "rape is not a half crime," she sat down pleased with having represented Washington to the best of her ability.

To rebut Barbara Trathen's argument that Tyson was a vicious rapist, Vincent Fuller began his speech to the jury with a slow pace. "Your role as a juror is the most important component of the legal system," he told the jury as he once again stood behind the podium instead of interacting with jurors used to his rather stoic demeanor. Why he did not "get it," that in the county courts lawyers needed to mix it up with jurors was hard to understand. Most walked and talked and moved about in the courtroom gesturing at will as their voices resonated with arguments in multiple tones designed to captivate jurors not put them to sleep. But Fuller could not, even if he had tried, acclimate himself to any other method of argument than from behind a podium. He had used one in Federal Court and if that worked there, it would work in the county courts. He was wrong, but no one could change his mind. There thus appeared a "wall" between Fuller and the jurors and he appeared to be talking to that wall instead of each individual juror. Instead of a conversation with the jury, he preached and lectured like the college professor who intends on convincing students of his theory but cannot talk plain language they understand.

After his beginning thoughts about the legal system in general, Fuller finally told the jury that the "core issue" in the case was "consent." Would he finally focus on this defense, and only this defense, and let all others alone? Hopefully this would occur, but the promise of such happening was clouded as Fuller recounted for the jury the presumption of innocence, the burden of truth, doubt based on reason, and the need for a unanimous verdict. He said the need for "12-0 verdict is because we are terrorized by the thought of convicting an innocent man."

Turning to words about his client, Fuller told the jurors Tyson was "not a trained student, he's a trained fighter." In sharp contrast to Washington, Fuller said, the ex-champ is a "high-school dropout" while Washington had an "ability to interact with national people," including Vice President Dan Quayle and Elizabeth Dole, among others. "She's poised, mature for her age, one of thirty-four out of thousands chosen to go to the Soviet Union. She's young in years, but not young in experience." The State, Fuller argued, suggested Washington was "oblivious to Tyson's conduct. Even the 1:36 a.m. telephone call was an act of rudeness." In the limousine, Fuller said, Tyson moved over and "kisses and hugs her." It "insults your intelligence," the defense counsel argued, "to believe this woman didn't know of Tyson's intentions. The State would have you believe that Tyson lures her to the suite, lures her to the bedroom, lures her to the TV." How impressive this argument would have been if the witness the defense tried to call corroborating the "kissing and hugging" in the limousine would have been permitted to testify.

When Tyson said, "you're turning me on," Fuller told the jury, Desiree Washington says she went to the bathroom. "If she was unnerved," fuller said, "there was a quick exit route right out the door." This point was well-issued, but Fuller did not go further to discuss a most important point – why Washington took off the panty shield. Was there any stronger indication that Washington intended to have sex with Tyson? And that, arguably, when the sex became too rough for her liking, she was disappointed with being treated like a rag doll instead of a future Mrs. Tyson? This would certainly have explained her conduct when she left the room and entered the limousine in tears if this is truly what occurred. And then led to the feeling that "she might have been raped," but was uncertain due to the nature of the consent, one garbled by her wanting to have sex with Tyson but not wanting to at the same time. But Fuller left this alone, and the consent defense was now pushed into the background as Fuller unwisely focused on why Tyson was such a bad boy and Washington knew it based on Iron Mike's irreverent behavior. Fuller pointed to Washington's having sat on Tyson's lap, and that his remarks, ones she heard, were "raunchy." Fuller recalled the testimony of Fran Valentine who said Washington was "jocking" Tyson with sexual overtones; Kycia Johnson, who said she heard Desiree talk about "Mike Tyson's body," and Johnny Gill, who said Tyson say, "I want to f . . . you." Hearing this remark again only impressed it more into juror's minds. Was this a wise move, for them to hear Tyson at his worst with a degrading and filthy remark to a woman who was by all accounts a decent young girl? Fuller told the jury that Tyson's failure to mention these words at the Grand Jury was a "red herring" and that even if Tyson used the words, "I want you," this was enough to alert Washington to his intentions.

Regarding Washington's intentions, Fuller said she made that clear at the opening ceremonies when she said, "I'm going out with Mike Tyson. He's got a lot of money. He's dumb. Look what Robin Givens got." And, Fuller asked, what about Washington's claim that Tyson said he was going to pick up his bodyguard at the Canterbury Hotel when the bodyguard was right there in the limousine for her to see? It's naïve to believe he would fabricate such a story when the bodyguard was not only there, but went into the hotel with Washington and Tyson. These arguments would have been much more powerful but Fuller appeared confused with his thoughts. He misstated a date, was unable to locate an exhibit, mistakenly thought another exhibit was in evidence when it was not, and kept calling the "State," the "Government," a throwback to his days in Federal Court. This caused Fuller to seem less than a believing soul in his own arguments, leaving the jury to wonder whether truly thought his client was innocent. But he pressed ahead, and was given a gift when Steve, juror #5 surprised everyone by requesting a bathroom break. What a reprieve this was for Fuller who used the fifteen minutes to gather his thoughts as a confused Tyson watched him try to regain his composure as he moved toward the finality of an argument that needed to be first rate to prohibit Tyson from a conviction and imprisonment.

"What woman who didn't have sex on her mind would go to a bedroom at two a.m.?" Fuller asked, attempting to re-focus his argument toward the consent issue. But then he left that arena and turned his attention to the dress that Washington was wearing the night of the alleged attack. "She told you that the dress she was wearing was very important to her since it had been given to her by a pageant official in Rhode Island," Fuller explained. "Why then," he argued, "would she remove a panty liner and risk destruction to the garment?" As the jurors considered this point of interest, Fuller tried to make them reason as to Tyson's behavior and whether it squared up with the portrait of a rapist. The defense counsel said, "Rape is not a considerate crime," but Tyson had used his fingers. "Would a rapist to that?" How about her allegations that Tyson and was on top of her and withdrew before ejaculation? "Why would a rapist do such a thing?" "Tyson weighed 220, Washington 105," Fuller noted. "Dr. Richardson said there wasn't a bruise on her body."

Switching gears to point out Washington's differing versions of the alleged crime, Fuller said she told others, "she was on the floor," "that she screamed," to others "that she didn't scream because Tyson's elbow was in her mouth." To Kycia Johnson, she said she "thought she'd been raped." Fuller also recalled the testimony of Chaplain Kathryn Newlin that she "noted some sense of participation between Washington and Tyson." He also noted inconsistencies with the garment and the need for the jury to speculate as to whether it had been tampered with in Rhode Island. Jumping back and forth with unfortunately little continuity, Fuller argued that Washington was "comparing herself to Robin Givens." When a contestant said, "Here comes your husband," Washington replied, "He'll make the money, and I'll do the talking." Regarding future plans, Fuller said Washington replied, "They haven't met you yet," when Tyson asked "Does your family like me?" But Fuller did not emphasize the importance doing his job as a prosecutor or simply wanted to add a notch to his belt as the one who whipped the ex-heavyweight champion of the world and sent him to prison. Had Garrison's quest become too personal for him to understand the difference?

To begin, he defended Washington instead of prosecuting Tyson: "The innocence of the defendant has become secondary to the guilt of the victim. This law platoon from Washington D.C. has sought to massacre the victim, and denigrate a courageous young person." "Let's bring a fan in here and blow away Fuller's smoke," Garrison roared. He then scrambled to a blackboard positioned for the jurors to clearly see. He pointed to statistics: "Dr. Richardson told you in 20,000 exams that injuries such as Washington's involving consensual sex are 'rare as hen's teeth.' Even the defense witness, Dr. Watanobe, told of the extreme rarity of such injuries where consensual sex occurred." All the doctors, Garrison argued, that "the chances [of consensual sex] are very small, around .03 percent." Labeling the defense tactics "a week-long barbeque of the victim," Garrison admitted that sure, his client's testimony had been inconsistent. "Coach Knight," the prosecutor said referring to Indiana University's infamous basketball coach, "calls his players kids. One minute, they're great, and the next they can't find the gymnasium." "Corroboration is the key," Garrison told the jury. The telephone call to the limousine and "C'mon, I just want to talk" comment by Tyson were, he told the jury, corroborated by Virginia Foster. "These are like a fingerprint," Garrison said. "A woman of the world doesn't go out on a date like this in her pajamas," he continued, referring to the underclothing that Washington had worn.

Garrison, without any objection from Fuller, who seemed mesmerized by the lead prosecutor's argument, then referred to the absence of the bodyguard, Dale Edwards. "Where is he?" the prosecutor asked, providing the inference that his never being called to testify was due to his inability to back up Tyson's story. Garrison then asked the jury, "Does it make sense to talk about pigeons for fifteen minutes after supposedly hugging and kissing in the car?" A fatal blow to Tyson's story, he said, was his testimony that he asked Washington to stay the night. "How is she rejected if he's asked her to spend the night?" Garrison asked. "She's hit a home run," implying that if Washington was really after Tyson, she would have been thrilled to spend the night with him. He then mocked the defense's contention that Washington was a "golddigger." It's a "ridiculous fairy tale," Garrison said, pointing out that if Washington had truly been after Tyson's wealth, she would have accepted his invitation to spend the night as a prelude to a more enduring relationship. "If she really wants his money . . . she's won the ballgame . . . when she can sleep with him."

Turning to Washington's behavior after the alleged sex act, Garrison asked whether Washington would have messed up her own hair and faked being frightened and scared after the alleged attack. "'Anxiety and fear,' that's what Virginia Foster told you Desiree Washington was like when she came down to the limousine," Garrison reminded the jury. "Vincent Fuller keeps say how smart Desiree Washington is," he asserted. "But next time you [pointing to Washington] frame someone for money, Desiree, do a better job." He then told the jury what he felt were the three important measurements they should use to make its decision: corroboration, character, and the persona of those who take the witness stand." Regarding the character issue, Garrison said Tyson "practices being deceptive by profession. He's aggressively deception." "Is he honest?" the prosecutor asked, "He even lied to Jesse Jackson."

Looking each of the jurors in the eye and he wrapped up his argument, Garrison said, "The world's eyes want to know if the citizens of Marion County have the courage to convict Tyson. A beautiful, honest kid came to town and got deceived by a professional deceiver who isolated, defeated, and raped her."

What was the effect of Garrison's emotional plea to the jury? Barbara Trathen had been methodical with her argument. Vincent Fuller seemed lost at time but made important points. And the Garrison took over and basically challenged the jury to convict Tyson. Who were the winners and losers among the three? It didn't matter, for the only one at risk was Iron Mike, Michael Gerard Tyson. Soon twelve people would decide whether he resumed his boxing career, or was known as a convicted rapist sent to prison.

Chapter Twenty
Guilty as Charged

Heading into jury deliberation as the definite underdog based on their many miscues, Vincent Fuller and defense team focused in on the defense of consent as their chief weapon against Mike Tyson spending years in prison. To that end, a final instruction dealing with the issue of "implied consent" was filed with the court.

The essence of the filing read:

> ... the defendant cannot be guilty of rape ... if the conduct of the complainant under all of the circumstances should reasonably be viewed as indicating consent to the acts in question." To bolster the argument that the instruction should be provided to the jury, the motion stated, "defendant has presented considerable evidence that Washington manifested her consent to the sexual acts in question through a consistent course of conduct leading up to, and including the acts themselves. A number of witnesses had testified that the defendant's intentions were made plain while he was in the complainant's presence, that she accepted an explicit sexual invitation from him, that her consent toward the defendant was at all times consistent with a desire to engage in consensual sex with him, and that she herself described consensual physical contact prior to the alleged rape.

Legal precedent was then cited with the closing remark: "The jury should be instructed that it must find Mr. Tyson not guilty it if harbors reasonable doubt on this issue."

Despite the defense plea for the instruction to be provided, Judge Gifford denied it. The defense was jolted with the decision believing it quite unfair and against the precedent they had cited. Was prosecutor Jeff Modisett smiling again with the decision? He and Greg Garrison had to be. But another instruction did cause them some concern since although it was not as concise as the one the defense had proposed regarding consent, it did provide guidelines for how the jury should evaluate whether consent had occurred. In part, it read: "It is not the law of this State that a person who is raped be required to resist by all violent means within her power. The law requires only that the case be one in which the complaining witness did not consent. The complaining witness' resistance must not be mere pretense, but in good faith."

The lack of any mention of the words "implied consent" in this instruction still concerned the defense as Judge Gifford provided the final instructions to the jury. All sat attentively as she spewed out guidelines that specified what the jury could decide and what they could not decide. When the judge had finished her instructions, the solemn twelve filed toward the back of the courtroom and past the witness stand where critical evidence had been heard during the trial. None glanced at Tyson. He sat calmly watching as they filed one by one through the door toward the jury room. His attorneys then escorted him out the front door as the prosecutors, supremely confident, ambled into the courtroom office and then into the hallway.

Predications ran rampant among the media. Some believed the prosecution's case was too weak, others predicted Tyson would be found guilty and sent to prison. This author, based on two main factors, an inept defense especially with regard to competing medical testimony, and Judge Gifford's pro-prosecution rulings and demeanor, especially when she told Tyson to "help yourself," when he asked politely about whether to use bold language, joined the latter camp with the belief that Tyson was a goner. But the jury was the decider of the facts and the law, and it remained to be seen what verdict they would return.

Less than nine hours later, the jury foreman, Tim, sent word to Judge Gifford that the jury had reached a verdict, there was bedlam as court personnel scurried around attempting to locate Tyson, defense lawyers, and prosecutors. Word spread quickly among the media and those attending the trial on a daily basis and all took their seats in anticipation of the boxer's fate. At 10:29 p.m., Tyson appeared in the courtroom flanked by Don King and his bodyguard and confidant, John Horne. No defense lawyers were present. His face stoic, his body motions slow and deliberate, Tyson walked to the defense table and sat there by himself. The image of Tyson alone was one that would remain in the minds of many who felt compassion for the ex-champion's plight. It was a sad moment.

At 10:35, Tyson's local defense counsel James Voyles and then Tyson's chief trial lawyer Vincent Fuller joined Tyson at the counsel table. Prosecutors Greg Garrison and Barb Trathen were already seated. As the bailiff called the courtroom to order, Judge Gifford entered through a side door. Her footsteps were the only sounds damaging the silence.

With the various media poised to write down every word, spectators leaning forward to gain a glimpse of Tyson, and the defense lawyers and prosecution team listening intently, Gifford began: "State of Indiana v. Michael Tyson. Show State by Greg Garrison and Barb Trathen. Defense by Vincent Fuller, Kathleen Beggs, Lane Heard and James Voyles. I understand the jury has reached a verdict. State ready? Defense ready? Al right, bring in the jury."

Four minutes later to the second, the first juror entered the courtroom. Each presented a stone-faced expression and none looked directly at Tyson. He must have known gloom was the air as his heart beat faster than during any of his heavyweight championship bouts.

When the jurors were seated, the judge asked, "Have you reached a verdict?" Tim, juror number nine, rose from his seat in the back row and announced in a rather weak voice, "Yes, we have." He then handed the three verdict forms to the bailiff.

Judge Gifford accepted the forms and looked at them one by one. Then at 10:46 p.m., as a hushed tone pervaded the courtroom and all those present held their breath during one of the most dramatic times anyone may imagine, the former prosecutor of sex crimes read the verdicts one by one.

When Tyson first heard the word "guilty," Iron Mike's head cocked slightly to the side as if he had been hit with a thunderous right cross to the chin. He whispered, "Oh, man," and then slumped down in his seat. Instead of being a free man with aspirations to recapture the world championship, he was now a convicted felon headed directly for prison.

    The world may have been shocked following the acquittal in the state trial of the four police officers who allegedly beat Rodney King, but there was a rather subdued reaction when Iron Mike was branded a rapist for the rest of his life. When he heard the words, "guilty," he looked as if he wanted to escape from the planet as he pondered how this decision could have been reached when he had purposely, at least in his mind, made it clear to Desiree Washington that he wanted to have sex with her and in return, she had joined him in his hotel room. Common sense, he must have believed, pointed directly to her consenting to have sex. Were the jurors crazy; did they simply ignore all of the evidence? Certainly his comment "Oh man," must have been the result of the word "guilty" pulsating in his gut harder than any punch ever thrown by Evander Holyfield or any other of the multitude of boxers he faced in the ring.
    Unlike the four officers in the Rodney King state case, William Kennedy Smith, Lemrick Nelson, Jr., or even Clarence Thomas, Tyson had been convicted. Why had this occurred, why had Tyson been the only one determined to be guilty? In celebrity trials, unlike those occurring thousands of times in cases around the world each day, a jury knows it is in the limelight and after the verdict is reached, they will asked why they ruled as they did.

As noted, it may be family, friends, fellow workers, or even simply the man or woman on the street who knows of their being a juror, but every day they will be asked about their decision. Faced with this occurring, as mentioned, defense lawyers and prosecutors must give a jury one or two single factors they may point to as to why they decided as they did.

      In the Tyson trial, the prosecution did their job; the defense did not. Greg Garrison and Barbara Trathen, with an assist from a friendly judge, basically provided the jury with their "out" through the unquestioned medical evidence provided by Dr. Stephen Richardson. If asked why they found Tyson guilty, a juror could easily point to this piece of evidence as being decisive. But, more important, the ineptness of Vincent Fuller's defense caused a more severe penalty for Tyson since because they did not defend him properly and professionally, there exists, and will always exist, the belief that Iron Mike did not receive a fair trial. With the playing field being so tilted toward a good prosecution with little defense to counter it, the truth will never be known causing speculation as to how the trial verdict would have differed with the prosecution had faced stiff opposition. To support this strong assertion, that Tyson did not receive a fair trial, the following points are relevant when assessing the defense performance and why, in effect, the guilty verdict was foregone conclusion. To recapitulate, first, the decision of Don King to hire Vincent Fuller was a disaster; second, Tyson's ill-fated appearance at the Grand Jury; third, Fuller hired local defense lawyer James Voyles and never utilized his skills; four, the defense did not request a change of judge thus disqualifying Judge Gifford;

five, the defense did not employ a jury selection expert familiar with the Indianapolis panel; six, Fuller did not strike Tim, juror number nine, from the panel, a mistake permitting the ex-Marine, one ground in matters being right and wrong with no in-between, to become jury foreman and highly influence the guilty verdict (this mistake was akin to the one committed by famed attorney F. Lee Bailey in the Patty Hearst case when Bailey permitted an Air Force colonel to sit in judgment); Fuller's opening statement was totally incompetent when he promised the jury Tyson would testify; eight, Fuller's cross-examination of Washington was highly ineffective due to Fuller being way too polite and not digging for the truth when his client's freedom was on the line; nine, Fuller's impersonal, federal-courtroom manner caused him to be the ultimate "outsider" and appear disconnected to the judge and jurors; ten, Fuller and company portrayed Tyson as a bad boy, unruly and dangerous so as to be a warning to Washington but this permitted jurors to finally decide he was right and Tyson needed to be removed by society due to his past bad behavior as well as that with Washington; eleven, Fuller's characterization of Washington as being "money-hungry" backfired; twelve, the defense decision to permit Tyson to testify permitting jurors to hear his ill-fated "I want to f . . . you" comment, a true turn-off for all that heard it; thirteen, Fuller's rambling final argument where he did not provide the jury with a single factor upon which to render Tyson non-guilty; and fourteen, as mentioned, the lack of medical testimony to counter the powerful testimony of Dr. Richardson. Together these factors doomed Tyson to defeat; in effect he never had a chance.

Would the verdict have been different if the three witnesses who said they saw Washington and Tyson together in the limousine and at the Canterbury Hotel, especially the one who saw them "hugging and kissing," had been allowed to testify? Even if this information had been provided to the jurors along with further facts uncovered later, the bottom line is that, in all likelihood, Tyson would still have been convicted due to the plethora of defense mistakes made in his behalf. With Judge Gifford in the driver's seat, Garrison and Trathen in the back seat, and Fuller on the street outside looking in, the only question was how long it would take the jurors to decide he was guilty. It didn't take long, but the defense was still in denial regarding the eventual outcome since Fuller and company actually believed a "not-guilty" verdict was forthcoming. At approximately 8:45, while the jury was deliberating, the defense team was enjoying a lavish dinner at a restaurant atop the downtown Hyatt Hotel. When this author approached Fuller and suggested that Tim, juror number nine, might be a problem, he responded, "Oh, we're not worried about juror number nine, maybe number five and number six, but not number nine." To the end, the well-meaning Fuller didn't have a clue. He should have never accepted representation of Tyson.

In the end, the jurors spoke to the media and basically provided a consensus that none believed Tyson had told the truth when he testified. This ended up being the most consistent reason given, the "hook" upon which to hang the verdict. Other factors were explained, but this reasoning pointed to wondering if the outcome would have been altered if Iron Mike had never spoken a word in court.

In the end, perhaps the verdict caused reflection about the type of choices people have in life, ones where they reap what they sow whether at the time of acting morally, ethically and legally wrong, or later when they pay the piper. Tyson decided he wanted to have sex with Washington during the early morning hours of July 19, 1991. But this time, he picked the wrong woman, Don King picked the wrong lawyer to represent him and the attorney picked the wrong strategy to defend him at trial. Don King and Vincent Fuller went home. Mike Tyson was on his way to prison.

Did the guilty verdict mean that Desiree Washington had told the truth about Tyson's having raped her? Or had she simply "thought she was raped," and then, after some consideration and a talk with her mother, began to truly believe she was even if she wasn't. But she was the clear winner in all of this, ready now for her lawyers to go after Iron Mike's money. She returned to the east coast to being her "post-Tyson trial" life, while Tyson had a date with the judge to learn just how much time in prison he would spend.

Chapter Twenty-Three
Judgment Day

On March 26, 1992, 252 days after the alleged rape of Desiree Washington, a stone-faced Michael Girard Tyson appeared before Judge Patricia Gifford for sentencing.

Tyson's appearance was somewhat of a shock to those who believed he would flee the country to some unknown destination where there was no possible extradition to the United States. Judge Gifford's having permitted the boxer free on bail after the conviction surprised some, but instead of considering leaving the country, he had spent much of his final days of freedom apparently holed up in his Cleveland mansion. No one knew what was going through his mind, and the only time the media reported anything unusual occurred when he received a speeding ticket. Now, Tyson appeared before the judge that would sentence him to prison. This was a reality with the only question how much prison time he would receive.

Beside Tyson was the dour-faced Vincent Fuller, dressed immaculately as usual, but with much less of a swagger than before. Like his client, he had gone down for the count with the savvy Greg Garrison having beaten him like a child. Even Don King had badmouthed Fuller's trial strategy attempting to shift the blame as always. He was in the courtroom to support the ex-champ as were twenty-five others including Camille Ewald, Tyson's mother. Dressed in the same gray pin-striped suit he had worn on the first day of the trial, Tyson sat at counsel table between Fuller and James Voyles. Seated a few feet behind them was newly acquired appellate counsel, Alan Dershowitz, the famed Harvard University law professor whose clients had included Leona Helmsley, Claus von Bulow, and Michael Milken. The fuzzy haired legal beagle with the glasses and a quick quip for anyone he felt could get his name in the media watched intently Judge Gifford, whom he planned to publicly assassinate with legal arrows in an appeal ready for filing the moment Iron Mike was sentenced.

Prior to sentencing, speculation arose as to the contents of the pre-investigation report filed by the Marion County Probation Department. Two items had leaked, 1) that the probation officer preparing the report believed that Tyson, if not treated for his psychological problems, "probably" would commit the same crime again, and 2) that the ex-champ's net worth had dwindled to a mere $5 to $8 million dollars. If the former were true, Judge Gifford had all the ammunition she needed to speed Tyson off to prison. Regarding the latter, Garrison told *ESPN's* Charley Steiner that Tyson's assets still totaled "eight figures." The probation department report apparently supported Tyson being wealthy but concluded all of his assets were tied up with Don King. A defense filing suggested Tyson's worth at about $5 million with assets including a fleet of thirty luxury cars, including a Ferrari and a Lamborghini, the 30,000-square foot mansion complete with a movie theater, and a multimillion-dollar jewelry collection.

Regarding the potential sentence Tyson could expect, records indicated that Judge Gifford's average sentence for such offense ranged from 10.7 in 1990 to 7.0 in 1991. She could suspend the sentence based on Tyson's having no excessive criminal record. Also available was the judge deciding to place Tyson in an alternative sentencing program involving a work release center of community service facility.

During the sentencing itself, Desiree Washington would not appear. Instead, she sent a letter to the judge. This appeared odd since throughout the proceedings, Washington had been front and center even through the final argument. Now, when Tyson was about to learn whether the punishment fit the crime, she had decided to relinquish her chance to face him one more time as Judge Gifford decided his fate.
For the defense, Fuller had listed five potential witnesses for Tyson: Lloyd Bridges, head of the Riverside Community Corrections Center, an Indianapolis work release program, Camille Ewald, Rita Akins and Steve Brock, owners of a private sentencing group who had been hired to conduct a "private" pre-sentence report about Tyson, and Jay Bright, Tyson's longtime friend. Noticeably absent on the list was Don King.

Anxious to proceed with appellate procedures to overturn the conviction, appellate lawyer Alan Dershowitz had filed an extensive motion with the court. Among the items he listed in behalf of Tyson's plea for a new trial were: exclusion of an African-American potential juror from the special grand jury that indicted Tyson; Judge Gifford's refusal to dismiss the indictment based on defense allegation that the indictment resulted from a system utilized to select a jury not unrepresentative of a cross section of the community, denial of three defense motions for continuance, denial of a defense motion to admit evidence of domestic problems between

Washington's parents that triggered domestic violence and the arrest of Washington's father; improper selection of a trial judge, the exclusion of three witnesses who would have testified that Washington and Tyson were "all over each other" in the limousine prior to the attack; the court's admission into evidence of the "altered clothing" worn by Washington the night of the alleged attack, and prosecutor Garrison's improper rebuttal argument summation.

Whether any of these allegations of impropriety might gain merit with an appellate court was subject to debate, but the exclusion of the three witnesses appeared to be Dershowitz' best shot.

The Harvard lawyer's appearance provided another element to the celebrity case and positioned him against not only Tyson but prosecutor Jeffrey Modisett who suddenly appeared ready to soak in the spoils of victory over the ex-champ. He decided to weigh in since the question existed as to whether Judge Gifford would permit an appeal bond if Tyson were sentenced to prison. Addressing this issue, Modisett said the pre-investigation report concluded, "Tyson is capable of doing it [rape] again" and that "as a prosecutor, the number one goal is safety." He also stated that the State would seek a six to ten year prison term, a $30,000 fine, and $150,000 from Tyson for court and related causes. Modisett's hard line and Dershowitz' appearance had certainly increased media attention to the case to the extent that Judge Gifford decided the twelve jury seats could be occupied by members of the media through an arbitrary system. As she rendered her decision as to Tyson's punishment, reporters from the *New York Times, Newsday,* the *New York Daily News*, and *Fox* television would be among those following her every word. Others would watch from the media viewing room. Spectators gathered early outside the City/County Building hoping to gain one of seventeen public seats available. Twenty-five Tyson supporters attempted to enter the courtroom, but deputy sheriffs turned them away. Many gawked as the diminutive Dershowitz entered the hallway. The fifty-three-year-old lawyer known for his passion for the downtrodden had been involved in several high-profile cases but his record did not bode well for Tyson. Over the past twenty years, he had filed nearly sixty appeals with success earned in less than ten of them. Dershowitz disputed these numbers arguing that he, and his brother Nathan, had a better record than reported in the media.

Dershowitz had become a Harvard professor in 1964, and the youngest tenured law faculty member in its history three years later. He had graduated at the top of his Yale class and then achieved some notoriety when he assisted Supreme Court Justice Arthur Goldberg with an opinion striking down certain existing death penalty laws deemed unconstitutional. Later, he would represent a string of rather unpopular clients including evangelist Jim Bakker and Leona Helmsley, known for her controversial quote, "Only the little people pay taxes." Some admired Dershowitz' savvy while others believed he was more a media hound than a sound defense appeals lawyer. In the Tyson case, he made it appear that he was the saving grace, the white knight, who would rush in on his white horse and prevent Iron Mike from being imprisoned. As to why he decided to help Tyson (the fee was unknown), Dershowitz had told some colleagues the "date rape" issue interested him because of the need to balance "feminist interests with civil liberties issues." He told a reporter that even while the Tyson trial was progressing, he believed he would be involved "sooner or later" and thus had honed in on the "state of mind of Tyson as to whether the boxer possessed the requisite intent necessary to commit the crime." Apparently Dershowitz had been informed that questions existed regarding the competence of Tyson's lead defense lawyer, Fuller. His response: "He had heard that they [the defense] were bad," but "he didn't know if they were *that* bad." Whether this was simply professional courtesy toward Fuller no one knew, but when the time of sentencing occurred, there Dershowitz was standing toe to toe with the defeated Fuller.

Having convicted Tyson without exhibiting his fiery temper, Greg Garrison was now poised to argue that the ex-champ required imprisonment to save society from his menacing ways. Since the jury verdict had been rendered, he pranced around with a proverbial smile on his face savoring his victory. Some in the legal community challenged the merits of his case, and whether he truly would have been successful had he faced a stiff challenge from competent defense lawyers, but this did not matter to Garrison. Enjoying the national and international spotlight, he had become the flag-waving symbol for justice. Fuller had never been able to dent the armor Garrison wore to protect this egotistical manner and expose the temper. But Kathleen Beggs finally did, albeit too late for the jury to witness. Before the sentencing hearing began, she challenged him regarding the filing of a motion without serving the defense with a copy. Beggs: 'You ever hear of serving notice on counsel?" Garrison: "Maybe you should return those phone calls at Williams and Connolly." After the exchange, each cooled down a bit but then the matter escalated when Beggs threatened to bring the matter to the court's attention. Garrison, sitting next to Modisett at the prosecutor's table, said in a tone loud enough for all to hears, "Well, you've been successful thus far, go ahead. Grow up." Even Modisett appeared embarrassed by the unprofessional comment. He motioned for Garrison to take it easy.

Moments before Judge Gifford made her appearance, Tyson sat at counsel table speaking to James Voyles. The ex-champ had seemed closer to Voyles than the other attorneys and this caring attorney really was disappointed for his client. But Voyles had been strictly second fiddle and though he was poised to attack several times during the trial, Fuller had, in essence, muffled him. Voyles was like a caged tiger hoping to be un-caged but the door was never opened by the arrogant Fuller, who had made it clear he ran the show. During Tyson's talk with Voyles, he held in his hand a white sheet of paper some three to four inches in size. It featured some indistinguishable words at the top, and a diagram with boxes containing the numbers one and nineteen below the words. Arnold Baratz, a public defender in Judge Gifford's court, and just one of several outstanding attorneys who would have provided Tyson with a much more competent defense, believed the words indicated some sort of Islamic prayer, but no one on Tyson's defense team revealed the meaning. Perhaps these were words of comfort that Tyson had been given to help him make it through this dark day since instead of a heavyweight contender 200 pounds or more armed with the power to punch his to the floor, his

245

opponent this morning was a slight, gray-haired, lightweight judge who was about to throw him a knockout punch.

Chapter Twenty-Four
Going, Going, Gone

Forty-four days had passed since twelve jurors had rendered Mike Tyson a convicted rapist. Now, at precisely 9:13 a.m. on March 26, 1992, Judge Patricia Gifford entered her courtroom through a side door and walked the ten steps or so to her chair, one stationed just a few feet from where witnesses had testified during the Tyson trial. Once again she uttered the words that began each day's proceedings, "State of Indiana vs. Michael G. Tyson, case number 01116245."

Judge Gifford, a devoted mother, told friends she longed for normalcy to return to her life but she had clearly enjoyed the limelight triggered by her presiding over the celebrity trial. This was a case every judge, faced with the mundane daily ritual of viewing people who had either hurt others or been hurt by others parade before her with only the faces changing instead of the circumstances, relished. Criminal courts were where lives changed in an instant for better or worse, but the rigorous schedule due to overcrowded calendars made the job a laborious one that seeped the very life blood out of those who chose to wear the robe and institute justice. Judge Gifford's life had been transformed by the Tyson case for she would forever, for better or for worse, be known as the judge who sent him to prison if this is what she chose and there was little doubt she was going to choose that option. But once Tyson was gone, she would return to her usual rituals, including time in the kitchen that she told others was therapeutic for her.

While William Kennedy Smith would become a medical student in Arizona, Clarence Thomas a Supreme Court justice, Lemrick Nelson, Jr. free to choose his destiny until indicted in federal court, and the four Los Angeles police officers able to return to duty pending further charges, Tyson's life was about to become a resident of an Indiana prison. But for how long? Only the fifty-five-year-old Gifford knew the answer. Was Tyson to be treated as simply another face of many, or would she attempt to make an example of this celebrity so as to deter others from a similar fate? Regarding the appropriate sentence, everyone had an opinion and the contrast was noticeable since no one was wishy-washy about Iron Mike. Some believed he should be locked away for twenty years. They believed he was a dangerous animal poised to rape again, and that the judge should "throw the book at him." Doing so would teach him, and other celebrities considering breaking the law in Indianapolis or anywhere else, that a stiff penalty awaited their actions if they were caught and convicted like Tyson. A stiff sentence would also put people on notice that Indianapolis was tough on crime, tough on defiant souls like Tyson who believed they could get away with raping an innocent teenager like Desiree Washington. To the contrary, Tyson's supporters believed he had gotten a raw deal from the get-go, that police and prosecutors were out to get Iron Mike and do so without regard for actual evidence in the case. Some still asked what Washington was doing in Tyson's room in the middle of the night if she did not want to have sex. To them, Tyson was the victim, not Washington. He thus should receive either a suspended sentence and probation or a year or two in prison at most.

Many Tyson supporters also believed race had played a part in Tyson being indicted. If he had been white, they said, the case might never have been filed or the least, plea bargained to a misdemeanor assault charge with the victim receiving a civil settlement. But because Tyson was African-American, the theory went, he had been persecuted not prosecuted by people who still held racial prejudice. One target was certainly Greg Garrison, but it appeared he had accepted the case for its celebrity nature and what it could do for his career. Certainly the Tyson victory propelled him into the spotlight, and besides being retained for some high-paying cases in the future, he rolled his celebrity status into becoming an Indianapolis radio talk-show host where his conservative bent was popular with those of like mind in the conservative-prone communities surrounding Indianapolis.

By all accounts, Judge Gifford had made up her mind regarding the sentence to be imposed, but she was required to go through the motions of hearing argument on both sides of the aisle regarding any important considerations that might affect her decisions. She had read the pre-sentence report prepared by the Marion County Probation office as well as the private one offered by the defense. She had also received opinions from colleagues and friends, and hundreds of letters from people around the world either pro or con Tyson. But one letter stood out from all the rest, the one submitted through the prosecution from Desiree Washington.

To present support for Tyson receiving probation, Vincent Fuller called to the witness stand Lloyd Bridges, the executive director of the local Riverside Correctional Facility. An ordained minister, he noted that Riverside was akin to a halfway house, a "minimum security" facility. Only two convicted rapists had ever been stationed there, but he wanted a third, Tyson, with whom he had spent three hours at the ex-champ's Cleveland mansion. Bridges said they spoke about "Tyson's background," and his "religious beliefs." According to a "point system" he used to evaluate potential inmates, Bridges determined that Tyson would be eligible for RCF. Hearing this, Fuller turned over the witness to Barb Trathen who destroyed any creditability Bridges had by having him admit that there had been four recent escapes from his facility, something Fuller should have noted in his direct examination to blunt its effect and provide an explanation. All Bridges could say was that, in his opinion, Tyson "was not an escape risk." Asked about Tyson's religious thoughts, Bridges testified that the former champion had "truly been touched by the Lord." Trathen countered this remark by questioning whether this was simply a "jailhouse conversion." Bridges said he thought Tyson was sincere. "If what Tyson expressed to me is real," he said, "and I believe it is, he will be okay."

Bridges would be the only defense witness to appear for Tyson. Even Camille Ewald was left out. But Vincent Fuller was ready to offer his two cents, still believing that he had any sort of creditability in the courtroom. Could he somehow pull an argument together that would save his client? Could he work some of the big city magic to convince Judge Gifford probation for Tyson was the right avenue to pursue? Was he finally going to show why he was worth $5000 a day?

Fuller began by pointing out, "Tyson came in with a lot of baggage. The press has vilified him.

I have never seen an athlete that has so offended the press. Not a day goes by that the press doesn't bring up his faults." Defending Tyson, he continued, "This is not the Tyson I know. The Tyson I know is a sensitive, thoughtful, caring man. He may be terrifying in the ring, but that ends when he leaves the ring." Fuller then chronicled his client's early life of petty crime on the streets of Brooklyn, ones that had landed him at the Tryon School for Boys in upstate New York. There, Fuller told the court, he met a guard named Bobby Stewart who taught him the boxing basics. When Tyson turned thirteen, Steward introduced him to Cus D'Amato, the legendary trainer who lived an hour or so south in Catskill. D'Amato took a liking, Fuller said, to Tyson, a "man/child," and, after watching him spar with Stewart, proclaimed he could make Tyson "the youngest heavyweight champion of the world." Earlier in his career, D'Amato had earned similar honors for Floyd Patterson. "But there was tragedy in this," Fuller continued. "D'Amato was only focused on boxing. Tyson, the man, was secondary to Cus D'Amato's quest for Tyson's boxing greatness." What Judge Gifford thought of Fuller's diatribe was unclear, but certainly his questionable comments about D'Amato's intentions with Tyson must have galled people like Camille Ewald, who loved Tyson but also had lived with D'Amato for almost forty years. In effect, Fuller was spitting on the legendary trainer's grave.

"In 1985, Tyson became champion," Fuller told Judge Gifford. "And, except for Camille Ewald, he was in a male-dominant world. [He never had] peer interpersonal relationships with women. His entire world was that of boxing." More was expected along this line, but Fuller, appearing to be a bit confused as to the message he wanted to convey, then said, "This case calls for a suspended sentence with probation and therapy, in a place like Riverside. To put Tyson in prison repeats the same experience he's gotten before. He needs to go into the work force with women, and see how he's expected to behave." In a final plea, Fuller then told Judge Gifford, "You are in a difficult position. I am not asking for irrational leniency. Only for compassion." Instead of stopping there, he felt the need to invoke the name of Desiree Washington and made the outlandish claim that she would no doubt join in asking that Tyson "be sent to a place like Riverside as well." What? Had Fuller spoken to Washington and learned of this wish on her part? If he had, he certainly did not inform the court of the specifics of any conversation. The reason, he had never spoken to the victim outside the courtroom and his supposition that she wanted some sort of leniency must have sounded as ludicrous to Judge Gifford as it did to anyone who heard it. But Fuller still just didn't get it; he was still the Federal court, white-collar crime lawyer who had no clue about what a rape case was all about. And instead of suggesting remorse on the part of his client without admitting guilt, or providing a comprehensive plan for psychological assistance in lieu of prison for a man who felt he could play by his own rules and not society's rules, Fuller had simply argued that Tyson should go to RCF, a facility where four prisoners had recently escaped. The rambling dissertation had probably hurt Tyson's chances more that they helped them as his remarks left the legal beagles, courtroom spectators, and those media present shaking their heads. Could it be that Don King had hired the bumbling Fuller with the clear intention that Tyson would go to prison permitting King to steal any money from Iron Mike that he had not already stolen? One had to wonder since Fuller, instead of being the stalwart defense lawyer in the ex-champ's corner, had been more of an ally to the prosecution. But there was another gift coming for the prosecution, this time when the stern-faced Judge Gifford asked Tyson if he had anything to say in his own behalf. The battered ex-champion rose from his chair and stood behind the podium. It reminded onlookers of his rising from his corner stool and stepping to the middle of the ring to meet his foe, only this time it was not a huge man who wanted to punch his lights out but a diminutive judge who had the power to send him to prison. Certainly Tyson must have realized that he needed to give Judge Gifford some viable reason, some knockout-type excuse for permitting him his freedom. But for the next twelve minutes, Iron Mike joined Fuller in helping the judge make up her mind to send him to a penitentiary. First, he apologized to the media. Good start. Tyson then apologized to the court, and to the other Miss Black America contestants. Good idea. Now would come the apology to Washington, even if he still denied having raped her. Right? Wrong. Instead of apologizing to Washington for his conduct, Tyson only mentioned, "my conduct was kind of crass. I agree with that." Then in the high-pitched voice that was his trademark, the one that exhibited the lisp that had caused kids in his second grade class at Public School 78 in Brooklyn to laugh the first time he answered a question from his teacher, Doris Wilson, he said, "I got carried away, ending up in a situation that got out of hand. I'm not guilty of a crime. The situation that occurred was not in a harming meaning at all. I didn't hurt anybody. There was no black eyes, or broken ribs." Continuing on as Judge Gifford stared at him with a rather incredulous look on her face, Tyson said, "I didn't rape anyone. I didn't attempt to rape anyone. I'm sorry. I agree. I've done something, but I didn't mean to." Then he turned toward Greg Garrison, referring to him as "the big man," who had "said disdainful and distasteful" things about him.

Pausing as if he was out of breath, Tyson added, "My personal life has been incarcerated. I've been hurt. I was humiliated. I expect the worst. I don't know if I can deal with it. I'm prepared for the worst" before calling the trial experience, "one big dream. It was not real. I was quite devastated." Finally, Tyson, still clutching the white piece of paper he had shown Voyles before, said, "I don't come here to beg you for mercy, ma'am. I expect the worst. I've been crucified. I've been humiliated worldwide. I'm been humiliated socially. I'm just happy for all of my support. I'm prepared to deal with whatever you give me."

Twelve minutes. Tyson had stood before his judge and did his best to explain his conduct, but Judge Gifford appeared confused as to what Tyson had told her. After a quick recess to fix the sound system that had caused problems for those unfortunate souls in the media room to be unable to hear Tyson, the judge decided she needed to ask the convicted rapist a few questions. She began by asking him about being a role model. Tyson appeared to be a bit confused as to what he was supposed to say but uttered something to the effect that there will difficulties with his "celebrity status." "I was never taught how to handle it," he said. "I don't tell kids its right to be Mike Tyson . . . parents serve as better role models." "Gifford: "Do you believe people look at you as a role model?" Tyson: "Celebrity actions are different than other people." Realizing Tyson had not really answered the judge's question, Fuller quickly added "He was not prepared for the responsibility of being world champion. He just made money for them [Tyson's promoters, managers and trainers]." With this, Iron Mike and his mouthpiece had said their piece. If Judge Gifford had been impressed, she would have been the only one in the courtroom. Once again the defense had failed miserably. Certainly no extenuating circumstances had been presented providing the judge with a reason not to judge Tyson harshly. He had not admitted the crime, no surprise since he still believed he had not committed one. But Fuller could have devised a strategy designed to show the court that psychological help in the form of responsible incarceration might be possible, or at the very least that Tyson would accept a lengthy sentence but one suspended with the full knowledge that if he slipped up in any way, even a parking ticket, he could be sent to prison for years on end. The likelihood of the judge accepting such a potential was unlikely but it at least was worth a try. Instead, the rambling, defiant Tyson had appeared before the judge giving her no choice really than to send him to prison where he could not hurt anyone again. This was inevitable since he truly believed that celebrities played by different rules and since he had given Washington notice, at least in his mind, of his evil intentions, he was absolved of any responsibility.

  Certainly the demeanor of Alan Dershowitz made it clear that he was shaken with what he had witnessed from Tyson and Fuller. He appeared to be disbelieving the confused presentation, wondering what purpose Fuller had in mind. Of like mind was Dershowitz' associate Judy Woods. Her facial expressions made it appear that she wanted to stand up and say, "Wait a minute. Call a recess. Let Alan and me help this poor fellow because his lawyer is driving him into a prison cell for a long time." When quizzed later about the hearing, she simply shook her head in disbelief at Fuller's inept performance. Hadn't this clued Dershowitz and Woods into filing as part of their appeal incompetency of counsel? Didn't they now have firsthand knowledge of why Tyson never had a chance from day one after Fuller was hired?

When Vincent Fuller and Mike Tyson had finally sat down at counsel table, it was the victor's turn to enjoy the spoils. First to speak was Jeffrey Modisett, tall, with a receding hairline, appropriately gray at the temples with a straight up posture that portrayed the image of a serious man with a purpose in mind. Born to wear a gray, pinstripe suit, the canny Modisett knew the voters of Marion County were watching his every move unlike Greg Garrison who had no known political motives. "Your honor," he began, "there are two Mike Tyson's. There is the Mike Tyson that's a nice guy, the one who only occasionally goes astray. But in thirty-eight hours in Indianapolis, Tyson exhibited a pattern of behavior different from the nice-guy image. He displayed disrespectful behavior toward women." Continuing, he added, "He had a capacity to be nice. Just ask Desiree Washington. She saw the good side of him. She trusted him." Turning to Tyson's attorney's, he said they were "the best trial counsel anybody could ask for," causing several members of the media to shake their heads in disbelief. Then Modisett noted that he had been inundated with mail from many parts of the country. "Some tell me," he said, "that a heavy sentence should be imposed to send a message to those who would commit rape. Others ask for a lenient sentence. Tyson was convicted of a violent crime, and the woman was tremendously victimized. It's an outrage to every person in the community, and I'm stunned that people say that she got what she deserved for going to Tyson's hotel room. There is no excuse for criminal behavior, but it is a time for healing."

Having now assumed the posture of the consummate politician, Modisett, his voice rising and falling with emphasis as he suddenly became the symbol for justice around the world, said, "The defense wants you to handle this defendant differently, and allow probation and a trip to Riverside. They want to perpetuate the myth that males with money and power don't know how to deal with women. Draw the line. The law says there a presumption of ten years, and that is then affected by either aggravation or mitigation." As to mitigation, the prosecutor explained, "The defendant doesn't have a prior criminal record. The 'he rose from the ghetto argument' is not a mitigator, and it is no comfort to Desiree Washington. It's not going to take away the nightmares. [She] is in prison permanently." Regarding Tyson's current status, Modisett said, "From 1988 to 1990, Tyson made thirty four million dollars. He has millions left. But being rich and famous doesn't make him a hero or a role model. Tyson had everything, but he continued to take what he wanted."

Pausing, Modisett then stated that he would read from Washington's letter to the court: "In the place of what had been me for eighteen years is now a cold and empty feeling. I can only say that each day after being raped has been a struggle to learn to trust again, to smile the way I did, and to find the Desiree Lynn Washington who was stolen from me, and those that love me, on July 19, 1991. Although some days I cry when I see the pain in my own eyes, I am also able to pity my attacker. It has been and still is my wish that he be rehabilitated." What else Washington told the court would never be known since the letter was never released to the public.

Apparently spurred on by Washington's strong words, Modisett was strong himself stating, "From the date of his conviction, Tyson still doesn't get it. The world is watching now to see if there one system of justice." He then told the court that eight to ten years was the recommended sentence since anything less "depreciates the seriousness of the crime. It his responsibility to admit his problem. Heal this sick man. Mike Tyson, the rapist, needs to be off of the streets." With this plea, Modisett sat down apparently pleased with his presentation. He had carefully skirted the edge of the prosecutor/politician tight wire, hoping to please everyone as he cried out for justice. Unlike Fuller, he had played to Judge Gifford's passion, given her a reason to send Tyson to prison for up to ten years. He was organized and he said all the right things in contrast to his adversary.

Would Mike Tyson's rape conviction had been avoided if Indianapolis attorney James Voyles had been lead counsel? Probably not since it appeared Iron Mike was convicted more for the type of man he was, the disrespectful, downright crude boxer who looked at women as playthings, than hard evidence that he had raped Desire Washington. But there existed little doubt that if Voyles had been in Tyson's corner, the prosecution would have had a much more difficult time from day one. Greg Garrison so much as admitted this to friends realizing that Tyson would have probably never testified before the Grand Jury, Voyles would have certainly never promised that Tyson would testify during opening argument, and in all likelihood, never testified at trial. Instead of making these decisions, Voyles' advice was ignored and Tyson paid dearly for King's non-decision to replace Vincent Fuller when it was clear he was over his head in a county court sex crimes trial. Perhaps more important, the good-humored, heavy-set Hoosier with the friendly smile was the only one on the defense team who appeared to have a close relationship with the ex-champ. And Voyles knew how the legal game was played in Indiana. He knew Judge Gifford and there was a mutual respect between the two. As a local boy, he also would have bonded with the home court jurors much more than Fuller, the outsider. Together, Tyson and Voyles would have been a formidable team with Voyles in the driver's seat calling the shots. But this had not occurred, and now the only thing left for him was to plead for a lenient sentence in front of Judge Gifford. The team player would now have his say and he began by telling the court, "Incarceration is the easy answer. You can step up now . . . and do what's right for the person, Mike Tyson. We can't build enough prisons. Plainfield, Westfield, the rehabilitation won't be there." He then explained that the halfway house was the best bet for Tyson because "what we can do as a society for people . . . is to deal with the problem. You have a unique opportunity, your honor, to do something for Mike Tyson." With this, Voyles sat down, having provided a passionate plea for his client albeit one that did not impress most onlookers. Why should Judge Gifford reach out and "do something for Tyson?" Had Voyles forgotten that Iron Mike was a convicted rapist?

Perhaps believing that he needed to have the final say as lead counsel, Vincent Fuller rose with the words, "In the Department of Corrections, Tyson is a marked man. A target of abuse. It's not the kind of environment where he should be." Whether this was a consideration Judge Gifford would take into account was unclear, but there was no doubt Fuller was correct. Certainly anyone coming in contact with Tyson in prison might want to make a name for himself by assaulting or even killing the ex-champ, the so-called "baddest man on the face of the planet." But prison officials did not have much concern with this possibility, believing they could regulate Tyson's visibility and keep him from harm. To them, he would be "just another prisoner," but one watched carefully so that his every move was recorded.

When Fuller had completed his last words, it was now the time for the most important words of the day, the only ones that really counted. Judge Gifford shuffled some papers before she spoke, but when she did to more than 70 people crowded into the courtroom, they were strong words beginning with her signaling her disgust for the term, "date rape." Now, the judge who had for the most part kept her emotions in check, became not only the judge, but a woman, a mother speaking as she stared at Tyson with a glare that burned right through him. "It is not all right to proceed if you are acquainted with or dating a person," she began. "The rape law doesn't mention anything about acquaintance. We have managed to imply that it is all right to proceed to do what you want to do if you know or are dating a woman. The law is very clear in its definition of rape. It never mentions anything about whether the defendant and victim are related. The date, in date rape, does not lessen the fact that it is still rape." Gifford then added that Something needs to be done about the attitude you displayed here. I feel very much like I am seeing two different people, which makes my decision more difficult."

Having made her point, Judge Gifford then spoke about Tyson. "I feel he is a risk to do it again because of his attitude. You had no prior record. You have been given many gifts. But you stumbled." And then she said the words Tyson never wanted to hear: "On count one, I sentence you to ten years." Tyson winced at the word "ten." Judge Gifford continued. "On count two, I sentence you to ten years," and then "one count three, I sentence you to ten years. The sentences will run concurrently. I fine you the maximum amount of $30,000." After hesitating as the lawyers, media and spectators attempted to understand the full impact of Tyson going to prison for ten years, the judge added, "I suspend four of those years and place you on probation for four years." And then, "During that time [probation], you will enter into a psychoanalytic program with Dr. Jerome Miller, and perform 100 hours of community work involving youth delinquency."

Not satisfied with the punishment, Jeff Modisett ask that Tyson pay $150,000 for the cost of the prosecution's case but Judge Gifford denied this motion stating that nothing in the law permitted her to levy such an amount "even though the defendant has offered to do so." In effect, the judge saved Tyson from having to pay for the prosecution that sent him to prison, an irony not lost on many members of the media. Regarding bail, Judge Gifford said there would be none. Earlier, she had noted that in retrospect, Tyson should have been incarcerated after he had been found guilty thus agreeing with the State's contention that he was flight risk.

In quite a disturbing and rude manner, the moment Judge Gifford denied bond, Alan Dershowitz and his son Jamie, loudly and abruptly left the courtroom. It was embarrassing for all to see as they stampeded toward the Court of Appeals as if they could somehow free their embattled client. Following them was the media horde, and all snaked down the nearby stairs, into the lobby, and out the revolving doors, no small feat for cameraman attempting to negotiate the close quarters with their expensive equipment. All noted that if Tyson gained credit as model prisoner, the sentence would be cut in half under Indiana law. That meant he could be free at age twenty-eight in 1995. But if he had to serve the entire sentence, then a release date of 1998 was possible when he would be thirty-one. Whether he could ever resume his boxing career was doubtful, but Tyson had more to worry about than that as Judge Gifford ordered him released to the Department of Corrections. After her banging of the gavel ended the proceedings, Tyson, wearing the same confused look he had shown since his trial had begun as if to say, "I still don't understand what I did wrong," handed his Rolex watch, his belt, his tie pin, and his wallet to the waiting Fuller. Two women friends of Tyson seated in the front row of the gallery sobbed, and said loud enough for the former champion and everyone to hear, "We love you Mike." But the only one to hug Tyson was a teary-eyed Camille Ewald. Once they parted, Marion County Sheriff Joe McAtee escorted the convicted rapist out the courtroom back door to the booking station. Tyson was then searched, fingerprinted, and processed through before emerging handcuffs high in the air with a smirk on his face while he headed for the prison in nearby Plainfield. All of Tyson's attorney's, handlers, managers, and friends headed home. Tyson, still clutching the white piece of paper he had by his side during the sentencing, was headed for prison.

Chapter Twenty-Five
The Appeal Begins

During the debate as to whether to release Mike Tyson on bail after sentencing, Vincent Fuller reminded the court that his client had shown up for every proceeding. And he decided to get in a final jab at the prosecution by mentioning their continuing reminder that they had "pursued the truth" while at the same time denying the defense the right to call the three witnesses who had been prohibited from testifying by Judge Gifford.

Greg Garrison, whose demeanor showed his true disdain for Fuller, decided it was once again his moment in the sun. As the victor in a fight that was a mismatch from the beginning, he had become the dandy of the media whenever and wherever possible. But most chuckled when he made a fool of himself on the ABC program, "20/20" when he bungled a question from Barbara Walters about what constituted "deviant sexual conduct" Intent on resuming his stature as the "man who got Tyson," he told the court, "Tyson's a potential threat, possesses an on-going practiced pattern toward women. He possesses the desire of an opportunist." Regarding Fuller's assertion that the appealable issues implied that both the "State and the Court were incompetent," he replied, "This defendant got a bucketful of due process." Regarding Tyson being on bond, the prosecutor noted, "We shouldn't let this defendant out when the issues for appear are an exercise in fiction" especially when Tyson is a "guilty, violent rapist who may repeat. If you fail to remove the defendant, you depreciate the seriousness of the crime, demean the quality of law enforcement, expose other innocent persons, and allow a guilty man to continue his lifestyle." Judge Gifford had agreed with him, stating that bail was denied based on the seriousness of the crime, the risk of flight (she noted that five years earlier a drug dealer had fled to South America even when a very high bail was imposed), and the potential that Tyson would commit a similar act.

Alan Dershowitz' flight to the Court of Appeals to rescue Tyson did not impress the panel regarding it needing to hear the case post haste. Instead, it set down a hearing for Friday, March 27th. The hearing, before Judge Sue V. Shields, John G. Baker, and Patrick D. Sullivan would last less than two hours as Dershowitz pled not only for bail but for reversal of the guilty verdict as well. His adversary was the quiet, polite, low-key deputy prosecutor David Dreyer, a far cry from the bombastic ways of Garrison. He showed no fear of the great Dershowitz who had once told *ESPN* that he entered "cases as a coroner doing an autopsy and tries to bring the patient back to life." But there was no discounting the famed Harvard lawyer's skills as an appellate attorney since his presentation was smooth and persuasive. To quell the belief that Tyson might commit another crime if permitted bail, he promised his client would submit to house arrest "to allay fears that he would be a danger to women. He would promise to live at his Cleveland estate under supervision of local law enforcement and keep out of trouble while on bail." He even agreed to stand by Tyson and if he got into trouble, withdraw any appeal rights. Whether Tyson knew this or not was unclear. David Dryer responded logically, but strongly, by calling Dershowitz' statement, "flamboyant hyperventilation." He asked, "How would any this help another rape victim?"

The three-judge panel avoided much debate on this issue instead focusing on the strength of the appeal issues since they were one measure of whether bail might be granted. Ready to attack, Dershowitz told them, "In my twenty-eight years of practice, I've never seen a case with so many good issues for appeal, and I've never made that statement in any court about any client before." Whether he had or not, no one could prove, but regardless, the statement was an indication of his that the conviction would ultimately be overturned on appeal. To accentuate this belief, he focused on three main issues, 1) exclusion of the three witnesses; 2) exclusion of the defense jury instruction regarding "implied consent," and 3) that Judge Gifford erred when she permitted Garrison to read from a partial Supreme Court decision that "the job of a defense lawyer is not to seek the truth, but to defend their clients." Concerning the former, the Harvard lawyer said that Tyson's constitutional rights had been violated since the anticipated testimony "backed Tyson's claim that he believed [Washington] had consented to have sex." David Dreyer retorted that such evidence would have severely prejudiced the state and that Dershowitz was still attacking Washington: "She still continues to be battered by the defense. We still have Desiree Washington on trial here." Regarding the latter, Dershowitz believed this implied that defense lawyers were not to be believed by jurors. After argument was concluded on both sides, Judge Shields, a former prosecutor and friend of Judge Gifford's, recessed the hearing until a certified copy of the testimony could be filed with the court. Why this had not been completed before was anybody's guess.

Meanwhile, Mike Tyson had spent his first night in prison. "Tyson has been out of his cell," prison system spokesman Kevin Moore said. "He is playing it very low key. There have been no confrontations or difficulties." But a few days later, a different story appeared as it was reported that Tyson had refused to eat and would only drink liquids. He had also apparently refused to participate in an educational assessment but had the right to do so. Tyson also faced his first disciplinary action after two inmates were discovered in possession of Tyson's autographs. Moore said Tyson "was warned that it is a violation of prison rules to give anything of value to another inmate, and his autograph is considered valuable. Mike Tyson was specifically counseled about this prison rule, and we found a couple of inmates who had autographs." At a disciplinary hearing, Tyson received a reprimand, one that would not affect the length of his sentence.

On March 31st, Judge Sue Shields issued a terse, three-sentence opinion to the effect that Tyson's request of the appeal bond was denied. Like Vincent Fuller before him, Alan Dershowitz had failed.

Chapter Twenty-Six
A Juror Speaks Out

After Mike Tyson was sentenced to prison, comments from those surrounding the case abounded. Tyson's sparring partner, Hakeem "Hurricane" Muhammad, who had been with Tyson throughout his trial, said, "I looked at it from the onset as being a circus. I thought for sure he'd be found innocent." Outside, Tyson supporters had yelled, "Black men can't get a fair trial in Indianapolis" as others wandered about wearing "Free Mike Tyson" buttons.

From the prosecution side, Greg Garrison told reporters, "We're not going to pop any champagne corks, but we're profoundly grateful the system has worked again." He then added, "Criminals always convict themselves. Tyson would have had a harder time with the jury had he not taken the stand," leaving the media to wonder the true meaning of his words.

To gain more of a perspective of one juror's impressions of the Mike Tyson trial, and how the ultimate guilty verdict was arrived upon, juror Michael Wettig agreed to an interview with this author in his hometown of Greenwood, Indiana. None of this book text was shown to him, and none of the analysis or conclusions heretofore reached in the book were based on his observations.

The forty-five-year-old Wettig, an Indiana Bell employee, said he was proud to have served on the jury. His wife Pat, a senior clerk at Merchant's National Bank, was fearful that he might be selected since he would be away too long if the jury was sequestered. But on January 14, 1992, Wettig's birthday, he had received noticed that he was among the jury pool selected and provided with a twenty-five page jury questionnaire to fill out. Then, when he reported for duty, and Judge Patricia Gifford popped into the room and said, "You all know why you're here," he knew the case he had been selected for was the Tyson trial.

On the 29th of January, Wettig took the bus to the City/County Building in downtown Indianapolis, and reported to room #260. It was almost two full days later when he was called into the courtroom where he took a seat in the front row as jury #631. He said he was "nervous," and didn't know what to expect. He recalled glancing at Tyson and that "he didn't look as tall as I thought he would." Judge Gifford, Wettig said, "didn't seem as tough as she would later turn out to be." Wettig was first questioned by prosecutor Greg Garrison, whom he described as being "very confident, and not intimidating." He recalled Garrison telling him about "Tyson's right to be judged innocent until proven guilty," and also that "even if a person is in the wrong place at the wrong time, there is still a crime if the person is wronged." Regarding questioning by defense lawyer Kathleen Beggs, Wettig said she "wore the same thing all the time . . . skirt blouse . . . It wasn't very attractive." Wettig could not recall the questions she asked him.

Wettig said he noticed that there ten to twelve blacks on the jury panel among the fifty or so jurors called. He said it appeared to him that "none of the black jurors wanted to touch the Tyson case with a ten-foot pole, apparently because they did not want to sit in judgment of one of their heroes." He also believed that some of the black jurors were "scared" of being on the jury. He told of one black man who said he was going to tell the judge "he had a bad back" and couldn't serve. "If that doesn't work," he told Wettig, "then I'll tell the judge I have an opinion about the case." When this juror appeared, Wettig said, he was true to his word, and excused from serving on the jury.

After being questioned, Wettig said he sat with five other potential jurors, and then each of the others was excused. The judge then asked him to return to the jury room, and he said he walked there in "a state of shock." One of the bailiffs then asked him whether he could be at the Indianapolis Athletic Club by 3:00 p.m. He said he called Pat and asked her "to pack a bag" and then took a taxi home. After calling his supervisor at work, and another friend at Bell, Pat drove him to the Athletic Club. He was directed to the sixth floor where the chief bailiff, "Big Ed," assigned him room 651. He described the accommodations as "nice," and said that jurors were permitted to watch television in the parlor, play pool, and enjoy use of the basketball court and other athletic facilities. A deputy sheriff stood by when the television was on to make certain that no newscasts about the Tyson case were being shown. Only once during the trial, Wettig said, did he see Tyson's name on the screen. The jurors were permitted to read newspapers, but any reference of Tyson, the Tyson trial, rape, the ongoing Jeffrey Dahmer trial, or the subsequent fire was cut out. One day, a photograph of Indiana University basketball star Damon Bailey was excluded, and the jurors laughed, Wettig said, since they could not figure out why. To show how careful the bailiffs were about making certain the jurors did not see or discuss any matter relating to the trial, Wettig said some were stopped when a question occurred about boxing during a game of Trivial Pursuit. He said family visits were permitted for two hours on Sundays, and that "meant exactly two hours and no more." Wettig said one black juror, Chuck, who was ultimately excused from the jury after the fire, was apparently married to a white woman and didn't want anyone to know. He told the bailiffs, Wettig said, that his kids had the chicken pocks as an excuse for them not visiting. "Chuck was also really the only one who didn't get along with everyone else," Wettig said. "He didn't seem to fit in with the others. He was a picky guy, didn't like cold sandwiches and the other food we had. He also would just flip the channels on the television whenever he wanted to without asking. Deep down, he seemed kind of scared."

Regarding the Athletic Club fire on the fifth day of the trial, Wettig said "I was sleeping in my room, when I thought I heard something. I went to the door, but I didn't hear anything, so I went back to bed. I heard some commotion, but no alarm, it was sort of a hum. I went out of my room and to the main area, and I smelled smoke. And then I saw a fireman and a security guard." "Are you a member of the jury," Wettig said he was asked, and when he said, "yes," they led him down the stairs, and when they got to the third floor, "the smoke was very bad and I couldn't see. I was the last juror out, and the other jurors across the street began clapping for me." Wettig said "a bailiff, a husky guy, wanted to go back in, but a fireman wouldn't let him. Everybody was pretty calm, but juror #3, Beth, broke down and cried right there on the sidewalk." The jury, Wettig said, was taken to by bus (it was called the "prison wagon" by jurors) to the downtown Hilton Hotel where they spent the remainder of the trial. "We were allowed to have a drink (alcohol), per the judge's permission," he said. The next day, Wettig said, "we were taken to the City/County Building and one by one were escorted into the judge's chambers. The judge was there, and Mr. Fuller and Mr. Garrison, and a court reporter. The judge apologized for the fire and I told her, 'its' not your fault.'"

Regarding the cause of the fire, "the judge then told me that the preliminary investigation indicated that the fire started in the refrigerator on the third floor. And then asked me whether the fire affected me in any way. I told her that there would be no more birthdays in our family this year because I had been called for jury duty on my birthday, and then the fire occurred on my daughter Tanya's birthday. Fuller and Garrison and the judge all laughed, and neither Garrison nor Fuller ask any more questions of me. In fact, that very night before the fire at about 7:30 p.m. the bailiff called up Tanya, and a group of jurors and I sang happy birthday to her." When the questioning was done, Chuck was excused, and Michael, juror number 13 was now a member of the jury.

When the trial began in earnest, Wettig had been "impressed with Greg Garrison's explanation of what he was going to prove during his opening statement to the jury. He had a fluid delivery, was animated, and presented himself well. I knew that it was just his opinion, though because I've read a lot of books that are true stories about trials."
Regarding Fuller and his opening statement, Wettig said, "What is he doing here, I asked myself. He's stumbling and has lost his place a few times. He's also calling his own client manic depressant, crucifying his own client. He's starting off bad. I

hope he's better at asking questions than giving statements." Concerning the prosecution's case in chief, Wettig believed that "Desiree Washington made a very credible witness and handled herself very well. I believe she told the truth, that she was just going out to have a good time. She said she was just going to take pictures, and she took her camera. In my mind, she felt she was going out to see the city." Fuller's cross-examination, Wettig said, was disappointing because he "didn't get of the jugular . . . didn't grill her . . let her off easy . . . and therefore she only got rattled a couple of times. If she could handle cross-examination and stick to her original story, I figured she must be telling the truth."

Turning to the issue of consent, Wettig said, "All along, it was question of whether she consented to have sex or not, and if I had been Fuller, I would have come out more strongly. He more or less accepted her at face value. She felt she was raped, and that part about her waiting two days to call 911, well, women think it is their fault. It takes a lot of courage to call 911 . . . and file charges against a guy of Tyson's stature." Wettig also believed Washington's testimony about the panty shield, and her answers concerning "how she got on top and tried to escape." As for Tyson, Wettig explained that "he acted during the whole trial like he didn't give a shit. He had the same expression all the time. I glanced at Tyson, expecting a reaction, but he looked the same." The State's most compelling witness, Wettig believed, was Virginia Foster. "She was a strong witness. In the end she made the case against Tyson because she was hired by them to drive him around, and if anyone would have contradicted Desireee, it would have been Foster because she worked for them. She corroborated Desiree as far as the actions in the limousine and the telephone call." Wettig also believed that Foster contradicted what Tyson later said about Washington's appearance when she left the hotel after the alleged rape. "When Tyson testified about how Desiree prettied herself up, that didn't coincide with what Foster said her looking like hell," he said. Also impressive to Wettig was the testimony of the night manager at the Canterbury Hotel "He and Tyson's story didn't work," Wettig said. "Tyson said the bodyguard was outside the room during the sex act, but the night manager said the bodyguard was in the parlor making plane reservations. Besides, they said they made the room reservations for the whole weekend, and the bodyguard is making reservations to get out of town. Why are they cutting out within a few hours unless he [the bodyguard] knew something was going on that shouldn't have."

Regarding the medical testimony, Wettig stated that only one doctor really impressed him and that "was the young one from I.U. with glasses [Richardson]. He pointed out that injuries like she did have were very race in cases where there was consensual sex, but in the deliberations I don't think that really made a difference because there was at least a slim chance that injuries like that could be caused with consensual sex." "One of the most ironic moments in the trial," Wettig said, "Came when we found one of the sequins from the garment worn by Desiree Washington on the floor of the jury room. We called Ed, the bailiff, and told him we didn't know how it had gotten there and asked him what to do with it. He simply took it with him."

Despite the evidence to that point in the trial, Wettig said the State had presented a "strong case," but if "the case had ended there, he would have been inclined toward guilty, but couldn't have said 'yes' . . . couldn't have voted guilty." Turning to the defense witnesses, he explained that their doctor (Wantonabe) "kept changing her story as she went along . . . said she had seen all of these injuries when there was consensual sex . . . and then would change her answer. I could never figure out why they called her . . . They could have called somebody better." Overall, Wettig said, "the defense was boring. They had a list of questions . . . the same questions . . . and if the answer differed from what they wanted to hear . . it took all three defense attorneys to think of any retort. Heard couldn't think on his feet, and would walk back and forth . . . he was nervous." But "Johnny Gill was the worst," Wettig said. "Since they [he and Tyson] were good friends, I expected him to go along with what Tyson would say. But I didn't believe him because was too close with what Tyson said, like taking a test in school, and looking over somebody's shoulder . . . word for word with Tyson." Concerning Tyson's testimony, Wettig said, "He lied. That part about the bodyguard and where he was, and the fact that he couldn't remember screwing B Angie B. If it was me, I could remember B Angie B and not Desiree."

"Testifying before the Grand Jury was a mistake," Wettig said. "and the prosecutor made good use of it. They played it back and it so differed from Tyson's other testimony. That convicted him more than anything. Also, if Tyson is as crude as they [the defense] said he was, then why did he act so embarrassed when he had to say the F word in court. That didn't make sense at all." When he learned that three witnesses had been excluded from testifying, especially the one who allegedly saw Tyson and Washington fooling around in the limousine, Wetting said he didn't think that would have made a difference since "the windows were so tinted . . . so dark . . . that if Virginia Foster couldn't see anything, then how could anyone see anyone from the curb?" He added, "Tyson was all screwed up. If you take his story about getting all hot and bothered in the limo, and then stopping in the hotel for fifteen minutes . . . that doesn't make sense. If you start something one place, you'll finish, and Tyson came across as that type . . . that he goes after something 100%." He then added, "the fact that Washington didn't spend the night . . . if she was so interested in him, then she could spend the night and be around him and that type of life . . . But she said 'no.'" This latter fact was most important to Wettig who said, "The defense painted him as a crude, bad guy, but it worked the wrong way for them . . . gave the impression . . . that no matter what . . . if she said 'no' . . . he wouldn't take 'no' from anybody. I wouldn't have degraded him as much as they did."

    As for final arguments, Wettig discussed Garrison's use of the blackboard to "show us percentages concerning Washington's vaginal injuries, and whether they were possible with consensual sex or not," but that "the percentages did nothing for me, because they left room for doubt." But "I would have liked for someone to tape the rest of his argument though," Wettig said. "because it would really be good for law students to hear." Regarding Fuller's argument, Wettig explained, "he lost track too easily. He really got flustered when

Steve [juror #5] asked to go to the bathroom. The rest of his argument was a waste. He also made Tyson out to be such a bad guy and talked about Desiree's desire for publicity and money. That was a mistake. Also Fuller stayed at his podium. He didn't seem to want to get close to the jury." Concerning whether it would have made a difference if the jury had seen the attorney retainer agreement Washington signed with Rhode Island lawyer Ed Gerstein, Wettig said "We knew she had an attorney . . . It made no difference. . . More power to her if she can get money from him."

When deliberations began, Wettig said the jury had lunch and then chose Tim as foreman."He was one heck of a nice guy," Wettig said. "Once we got his suit and tie off, he relaxed more, and was more like the rest of us." "Right away," he explained. "I spoke up and said that we needed to get it out of our minds that this Mike Tyson vs. Desiree Washington. Look at it like it is John Doe vs. Mary Smith. Some discussion was held regarding how we should discuss the evidence, but someone spoke up and said we should take a vote first." Regarding the procedure, Wettig said, "Small slips of paper were passed around, and we all wrote down our verdicts. Then we gave them to the foreman, and he put them in a bowl. He undid the slips, and laid them on the table for everyone to see. Then he told us that the vote was six for 'guilty' and six for 'not guilty' on the rape charge, ten for 'guilty' and two for 'not guilty' on the first criminal deviate conduct count, and six for 'guilty' and six for 'not guilty' on the second criminal deviate conduct charge." "We then decided that we would list a bunch of ideas on the blackboard that we wanted to discuss, but we weren't getting anywhere, so we decided that each of us would explain why we felt the way we did." Then "one by one we went around the table, and eleven of us did that, but juror #5, Steve, wouldn't do it, so we didn't know how he had voted. I learned that besides me, the foreman, Tim, the T-shirt designer, Neil [told by the bailiff that he was not dressing professionally enough by wearing T-shirts in the courtroom), the Pizza Hut driver Walt, and Dave [nicknamed Coach], had voted 'guilty' on the first ballot.

Assessing the women on the jury's feelings about the evidence, Wettig said "They didn't care about the evidence, only that they wouldn't have gone up to the hotel room at that hour . . . wouldn't have put themselves in that position . . . It was simply not the way they would have acted." The pivotal juror turned out to #2, Ken, Wettig said. "He was against voting guilty on the first ballot, but only for a few minutes. After that, he came over to our side and was very vocal. Helped to turn the others around when he broke down Tyson's testimony and irregular answers with the Grand Jury testimony." After two or three hours of discussion, the jurors decided to take a second vote. True to his word, Wettig said, Ken came around, and so did Beth and Chuck, who worked for a medical equipment company. Now the vote was nine to three for guilty regarding the rape count, the only count the jury decided to vote on. The final holdout then, Wettig reported, was Rosie, juror #8, an insurance underwriter. "She was the last one to come around because she didn't care who it was, she wouldn't have gone out with him. When juror #2 started picking Tyson apart, however, it helped. And soon she came around too." "The women weren't that strong, but we kept rehashing the evidence," Wettig added. "And Steve kept playing the devil's advocated so no one was sure where he stood although they thought he favored 'guilty.'"

Regarding the ultimate decision, Wettig said, "The jury then took the final vote, and after laying out the small pieces of paper on the table, Tim, the jury foreman, very calmly announced that the vote was twelve to zero for conviction on the rape charge. I was surprised at the vote because I was very uncertain as to what Steve was going to do. Then the bailiff arrived about ten o'clock, and said the judge wanted to send us home for the night. We told the bailiff that we were almost done, and that we would be done by eleven or we would go home. It took another half-hour or so to decide [the other two counts] once we got through with the big one. The 'finger' one was iffy but one of the jurors made the point that if Tyson was guilty of rape, then he was probably guilty of the other ones as well." The final vote was then taken, and it was twelve to zero for conviction on the two remaining counts. "Before the bailiff was summoned," Wettig recalled, "the foreman asked everyone if they were comfortable with the verdict, even after they had signed the papers. He told them they could back and vote again if they weren't comfortable, but no one did."

After the verdict was announced, Wettig said, "the judge came back to the jury room and she told us about the press conference potential and we asked her if she would do it if she were in our shoes. She told us she would just get it over with, and then a couple of jurors asked if they could get a lifetime exemption from serving on jury duty, but the judge said that was out of her control." Wettig also recalled that when he was returned to the hotel, he played pool with Ed, the bailiff, and most of the jurors went home, except Tim, who walked down to the hotel bar. Regarding his overall impressions of the main characters in the trial, Wettig said he was most impressed with Judge Gifford who "did a very good job, and never favored one side of the other." As for Garrison, he said "he was very well prepared for his questions and his arguments. He didn't use many notes, and didn't have a list of questions . . . only a list for cross-examination." "Barb Trathen," Wettig observed, "gave a good perspective from a woman's point of view. She was a good partner for Garrison. Vincent Fuller was out of his league. He lost his place and made Tyson look bad. He got flustered when he got answers he wasn't expecting, and it took him too long to rebound. His presentation was boring, and he spoke in a monotone." Concerning the sentence, Wetting thought it was "fair" and would have been disappointed if Tyson had received probation. "Just because he was Mike Tyson . . . he shouldn't be [treated] differently. Tyson was in over his head with King and the others, and he's got all this money and thinks he can do whatever he wants. I feel sorry for him in that regard. He has no control over his finances . . . he'll be broke when he gets out. But I feel the same about the verdicts today as I did then. Mike Tyson was guilty."

In early December, two more of the Tyson jurors spoke up during radio interviews with Philadelphia radio station WHAT-AM talk show host Ted Watley. Both discussed the verdict after media reports confirmed that Desiree Washington had discussed film and book deals with lawyers before the rape trial. Speaking to the point raised by Alan Dershowitz that Washington had perjured herself by not revealing this information, Dave Vahle (juror #10) told Watley, "I cannot see her as a credible witness from I know now. We [the jurors] felt that a man raped a woman . . . In hindsight, it looks like a woman raped a man. Right now, I would not believe anything she said. I would sign an affidavit that if we had known about the money, I couldn't have voted to convict him. Mike Tyson deserves a new trial." Juror Rose Pride (#8) said she would have been more skeptical of Washington's testimony if I had know about the alleged book and movies deals and reports that the nineteen-year-old had hung out in nightclubs since she was sixteen, and isn't the innocent young girl presented in court. When Washington went on Barbara Walters, she said she wasn't looking to make any money. I thought then we made the right decision." Pride then added, "I also think Tyson was poorly represented at trial by his high-powered Washington lawyer, Vincent Fuller. He wasn't very convincing. He was very aloof about everything, and had no rapport with Mike . . . his approach made me think his [Tyson's] own lawyer thought he did it" Both Vahle and Pride reported that they had sent letters to the Indiana Court of Appeals requesting that Tyson be given a new trial. To these statements, Michael Wettig observed, "For me, I don't think it would have made any difference . . . To me, it had nothing to do with what happened that night . . . the rape in bedroom . . . If she was so greedy, why didn't she take the million and run, instead of taking the chance with the trial."

Chapter Twenty-Seven
Post Trial Matters

    Most criminal cases end when the trial is completed, and if the accused is found guilty, when sentencing occurs. But the Mike Tyson case lives on even some twenty-years after Tyson was judged "guilty" by twelve Indianapolis jurors. Some people believe that the Tyson verdict and sentencing were appropriate; others that he was railroaded into prison by a prosecutor with a vendetta against him and a judge who wanted to show the world she was tougher than the ex-champ.

    The furor over new information about Desiree Washington that the jurors alluded to began as 1992 continued when Washington, whose identity had been kept secret during the entire judicial process, suddenly decided to go public. And how! Not only did she agree to appear on the cover of *People* magazine, but be interviewed by Barbara Walters on ABC's *20/20* program. There, bright and sassy in a multi-colored dress with hair as coiffed as possible, her brown eyes sparkled as Washington revealed: she was offered one million dollars to drop the charges after Tyson was indicted for rape; she would have done so if he would have apologized and agreed to get help; she called Tyson "sick" and said she agreed to prosecute not to destroy the former heavyweight champion's career but "because he needed help," and that she told Tyson "I did prosecute because you need help, and if your so-called friends weren't big enough to tell you, I was."

    Meanwhile, Tyson settled into this prison sentence, but trouble brewed when, while returning from the visiting area (visitors had included Arsenio Hall, Whitney Houston, M. C. Hammer, Spike Lee, Malcolm X's widow, and Shaquille O'Neal), he had an argument with a prison guard. Charges were filed that Tyson had threatened the guard. When confronted with the charges, he allegedly threatened another guard. He admitted the first charge, but denied the second. At an administrative hearing, he was found guilty of both. Prison officials decided he had thus violated prison rules, and an additional fifteen days were added to his sentence. One June 18th, Tyson broke his silence about the case by appearing for an interview with correspondent Ed Bradley for the *CBS* program, *Street Stories*. The convicted rapist was especially outspoken regarding comments about Greg Garrison: "The prosecutor, I thought he was a racist, weak, publicity-happy, little weak man." When Bradley asked Tyson "What do you say to the jury that convicted you? You think you got a fair shot," the ex-champ answered, "Well, there was no way I could. I knew I was innocent. But I knew what I was in that court, and when I was gonna get the verdict, I knew the verdict was gonna be guilty because of the mentality of the court, the mentality of the prosecutor." Garrison's response" "He was mystified by the charges of racism for prosecuting a black man for raping a black woman. It would have been racism not to prosecute him. That comment is pretty consistent with the denial he has lived in ever since he committed the crime and probably before. Once in his life, he's been required to face up to his deeds and it wasn't until he got to Indiana." During the interview, Tyson also spoke about the alleged rape itself: "She just sat on my bed and she was talking. We started kissing. And she started pulling off her clothes. She was getting hot. She was getting aggressive." He also said he couldn't understand why, if she had been raped, that she didn't seek help at the hotel and report him. "And if she really screamed," he asked, "why didn't someone hear her? It's just astonishing what people will believe." Responding to Bradley's question about Don King, Tyson said he supported his promoter despite a federal investigation in New York probing King's handling of Tyson's money. "He uses me. I use him . . . We never misuse one another . . . Don is my man."

The Desiree Washington camp wasted no time in striking back. Four days after the interview, her Boston-based attorneys filed a civil suit for unspecified damages in the U. S. District Court in Indianapolis. The suit charged Tyson with having caused Washington "immediate and severe physical pain, serious, and lasting physical harm, emotional distress, terror, and trauma, and psychological problems." Deval Patrick, Washington's attorney, alluded in a press conference that an unspecified communicable disease had also been transmitted to Washington during intercourse with Tyson. Chiming in about the reason for the lawsuit, Desiree Washington's father, Donald, told the *Associated Press*, that it was due to Tyson's lack of remorse. He also told *ESPN* that his daughter "wasn't after money, but after you beat somebody and you continually beat them, they got to fight back, so she is going through the justice system. Don King and Alan Dershowitz keep coming on television, going into the news media, insulting her, embarrassing her and calling her all kinds of names. How much torment can a person take?" Mr. Washington also confirmed Desiree's claim that at a time prior to trial, his daughter was offered a bribe that started as

$100,000 and quickly rose to one million dollars. "The bribe was done through a phone call," he said. "Rev. T. J. Jamison said, 'I have Don King sitting here in the room with me." When Mr. Washington asked Jamison, "Is Mike Tyson going to apologize and plead guilty," the reverend said, 'no," and Mr. Washington said he replied, "End of conversation. All you want to do is insult my daughter." Alan Dershowitz was quick to capitalize on the filing of the lawsuit to continue his attacks on Desiree Washington. He told reporters that the lawsuit, "finally discloses Washington's true motive behind accusation against Mike Tyson – money, and lots of it." He also said Tyson will not settle out of court, "we will fight it until the truth comes out." Don King added that Washington "has been lying all along . . . This is not a woman who was harassed, battered, confined, traumatized, terrorized, or more important, raped."

Post trial antics continued when it was divulged that the Rhode Island Supreme Court decided to investigate the appropriateness of the pre-trial retainer agreement signed by Washington with Providence attorney Ed Gerstein. This was the agreement the two jurors alluded to in the Philadelphia radio interview. Actually, Gerstein, concerned with apparent ethics violations, had asked the court for an opinion because the agreement had not been divulged at trial by either Washington or the prosecution. The Court had issued such an opinion stating that, while they will not ruling on whether Washington committed perjury at trial, the justices believed the matter should be brought to the attention of the Indiana appellate courts. Without hesitation, Alan Dershowitz called the *Indianapolis Star* and other news organizations screaming that this new development was the "smoking gun" that would free his client. He also called Washington, "a money-grubbing golddigger who is a liar to boot." Deval Patrick countered with a statement pointing out that "the continued character assassination against Ms. Washington, which is being waged in the media, constitutes a second rape. It is a second rape that should not and will not be tolerated. Dershowitz's campaign to impugn Ms. Washington's character and motives is a transparent tactic to shift the focus away from the real issue: Mike Tyson's guilt of a terrible crime."

Almost a year to the day after the rape incident occurred, the 1992 Indiana Black Expo opened in Indianapolis. Still under the leadership of the outspoken Rev. Charles Williams, the Expo promised an upbeat event that would drown out the unfortunate evens of the previous year. But, on Thursday, July 9th, nearly 500 people attended a rally in downtown Indianapolis in support of Tyson. Organized by the "Justice Coalition for Tyson," its purpose was to seek immediate release for Tyson on bond, ensure that would obtain a new trial, and make certain he could be given a fair opportunity to prove his innocence if a new trial were granted. Among the attendees were Don King, and B Angie B, Tyson's former girlfriend. But controversial black leader Louis Farrakhan, the leader of the Nation of Islam, and Reverend Al Sharpton, the New York activist, did not appear as promised. Los Angeles city councilwoman Patricia Moore, did appear and said, "The Africa-American women throughout the United States are not happy about what's happening with Mike Tyson . . . We will not let Desiree get away with using us a tool to destroy one of the greatest men we've ever known."

One of Tyson's supporters, Rev. Jamison, found himself charged with a crime when a Louisiana court indicted him for perjury in front of a grand jury. This charge was triggered by his having told the jurors he did not offer up to one million dollars to bribe Washington to drop the charges against Tyson. In early August, former Tyson bodyguard Rudy Gonzalez told the *New York Post* and *Fox Television* that the ex-champ was a man with such "intense sexual appetites that he would have four to five girls, sometimes ten to fifteen, a night." Gonzales said Tyson had "thirteen hundred names of sexual partners filed on a pocket computer, including women whose names would be recognizable. "He knew how to please women . . . it was very important to Mike to make each woman feel special . . . to remember her name . . . her birth date," Gonzalez said. Regarding why Tyson was left alone to fend for himself when he was Indianapolis, the former bodyguard said "King and his employees insisted Mike get on the plane by himself . . . I had no choice . . . While I was arguing with them downstairs . . . the plane was boarding and ready for take-off." He then added, "Tyson returned home to Cleveland from Indianapolis earlier than expected, and depressed . . . he finally told me 'I met a girl' . . . we really hit if off . . . we went out . . . we had sex . . . but I really messed up . . . I didn't walk her to the car." Could this have meant Tyson might have been serious about Washington? If so, perhaps she blew it by filing the rape charges against him if she had any intentions of becoming "Mrs. Iron Mike."

On August 17th, Judge Patricia Gifford weighed in on the continuing fistfight over Tyson's trial with an eight page opinion denying Tyson's motion for a new trial and affirming an earlier ruling prohibiting Tyson's attorneys from the right to question Washington in a deposition about the disputed retainer fee agreement issue. She also took a shot at Alan Dershowitz for his misleading statements about the agreement stating, "This Court is both appalled and shocked that such an attempt to perpetrate a fraud upon the Court has occurred." But Dershowitz kept right on fighting through his answer to the complaint filed by Washington in Federal Court by counterclaiming against her seeking unspecified compensatory and punitive damages. The counterclaim stated, "Washington made false and misleading statements about the boxer with the intent to obtain money or property, and that such statements were made with an ulterior purpose and motive and not in the enforcing Indiana criminal law . . . Tyson has been and continues to be injured by Washington's statements." Shortly thereafter, documents were also filed denying that Tyson had transmitted any "venereal disease" to Washington "during intercourse."

In October, as the leaves turned multi-colored and the temperatures began to dip into the thirties in Indiana, the popular rap group Public Enemy denounced Tyson's conviction and the Indiana judicial system in general by comparing Tyson's plight to the 1930 lynching of two black men in Marion, Indiana. The cover of "Hazy Shade of Criminals" portrayed two black men convicted of killing a twenty-three-year-old white man, dangling from ropes while mob of smiling white Hoosiers looked on. Rapper Chuck D created the following lyrics for one album cut: "Never like what I was in the law/Indiana tress hangin' us instead of leaves/we hangin' from the rope." On the back cover of the album, the words "hanged for bulls . . . that they didn't do based on cracker racism, jealousy, envy and greed. In 1992, by no coincidence, in the State of Indiana . . . a good friend of mine, Mike Tyson, was hanged in the same G . . . way. Some things never change. Free Mike Tyson and the hundreds of thousands of black men and women who are political prisoners in the jail cells of the United Snakes of Amerikka . . . Hell is on earth. One Tyson supporter, viewing the album, said, "It's not as physical or as drastic . . . but the way they did Mike Tyson . . .they lunched him through the legal system. The only difference is he's not dead. Yet."

In early December, Deval Patrick and Alan Dershowitz continued their arm wrestling bout in the media. Patrick: "He continues to infect and taint prospective jurors in the civil case by attacking Washington's character and motives. This is the same man who has written books about using the media and manipulating public opinion to influence the minds of prospective jurors – or to beat down the other side to make it back down." Dershowitz: "Washington and her father talked about how she could get movie and book rights," citing interviews with Donald Washington as proof of his occurring. In other legal news, *USA Today* reported that Rosie Jones, the 1990 Miss Black America, had reached a settlement with Tyson regarding her $100-million lawsuit that claimed Tyson had propositioned her and acted lewdly during a pageant ceremony at

Black Expo in 1991. No financial terms were announced. Meanwhile, in keeping with a three-year tradition, Tyson representatives passed out 1,500 free turkeys to needy families in Indianapolis just prior to the Christmas season. Tyson had been criticized for his kindness the year before by those believing he was attempting to influence jurors prior to trial. And Alan Dershowitz filed a second appeal with the Indiana Court of Appeals stating, in part, that "Desiree Washington had a financial interest in the criminal trial's outcome" and the trial court "erred in summarily dismissing the petition for post conviction relief without permitting discovery, holding an evidentiary hearing, hearing oral argument, or even permitting the defense to respond to the factual claims and legal arguments set forth in the State's motion for summary disposition." He added, "that if the jury had been aware that the complainant and her parents had lied and misled to conceal their financial interest in the conviction, it probably would have reached a different verdict."

Regarding Tyson's prison days, Dershowitz reported that he was occupying himself by exercising and reading. "He had been reading biographies like that of showman Florenz Ziegfied and others involved in New York City in the 1920s. He is also reading a lot about ancient Egypt, and we have had a number of intellectual discussions about these things." Sources at the Indiana Youth Center said Tyson was doing a great many sit ups and other exercises, and that he had lost nearly forty pounds since the trial. Dershowitz said he believed that Tyson had thrown himself into the exercise program to take his mind off the death of his father in October. Tyson was not permitted to attend the funeral, and Dershowitz said that "since you can't grieve in prison, you can't show emotion, you can't shed tears, and you can't show any sign of weakness, even if you are Mike Tyson," he felt that Tyson was working harder than ever on exercising.

As the new year, 1993, dawned, reports confirmed the sale of Tyson's 17-room, all-stone castle in Bernardsville, New Jersey to Richard Hall, the mayor of nearby Bound Brook. Price: $3 million. Once listed for $8, the Victorian Gothic home had once been occupied by Tyson during his tumultuous marriage to actress Robin Givens. Meanwhile, the early January issue of *People* magazine reported that Desiree Washington "spends most of her time alone in her room at Rhode Island's Providence College where she is plagued by nightmares that have been worsened by the split-up of her parents in June 1992. Deval Patrick said Washington still dreams of going to law school, but "her plans these days are to get through tomorrow." Her reputation was battered when the infamous *Globe* magazine presented statements from some of Washington's acquaintances in their January 12th issue shedding a bit of a different light on Tyson's accuser. "Desiree was very sophisticated when it came to boys and sex," said longtime pal Heather Anderson, 18. "Very early in our friendship she told me she was not a virgin, and she spoke in intimate terms about her lovers . . . to be frank, I was shocked." The *Globe* stated that another "friend" said that Washington only cried "rape" when her furious father discovered that she'd had sex with Tyson. Juror Dave Vahle was quoted in article regarding his comment he believed "a man had been raped by a woman" as was juror Rose Pride who said, "The panel was taken in by Desiree's performance, and that's . . . it's she who committed the crime." Indiana University School of Law professor Henry Karlson said, "the juror's statements are totally inappropriate and their testimony is not admissible . . . No jury's decision would ever be final if the jury were permitted to go back and change their minds." In late January, Alan Dershowitz continued his media parade by appearing on the *Maury Povich Show, the Morton Downey Program, ESPN,* and *This Week in Indiana.* On the latter program, prosecutor Jeff Modisett battled the Harvard professor saying "enough was enough" regarding Dershowitz' attempts to "drag [Washington] through the mud." Dershowitz countered with his belief that if the three witnesses had been permitted to testify about Tyson and Washington's conduct in the limousine, the verdict would have been altered. Modisett said this was an exaggeration, that only one witness had testimony relevant to this issue and that it would have made no difference. Dershowitz then hit Modisett with why the prosecutor's had withheld Washington's retainer agreement with Ed Gerstein from the defense and the jury, but Modisett denied this was so even though it had been discussed by prosecutors Garrison and Trathen with Washington's local counsel David Hennessey during a mock cross-examination by attorney Robert Hammerle one month before trial. Asked if Tyson would be retried if the conviction were reversed, Modisett said that would be up to Washington since "we cannot go forward without her." Asked if he was concerned that his adversary was now the highly-touted Dershowitz instead of Vincent Fuller, Modisett answered, "No one thought we could beat Fuller either." Dershowitz said that at least four jurors, in lieu of the new information about Washington, would now change their vote. Modisett countered by alleging that any appellate court decision would not be affected by this development. He also stated that he understood "why the Tyson case is a very difficult one. Mike Tyson was a hero, and still is to many. There is a sense of loss, not only in the country, but in our community. We never singled out Mike Tyson for prosecution."

Prompted by Modisett, Desiree Washington spoke to Jane Harrington, a local television station reporter and said she felt trapped by the publicity surrounding her since the trial one year earlier. "I think I was also tried and convicted," she said. "as long as Tyson is in prison, and maybe even longer, I will be in prison. I look at people my age having a good time, enjoying their lives . . . and I can't do that . . . I basically just lost my life. I know it [pressing charges against Tyson] was the right thing to do, but I can't say it was the easy thing to do." She added that the publicity had made it difficult to resume her private life. "I was attacked once, and now I'm attacked over and over again. I can't heal and I can't get better. I'm finding it hard to love and to open up." Regarding Alan Dershowitz, and his personal attacks on her, she said she would ask him "to think about what it would be like if it were his daughter who had been raped like I was, and how he would feel." Dershowitz responded, "I think it's in her financial interest to come forward now . . . Maybe she thinks . . . she'll have a better opportunity to get movie and book rights." He also said it was unfair to blame or other Tyson supporters for the publicity surrounding Washington. He told reporters that Washington lost her right to privacy when she agreed to disclose her name after the guilty verdict. "She made the decision to go public, and so she and her lawyers take any responsibility for her being the public eye. She is home free and going to college, and Mike Tyson is in prison. Who's the one who's been attacked?" With this in mind, documents filed by the Dershowitz team with the Appellate Court indicated it would argue that Tyson should be awarded a new trial since Washington was motivated to testify against him by a "well-developed financial agenda." Dershowitz wrote, "when the allegations is that the state knowingly, recklessly, or negligently promoted false testimony, a new trial is required . . . so long as the testimony could have affected the jury's verdict." If a new trial was granted, Tyson's attorneys requested that Judge Gifford should not be permitted to preside citing concerns about Gifford's comments that the impact of publicity in the case and public's cost for prosecuting were factors for deciding whether there should be a new trial."

Armed with the latest developments in the Tyson case, *NBC* decided to air a documentary called, "Fallen Champ: The Untold Story of Mike Tyson" on February 12th It was billed as "a coherent insightful view of the why and wherefores of Tyson." Included in the viewing were images of Tyson crying in trainer Teddy Atlas's arms prior to winning the 1982 Junior Olympic heavyweight championship, and Robin Givens infamous Barbara Walters interview where Givens characterized her marriage to the ex-champ as "pure hell." Donald Washington told the producers, "I idolized Tyson," but after his daughter told him she had been raped, "tears welled up in my eyes, my heart sank, and I want and put my arms around her. She used to give me a rally tight hug . . . but no more. She just held her hands like this, to her chest. I want my little girl back. I just lost her, and I'm not getting her back. She will try to come back to me, but I don't think I'll ever have the little girl I sent to Indiana back." Overall, producers said the documentary was intended "to put into perspective the enormous amount of sympathy that was given to Tyson after his conviction, and explodes a "lot of mythos about black athletes and their infallibility."

On Super Bowl Sunday, January 31st, the television program *Hard Copy* aired a one-hour special titled, "Reasonable Doubt." Among the highlights: a former middleweight boxing champion telling the interviewer that Tyson "was a master at cheating in the ring," an apparent reference to Tyson's ability to fool his opponents into believing he was going one way when he was going another; former Tyson trainer Kevin Rooney describing Tyson as "a black ghetto kid who moved to a white household" when he was taken in by the legendary Cus D'Amato; and Rooney's statement that "Tyson made $82 million in his career, and today, he's broke because of cars, women, and King." The special also included Robin Given's statement to Barbara Walters that "Tyson shakes, he pushes, he swings . . . trying to scare me." Most entertaining was the sparring bout between Garrison and Dershowitz, with the latter hammering once again at Washington's truthfulness regarding perjury during her testomony about intentions to pursue book and movie opportunities. Garrison defended his client calling her "Joan of Arc," and that she would have passed a lie detector test if given one. But Dershowitz fought back asking if it was credible to believe that Washington would have dropped the charges, as she stated, if Tyson had apologized. Dershowitz asked, "Can you image anyone saying they'd accept an apology for being raped?" When the subject of the retainer agreement occurred, Garrison again denied knowledge of such a document while stating that "defense lawyers knew she had a lawyer," but Dershowitz said the prosecutor's actions amounted to "prosecutorial misconduct."

As for Tyson, one the eve of heavyweight champion Riddick Bowe's first defense of his title against Michael Dokes (Bowe knocked him out in the first round), *ESPN* reported that the ex-champ had sent a message from prison reprimanding him for "weighing too much to fight." The letter also stated that Tyson looked forward to "some fighting" against Bowe, the first indication that Tyson hoped to resume his boxing career when he left prison. On February 7th, news reports stated that Tyson's prison days were rather routine. His schedule: awaking at six a.m. for breakfast, and either watching television, reading or receiving visitors before heading for the gym where he was paid 65 cents an hour for handing out gym equipment. "The fewer exceptions we make for him the better, "assistant superintendent Phil Slavins said." He also said Tyson received more than 100 letters a day, all of them subject to searches and prison restrictions. "Tyson can't have the many pieces of women's lingerie sent to him by fans because it would create jealousy among the prison inmates," Slavins said. Rev. Charles Williams, who apparently visited Tyson regularly, told him that "the trial was kind of a turning point in the sense that I think mike is more focused on who he is . . . his salvation, his piece of mind, and his relationship to God are the most important things to Mike Tyson right now." Boxing promoter Bob Arum told reporters, "Tyson doesn't need to worry about being replaced in the boxing ring . . . because nobody in the current crop of fighters has been able to match Tyson's skill in the ring or his celebrity status outside of it. Tyson was probably the premiere attraction in boxing while he was champion . . . He had that ferocity . . . and a menacing charisma when he came into the ring that people can't get enough of. If her come back and right into a title fight, I think there would be high interest. The public would be fascinated to see him fight the current champion."

Chapter Twenty-Eight
Another Day In Court

On February 15, 1993, the Indiana Court of Appeals convened to hear oral argument regarding the Mike Tyson appeals. Listed were seven main reasons for reversal of the guilty verdict. Foremost was Judge Patricia Gifford's refusal to permit the three witnesses to testify, the failure of jury instructions to include implied consent, the alleged error concerning Greg Garrison's reading of an excerpt from a court decision about defense lawyers not being interested in the truth, the admission of the 911 tape into evidence, and the selection process by which Judge Gifford was chosen to preside over the case. All were listed as reversible error compelling the need for a new trial. The State, represented by the Attorney General's office, countered that many of the arguments had been waived at trial or were harmless error. The fee retainer agreement was also listed in a motion for post-conviction relief based on the new evidence presenting regarding its existence and the State's failure to disclose this during trial. The State believed this had been waived since during discovery, since no question had been asked about the retainer agreement even though the defense knew Washington had hired a private attorney. To the notion that Washington had perjured herself at trial, the State said this was nonsense since questions about it had never been asked.

Some new evidence appeared that focused a different light on the trial. The defense stated that Donald Washington believed that a jury in a criminal case could award civil damages, which was not true, and that any criminal conviction could be sued in a civil trial, also untrue at the time. Regarding the retainer agreement, this author's name was cited in a brief since an interview by me of Modisett disclosed knowledge of the retainer agreement by the prosecutor's office and yet did not disclose it to the defense. About this point, Star Jones, *NBC's* legal correspondent, said, "That's sleazy. A prosecutor had a duty to turn over all of the evidence." Also a bit of a mystery occurred when three issues on appeal were under the seal of the court causing speculation that they dealt with further accusations by the defense that Washington had lied about her reasons for charging Tyson with rape.

Hearing the appeal was Presiding Judge Sue Shields, Jonathan Robertson, perhaps the most liberal of the three, and Patrick Sullivan, the legal tactician of the group. Two out of three votes were necessary for Tyson to receive a new trial. Opposing Dershowitz' team was Larry Reuben, described by former law partner James Atlas as "tenacious lawyer who is often retained by other attorneys as co-counsel and who has handled numerous federal civil rights cases." At 10:00 a.m., Dershowitz faced his adversary and the court, with more than two hundred people looking on, including reporters representing more than fifty media organizations. The bespeckled Harvard professor shot out of the gate by ripping Judge Gifford for not permitting the instruction regarding Tyson's state of mind at the time of the alleged rape. This involved the consent issue with Tyson being absolved of a crime if he believed Washington wanted to have sex with him. He pointed to the chaplain's testimony that she felt there had been "some participation" prior to the rape. Reuben countered this argument by asserting that Dershowitz' argument fell short since Washington had testified "I don't want to have a baby; I have a future," clear indications that she did not want to have sex. Judge Sullivan appeared to spark to Dershowitz' line of thinking stating that "the jury needs rules to work with," and indicating that absence of the instruction about consent prevented the jury from considering whether Tyson could be acquitted if he reasonably believed that Washington wanted to have sex with him. This issue having been debated, Dershowitz turned his attention to the three witness exclusion, arguing that the defense had done everything in its power to bring these witnesses to the attention of the State as soon as possible after their existence was discovered. Reuben said the defense interviewed the witnesses at least four times before alerting the State to their names. The Court appeared to buy Reuben's argument, a direct accusation that James Voyles had not done all he could have to notify the State of the witnesses and their possible testimony. Regarding the 911 tape, Nathan Dershowitz said this permitted Washington to "testify twice," that is was hearsay, and that the dispatcher's comments were prejudicial. The State replied that the defense had introduced evidence that Washington's motives were money and that the 911 tape was perfectly admissible to rebut such accusations. The justices appeared to side with the defense on this issue regarding the dispatcher's comments and the fact that the tape had been recorded almost forty-eight hours after the alleged rape. Regarding the selection process by which Judge Gifford was selected, the defense argued this permitted them to "judge shop," so they could find the most sympathetic judge for their case. The State countered by stating that the judge was selected through normal procedures and wondered why the defense had never asked for a change of judge as they had a right to do.

When the judicial bantering was completed, it was difficult to assess who had won and who had lost but there appeared to be sympathy with the defense from the justices. But the burden of overturning a jury verdict was huge, and whether there was truly reversible error of such a magnitude to order a new trial for Tyson remained to be seen. Asked his assessment, Don King told reporters, "I just hope the brother gets out, but it's probably a snowball's chance in hell."

Not content to discontinue their fight to free Tyson, his attorneys filed another post conviction relief motion on February 26th alleging that Tyson's conviction should be reversed due to new evidence that Washington had falsely accused Wayne Walker, a high school classmate, of rape in 1989, Court documents stated that Walker alleged that Washington told her father that he had raped her and that she did it "to cover myself . . . or I would have been in big trouble. Walker told *ESPN* radio that when he heard that Washington accused Tyson, "the first thing that came into my mind is she's doing it again." An angry Deval Patrick struck back, saying, "The charge is . . . categorically false and is totally irrelevant to the central issue of what happened in that hotel room with Tyson in July of 1991."

On March 23, Judge Larry McKinney of the United States District Court in Indianapolis ruled that all discovery proceedings in the civil case would be suspended until Tyson's' appeal was decided. He also prohibited release of any documents regarding Washington's private life.

Meanwhile, Tyson was having more problems in prison. On March 25th, Karen Grau, an Indiana Department of Corrections spokesperson, issued a press release reporting that Tyson had been ordered by a prison board to spend at least thirty and perhaps as many as sixty additional days in prison for allegedly disobeying an officer. Sources close to the prison indicated that Tyson apparently was "buying" other inmates' telephone time, and then argued with a guard when confronted over the rule's violation.

In later March, the *New York Post* reported that Desiree's relations with her father may have been a violent one. The newspaper stated that in October 1989, Mary Washington, Desiree's mother, had Donald arrested and charged with assault and battery against Desiree. Utilizing police reports, the *Post* quoted Desiree as alleging that her father "hit me and pushed me under the sink . . . He continued slamming my head into the wall and the floor. I freed myself and reached for a knife to protect myself." The article also said Mary Washington stated in the deposition that Donald "flew off the handle" when Desiree told him, "she had lost her virginity," and that she [Mary] "arranged for Desiree to undergo psychotherapy, because of severe depression, and suicide threats."

Countering the report that Desiree had falsely accused Wayne Walker of rape, Washington's lawyers filed a motion with the court that included the following statement from Desiree:

> Although Wayne and I have known each other since junior high school, and briefly

> dated in high school, I categorically and unconditionally deny that Wayne and I ever had sexual intercourse with penetration. I also categorically and unconditionally deny that I ever accused Wayne of having raped me. I never have never said such a thing or made such a charge to my father or to anyone else.

The defense then filed a motion stating that his statement was contrary to Mary Washington's testimony in the deposition to the effect that "Desiree lost her virginity in October 1989," precisely the time Wayne Walker said he had sex with her and she falsely accused him or rape. In the motion, the defense also produced a March 1993 affidavit of Mark Colvin, another schoolmate of Washington's. It read:

> I am very reluctant to come forward with this information because I still consider Desiree Washington to be a friend. She [Washington] called me on the telephone toward the end of 1989 and confided to me that she had sexual intercourse with Wayne Walker . . . She also said that after it happened she went into the bathroom and cried.

On April 1st, Florence Anthony and Tim McDaarrah reported in the *New York Post* that Mike Tyson had decided to embrace the Muslim religion, and change his name to Malik Abdul Azis (Servant of the Almighty). Tyson was not available for comment, but Alan Dershowitz denied the story, stating, "Mike Tyson will continue to be known as

Mike Tyson." In a telephone interview with this author, juror Michael Wettig reported that the jury planned a reunion for the weekend of April 4th. All of the jurors were expected to attend, he said, but there was a problem with locating "Kenny, the young black juror who made headlines after the trial by saying 'the case was rigged.'" On April 10th, fourteen months to the day when Tyson was convicted, twelve federal court jurors in Los Angeles returned a guilty verdict against the four LAPD officers alleged to have beaten Rodney King and denying him his civil rights. In the May issue of *Penthouse*, Alan Dershowitz took more shots at the prosecution, sating, "Mike Tyson was convicted of rape on the basis of testimony that we believe we can now prove, was known to be false and incomplete by prosecutors." He also provided a glimpse of Tyson behind bars suggesting that "the one subject Mike does not discuss is his future. Mike says, 'My life is in prison now, and dealing with prison one day at a time is a full-time job." Dershowitz further quoted Tyson as saying, "How could she have done this to me? She knows that I did not rape her; she knows she agreed to have sex. How can she do this to another human being?" Noting that Tyson was permitted to walk around in a fenced-in field, the Harvard professor said Tyson told him, "That's the worst . . . if I were locked in a cell all day, at least I wouldn't get myself thinking I was free. But when I walk in the field, I can sometimes forget for a minute or two that I'm not free, that I can't make any decisions on my life in here. I'm dying in here a little at a time."

Postscript

Three trials and one hearing with Mike Tyson the only one "convicted." What does this say about the American justice system during the early 1990s? The Clarence Thomas/Anita Hill confrontation, even though it was held outside the judicial process, permitted the world to see that accusations of impropriety may be leveled within the high levels of Congress when as important an issue as appointment to the Supreme Court is concerned. Because of Hill's courage in coming forward with her allegations, perhaps other women decided to call men to task for sexual harassment if the situation warranted such action. Who was telling the truth, Thomas or Hill? No one will ever know the truth, but perhaps it lies, as it often does, in the middle someplace, with each party viewing what occurred with their own lens as to what was proper and what was not. Hill has continued her academic career and, of course, Thomas his duties as a justice. If anyone thought his presence on the court was a win for minorities especially African-Americans, they were wrong as he has consistently voted a conservative bent some would call abusive to his own people. But one must respect his right to do so, and his legacy will prove the worthiness of the choices he has made. Books chronicling the confrontation abound, but each decided to tell their side of the story, Hill in *Speaking Truth to Power*, in 1998; Thomas in his 2007 memoir, *My Grandfather's Son: A Memoir*.

The not-guilty verdict in the Rodney King state trial caused riots, and the guilty verdict in the subsequent federal trial uproar with those who stood by the four policemen and the actions they took to quell King. Regardless, the conduct of police officers towards subjects being arrested was viewed with more scrutiny for a time before the King case was forgotten and subsequent "King-like" episodes prevailed in different parts of the country.

After his acquittal on the rape charges alleged against him, William Kennedy Smith earned his medical degree from the Georgetown University School of Medicine. He then moved to Chicago where he was physician at the Northwestern University Feinberg School of Medicine and founded the Center for International Rehabilitation, described as "a worldwide humanitarian network of individuals and organizations that promotes the full potential of people with disabilities." In 2004, a former employee alleged that Dr. Smith had sexually assaulted her five years earlier. She filed a civil action. Smith called the allegations "outrageous," but he resigned from the CIR. In January 2005, the lawsuit was dismissed. In subsequent years, Dr. Smith continued to speak out on the destructive nature of landmines and was active in assisting those rehabilitating from severe injuries. The truth as to whether he raped Patty Bowman will never be known but his innocence will continue to be clouded based on the exclusion of the testimony of the three women who alleged he had also sexually assaulted them.

There were certainly no winners in the Bensonhurst murders as the eye-for-an-eye attitude failed at every turn. Lemrick Nelson, Jr. was acquitted at the state trial and the family of Yakel Rosenbaum left to only cherish his memory. But Nelson subsequently paid for his crime when the federal government investigated the case and indicted Nelson, Jr. and Charles Price for their participation in the stabbing. Price pleaded guilty and was sentenced to more than eleven years while Nelson was convicted and sentenced to ten years in prison.

And what of the Mike Tyson case? What may be learned from it? Was Tyson truly guilty or was there a miscarriage of justice? Certainly Desiree Washington believed in her own mind that she had been raped while Tyson did not. This discrepancy permits several "What if?" scenarios to overshadow any jury verdict. They include: What if Tyson had walked Washington to the limousine as she had asked him to do? Would she have filed the rape charges? What if Tyson's handlers had retained a competent sex crimes lawyer, one familiar with county court procedures and the nuances associated with a rape trial? Would prosecutor Greg Garrison have had much more of a formidable battle on his hands; would the verdict have been different? What if Tyson had never appeared before the Grand Jury? What if Vincent Fuller had not promised during his opening statement that the jury would hear from Tyson, that he would testify? Was the evidence strong enough to convict Iron Mike if he had remained silent?

What if another judge, one less prosecutorial in nature than Patricia Gifford, would have presided over the trial? Would the three witnesses, one who swore she saw Tyson and Washington "all over each other" in the limousine prior to entering the hotel, have swayed the jury toward disbelief of Washington's story? Would another judge have made the flip remark, "help yourself," when Tyson was being courteous in court regarding his use of foul language? If not, would that have made a difference in the eventual outcome of the trial? What if the defense had produced a competent medical expert to offset Dr. Stephen Richardson's testimony? How might this have changed the juror's attitudes as to whether rape had occurred or simply rough sex, something Tyson was known for? What if there had never been a fire at the nearby Indianapolis Athletic Club resulting in the dismissal of an African-American juror who later indicated his doubt of Washington's story?

One may speculate all day long as to the proper search for truth in the Tyson case, but in the end, he was the one who was convicted and sentenced to six years in prison. He would serve three, either too few, some believed, for the rape, or too many to those who truly believed in his innocence. Once released, he vowed to pursue the Muslim faith, all while a rally was held in Harlem welcoming Mike back to his home turf. Reverend Al Sharpton, Don King at his side, led a crowd of well-wishers as Tyson stood with a look of disbelief at the fuss. Before his release, Desiree Washington had spoken of her feeling that she had convicted along with Tyson and was in prison as well. She said she had changed because of what Tyson had done to her, but also because of what society had done to her, being "attacked again and again" for her accusations against the ex-boxing champion. A source close to her indicated that she had suffered severe psychological trauma, had undergone extensive cosmetic surgery, and was working with special needs children. Her head attorney, Deval Patrick, who negotiated a final settlement with Tyson's appellate attorneys, would become the governor of Massachusetts while Tyson's lead lawyer, Vincent Fuller, continued to practice law with Williams and Connolly in Washington D. C. until his death from lung cancer in 2006. His courtroom successes had included defending John Hinkley and Don King, but he had lost the Tyson case as well as one involving financier Michael Milken. Asked about Fuller, Garrison said, "Coming out here and jumping in the mud with people who know how to swim in the mud and getting beat doesn't mean you're not still one of the great lawyers. I'm still in awe of the guy." An obituary notice quoted Fuller as saying, "Some people say trial lawyers are actors and the trial is like a play. I think that's misleading. It's really a battle, especially when the stakes are high and the value is liberty." How Fuller viewed his performance in the Tyson trial was never known as he refused to discuss it.

      The post-prison Mike Tyson continued on the daily rollercoaster he had ridden prior to going to prison. Everyone wanted a piece of him and he began by attempting to resume his boxing career. The so-called "Kid Dynamite" and "The Baddest Man on the Planet," Tyson regained a portion of the heavyweight title before losing it to Evander Holyfield in 1996 when Iron Mike was disqualified for biting off part of Holyfield's ear. At thirty-five-years-old, he fought to regain the championship but lost to Lennox Lewis in 2002. Finally, in 2005, Tyson retired from competitive boxing when he suffered humiliating losses to journeyman boxers Danny Williams and Kevin McBride. These fights were purely for money as Tyson had filed bankruptcy in 2003 despite having earned more than $300 million during his career. Tyson was successful in a lawsuit against Don King to the extent of recovering more than $14 million dollars but that money was already headed away from his pocket to pay debts including a huge one to the Internal Revenue Service.

Legal hassles continued to follow Tyson wherever he traveled. In February 1999, he had been sentenced to a year in prison for assaulting two motorists. He served nine months. But he had risen again, and with his name still a big crowd draw, the battle with Lennox Lewis in 2002 was set where Tyson said about Lewis, "I want your heart, I want to eat your children." But the boxing skills were mostly nil and in the eighth round, Lewis had knocked Tyson out with a right hook. At the time, the fight was the highest grossing one in history, triggering revenues of more than one hundred million dollars. But his past success still caused Tyson to be ranked number 16 by *Ring Magazine* in a poll of the greatest fighters in history.

In a 2005 *USA Today* interview, Tyson was quoted as saying, "My whole life has been a waste. I've been a failure. I just want to escape. I'm really embarrassed with myself and my life. I want to be a missionary. I think I could do that while keeping my dignity without letting people know they chased me out of the country. I want to get this part of my life over as soon as possible. In this country, nothing good is going to come of me. People put me so high; I wanted to tear that image down."

Residing in Phoenix, Tyson turned to his beloved pigeons for comfort while doing promotion and appearances to earn some cash. He also performed boxing exhibitions in Las Vegas. But in late 2006, Tyson was arrested in Arizona on suspicion of driving under the influence of alcohol and possession of drugs, and checked into a rehabilitation facility. In September 2007, he pleaded guilty to DUI and possession of cocaine. He was sentenced to 24 hours in jail and the performance of community service.

On the personal front, Tyson had been married three times while fathering seven children. The first two wives had been Robin Givens, and Dr. Monica Turner, the sister of Republican Chairman Michael Steele (the marriage ended when she alleged adultery). Tyson then married Lakiha Spicer in June 2009.

In 2008, Mike Tyson had once again had hit the headlines through the release of "Tyson," a documentary produced by gifted filmmaker James Toback. At the Cannes Film Festival, Tyson was a rousing hit with crowds cheering his every appearance. Of the reception, he said, "I've never experienced anything like that in my entire career." He added, "I lived a wild and extreme life. I've used drugs. I had all sorts of physical altercations with people. I've slept with guy's wives that wanted to kill me. I'm just happy to be here, you know."

The Tyson documentary was Tyson in his rarest form. Toback had persuaded him to be as open as possible about this life and his troubles. Memorable quotes abounded, but one stood out when it is placed in context with what occurred during the 1991 confrontation with Desiree Washington. Tyson said, "I never fit in with society. I had to be the beast." Later in the film, he added, "I'm an insane individual."

During the fall of 2009, Tyson appeared on the Oprah Winfrey program to once again bare his soul. Looking contrite and serious in a polished suit, his face tattoo obscuring an otherwise placid complexion, Tyson talked about everything from the demons that had haunted him to the loss of his four-year-old daughter Exodus, whom he called "my angel." Regarding the unfortunate accident that had killed her, Tyson said he first was looking for whom to blame, but decided he "didn't want to go there" since that would provoke animosity and anger, emotions he had attempted to quell through his rehabilitation. Although Oprah kept pushing to gain his true feelings about Exodus' death, Tyson sat stone-faced with tears in his eyes and refused to go there. On the program, he also apologized to Evander Holyfield for the biting incident and the two men shook hands. This was allegedly the new Tyson, the man-child acting as the man. Whether he could continue his non-violent ways, whether he could resist the temptation to become the old Tyson, remained to be seen.

Did Mike Tyson rape Desiree Washington, and if he did, why? Perhaps the partial quote, "I had to be the beast," says it all. Throughout his formative years, Tyson was taught, instructed to the villain, the enemy, the tough guy, the menace, the "baddest guy on the planet." This persona worked in the boxing ring and in the troubled world of boxing, but in society, that sort of behavior was condemned, against the law. When Mike Tyson met Desiree Washington, the former champ was called to the mat to reap what he had sowed for so long, the idea that he was special, that he was above the law, that he could treat women as roughly as possible and get away with it as long as he warned them first. To this day, he still believes that he did nothing wrong, that he did everything possible to let Washington know of his intentions. In his mind, he had warned her, but he picked the wrong girl to warn for any number of reasons. And his bad choice cost him his freedom and destroyed his boxing career. Did he receive a fair trial in every sense of the word? No, but it didn't matter, for in the end Tyson got what he deserved, a prison sentence if not for raping Washington then past conduct that was just as bad or worse. In the final analysis, he is lucky to be alive, lucky to still have a chance at surviving, lucky to not be in prison for the rest of his life. One may only help that he realizes his good fortune, and will count his blessings and make something of a life that he was right to say was mostly wasted. If so, then the trial that changed the course of his life will have been worth it, and he will finally discover peace and joy as the years pass.

About Mark Shaw

Mark Shaw is a former criminal defense lawyer turned author/journalist with twenty-one books. At the ripe young age of sixty-two, he earned a Masters Degree in Theological Studies from San Francisco Theological Seminary.

Published non-fiction books include *Road to a Miracle, Beneath the Mask of Holiness: Thomas Merton and the Forbidden Love Affair that Set Him Free, Melvin Belli, King of the Courtroom, Miscarriage of Justice, The Jonathan Pollard Story, Forever Flying*, the autobiography of famed aviator R. A. "Bob" Hoover, and *Larry Legend*, a biography of NBA superstar Larry Bird. He has also written *Down For The Count*, an investigative book about the Mike Tyson rape trial, *Bury Me In A Pot Bunker*, the autobiography of controversial golf course designer Pete Dye, *The Perfect Yankee*, a chronicle of New York Yankee pitcher Don Larsen's perfect game in the 1956 World Series, and *Clydesdales, The World's Most Magical Horse*. Mark has also written five books about writing and becoming published.

Novels published include *No Peace for the Wicked* and *Dandelions in the Moonlight*.

Thirty-one editions of Mark's books are in print. *Forever Flying, The Perfect Yankee, Larry Legend, Jack Nicklaus, Golf's Greatest Champion,* and *Bury Me In A Pot Bunker* have been published in paperback. *Bury Me In A Pot Bunker* has been translated in Japanese.

Mr. Shaw's background includes six years as a noted criminal defense attorney in the Midwest. He practiced entertainment law in Los Angeles and

Indianapolis. Mark remains a member of the bar in California and Indiana.

Mark co-founded the *Aspen Daily News,* a daily newspaper in Colorado. He has hosted radio talks shows in Bloomington and Indianapolis, Indiana.

Mr. Shaw began his career in the entertainment industry as an on-air television personality for *ABCs Good Morning America, CBS's People,* the syndicated *World of People,* and the Disney Channel's *The Scheme of Things.* He has hosted various talk shows including *A.M. Los Angeles* and *Mid-Morning L.A.*, and was a legal correspondent for the nationally syndicated program, *On Trial.*

Mark was the legal analyst who correctly predicted the outcome of the Mike Tyson and O. J. Simpson trials for, among others, *CNN, ABC,* and *ESPN.* He wrote several columns analyzing the case for *USA Today.* In 2004, he analyzed the Kobe Bryant case for *ESPN* and *USA Today.com.*

Mark created and produced the Television Special, A *Beverly Hills Christmas with James Stewart,* for Fox Broadcasting. He was co-executive producer for two motion pictures, *Freeze Frame* and *Diving In.* After co-writing the screenplay for the film *Hazel* for Universal Studios, Mr. Shaw became a member of the Writers Guild of America. He has written articles and columns for, among others, *USA Today, The Aspen Daily News, The National Pastime, The Bloomington Voice, Indianapolis Monthly,* and *Indiana Lawyer.*

An avid collector of Ernest Hemingway books and a longtime suffering fan of the Chicago Cubs, Mark is married to Wen-ying Lu, a librarian at the University of Colorado at Boulder. Mark, Lu, and their beloved dog, Black Sox, reside in nearby Superior.

Made in the USA
Lexington, KY
17 July 2012